CW01619376

TR
AGENTS

More scrapes, japes and narrow escapes

GRAHAM WILLIAMS
& LISA JACKSON

LITTLE BANDIT BOOKS

A LITTLE BANDIT BOOKS PAPERBACK
First published in Great Britain in 2020

Copyright © Graham Williams & Lisa Jackson, 2020
The right of Graham Williams and Lisa Jackson to be identified as the Authors of the Work has been asserted by them in accordance with the Copyright, Designs and Patents Act 1988.

All rights reserved. No part of this publication may be reproduced, stored in a retrieval system, or transmitted, in any form or by any means, electronic, mechanical, photocopying, recording, dramatisation or otherwise without the prior permission of the copyright owners, nor be otherwise circulated in any form of binding or cover other than that in which it is published and without a similar condition being imposed on the subsequent purchaser.

Printed and bound by Amazon.

Paperback ISBN: 978-1-9163537-4-9
eBook ISBN: 978-1-9163537-5-6
Audiobook ISBN: 978-1-9163537-6-3

Facebook: Little Bandit Books
Twitter: @lisajackson43

Other books by Lisa Jackson & Graham Williams
Travel Seekness (Little Bandit Books; Love Travel Series #1)

Other books by Lisa Jackson
Running Made Easy (Collins & Brown)
Adore Yourself Slim (Simon & Schuster)
Your Pace or Mine? (Summersdale)

PRAISE FOR *TRAVEL AGENTS*

Travel Agents is an absolute belter of a book. **Vassos Alexander, Virgin Radio sports presenter & author of *Don't Stop Me Now***

I'd never want to join a trip Lisa and Graham organised, but I'd absolutely help hold the Iranian nightmare guide Milad down while they strangled him. **Lonely Planet co-founder Tony Wheeler**

An awesome collection of travel tales that will enthral, terrify and perhaps appal you.
Jamie McDonald, author of *Adventureman*

A brush with death on one holiday is bad luck; doing it on four trips is either careless – or the basis of a fantastic travel book! **Helen Foster, Differentville.com blogger**

Cracking stories need a cracking storyteller, and they get them here. Graham and Lisa stuff you in their backpacks and take you on a journey that is warm, witty, wise and endlessly engaging. **Phil Hewitt, author of *Outrunning the Demons***

The world needs more travel writing like this; a surge of dromomania sprinkled with love and unexpected hilarity.
Dave Cornthwaite, founder of the YesTribe

Dramatic! Unputdownable! Riveting! Make a movie of this book! But please Lisa and Graham, don't ask me to go on 'holiday' with you. Ever. For once, I'd prefer to sit on the sidelines and cheer you both on! **Kathrine Switzer, author of *Marathon Woman***

Armchair escapism at its best. **Elaine Griffiths, Special Projects Editor, *Good Housekeeping*, *Red*, *Prima***

To our astonishing parents, Irene 'Ma' and Reg 'Pa' Williams and Anthony and Leoné Jackson, and to our loving and supportive family and friends

To all the welcoming, considerate, generous and kind people we've met in some of the world's poorest countries and in some of its richest.
It is they who turn travel into a life-affirming journey

The stories you are about to read are true. Only names, identifying characteristics, occupations, hair colours, blood groups and clothing choices have been changed to protect the guilty. If someone in our book sounds like you, they probably aren't

CONTENTS

INTRODUCTION

A single brush with death on one overseas trip could be seen as bad luck; four flirtations with The Grim Reaper in the same year would probably be seen as carelessness. Yet that's what happened to me and my husband Graham in 2003. For some unknown reason it became the year that death repeatedly came up close and breathed his hot, foul breath on us: in Rangoon we escaped a vehicle collision by seconds that tragically took the lives of eight unfortunate Burmese; Graham's work sent him to Kashmir, then the most dangerous place on earth; a few months later we braved burning barricades in riot-torn Bolivia; and, to round off our death-defying year, we nearly froze to death in a flimsy tent pitched on the snowy South Rim of the Grand Canyon.

In contrast, we'd spent the previous year in limbo, which the dictionary describes as 'a situation in which nothing happens for a long period of time, and in which it's difficult to make decisions because you're waiting for something else to happen first.' In Catholic theology, Limbo is an actual place, the abode of souls who've not been despatched to Hell but who haven't accrued sufficient Brownie points to enter Heaven either. The defining characteristic of living in both types of limbo is that it isn't fun – quite unlike the other definition of limbo: 'a Caribbean dance involving bending backwards under a stick'.

Throughout 2002 we'd been in turmoil over whether to emigrate to Australia and start a family – we'd chosen Oz principally because its outdoorsy lifestyle meant it would be ideal for bringing up children – or whether to stay put in London and continue travelling whenever we could. Our prolonged state of indecision meant we couldn't buy plant pots for our garden 'in case we emigrate' and we couldn't shop for a new sofa 'in case we go to Oz'. And we couldn't spend much on travel 'just in case'.

Instead, our new 'fun' evening and weekend hobby was to revisit the points system Australia used to manage immigration to its shores. Graham gained points for having three philosophy degrees – 'For the first time, having a philosophy PhD doesn't actually count against me,' he joked – but lost some for being 'old', in other words, northwards of 35. I gained points for having a second language, Afrikaans – 'This is the only time that's proved useful since leaving South Africa,' I quipped – and being younger. Australia wasn't crying out for magazine sub-editors like myself or research analysts like Graham, but it was prepared to let two educated 30-somethings in, provided we had behaved ourselves. A criminal record long ago ceased to be a requirement for entry. Our immigration papers had to be lodged before my 35th birthday in September, because after this I'd lose several 'age' points and we'd have too few overall to qualify for entry.

'If we went to live in Australia, we wouldn't have to put up with weather like this,' said Graham one wet and gloomy April day.

'We can't make a major life decision based on how much you love the sun,' I replied. 'I've told you a million times that I'm really worried about us living separate lives. There aren't any magazines in Canberra where you'd have to be based. Do you really want us to live apart five days a week?'

'Hmm, let me think,' teased Graham. 'A spotless apartment where no one hangs up their towels on the floor. Beautifully polished tiles. A bathroom mirror without any finger smudges. What's not to like?'

'Graham, I'm serious. Marriages fall apart when the little

things aren't shared. Even "squaddling" about whose turn it is to take out the rubbish or wash the dishes is bonding. I think if we emigrated we'd be risking our marriage.'

Our other major life decision was looming, too. It wasn't only my immigration points that would drop once I turned 35; I knew that female fertility declined significantly then, too, and so at 34 it was make-your-mind-up time. If Graham and I wanted to go forth and multiply – in the literal sense – then to give ourselves the best odds of becoming parents we had to start trying imminently.

'If we decide not to have kids, do you think we'll regret it?' Graham asked me as we ambled around the ponds in Crystal Palace Park where toddlers stood wide-eyed with delight at the life-size Victorian concrete dinosaurs.

'Who knows? I've been wrestling with this for years. We'll miss out on all those precious family moments – our child's first smile, first word, first steps, first day at school – but we won't have to worry about schools and university, and whether they'll find a good job or be able to afford their own home. These things would definitely keep me awake at night.'

'Lisa, you're fretting about things 10 to 20 years down the line. I'm concerned about the here and now. Only getting my first full-time job at 33 means salary- and pension-wise I've a lot of catching up to do. And you're not exactly paid a king's ransom.'

'I know. We definitely can't afford for one of us to give up work and stay at home.'

'If we both worked we'd spend a fortune on childcare,' continued Graham. 'Either way, we definitely wouldn't have enough money to continue travelling. I really don't want to give that up, do you?'

'No. I don't. But I also always thought we'd be parents. Every time I see photos of you as a baby or toddler it breaks my heart to think I won't be a mother to a son like that. Argh! It's just so hard to know what we should do.'

For months we went back and forth, endlessly examining

the pros and cons, the whys and the wherefores. As my September birthday drew closer and our discussions got longer – coming to rival the heated arguments we'd had when we'd first met, extending almost until dawn – we realised we couldn't stay in a state of limbo any longer. And so we took the biggest decision we'd ever make: we decided to give up the chance of a richer future life to stick with our present rich life. We would stay in London near family and friends in the small terraced house we'd made our home, keep the good jobs we'd worked so hard to get, and travel as much as possible rather than relocate halfway round the world, live apart, find new jobs and start a family.

It was a huge decision. One we took a long time to come to terms with. We grieved for Calvin, the little boy we'd now never have, and I often felt sad knowing there would be no one to whom I could pass on my love of marathon running and our shared passion for travelling.

But with the grief came relief. We were living in limbo no more. We could finally buy those garden pots, replace our knackered sofa and, most importantly, travel. Exotic and exciting destinations were waiting to be ticked off our wanna-visit list. We couldn't wait to dust off our backpacks. 2003 was going to be The Year of Making Up for Limbo. We never suspected that it would also turn out to be The Year of (Almost) Dying Dangerously.

CHAPTER ONE

2003: The Year of (Almost) Dying Dangerously
Burma, Kashmir, America, Bolivia

When we were beginner backpackers in the 1990s, Graham and I used to believe that death was more likely when we were travelling abroad. When we wander away from our comfort zone a very primitive fear kicks in: the fear of the unknown. And by going travelling, where *everything* is unknown, it's easy to think that you'd be less at risk if you stayed 'safely' at home. Nearly drowning on the Philippine island of Boracay had proved this point. Plus many of the tales we'd heard on the Taipei Hostel balcony – as well as from friends and fellow travellers – taught us to be wary. Our good friend John, for example, told us that he'd feared for his life when, as a thrill-seeking 19-year-old, he'd hiked Panama's Darién Gap. One of the most hostile places on the planet, it's a roadless and lawless 100km-long break in the Pan-American Highway that runs from Alaska to the southernmost tip of Argentina. It's the kind of place where, if drug runners, kidnappers, anti-government rebels and people smugglers don't do you in, the deadly snakes, venomous scorpions, crocodiles and bacteria-infested drinking water very well might.

On the fourth day of battling their way through the hot, humid and incredibly dense rainforest, John's group heard the sound of machetes hacking through the undergrowth ahead of them.

'Everyone, eyes on the ground! Don't look up, don't

fucking look up!' their guide had barked. Knowing that his life depended on it, John had obeyed. As the group passed to the right of them, in his peripheral vision John had glimpsed men in combat boots carrying AK-47s. Others, unarmed, shouldered buckets of cocaine. John lived to tell the tale. Many others didn't, including the Swede Jan Philip Braunisch who was shot after being suspected of spying and whose skeletal remains were returned to his family in a casket.

2003 seemed hellbent on making the point that we should never venture past our front door abundantly clear: death crossed our path in Burma, Kashmir, Bolivia and the Grand Canyon. If we'd remained at home we were unlikely to die in a head-on collision or a helicopter crash, get shot by soldiers, be burnt alive in a riot or freeze to death. But Graham and I knew by now that the Grim Reaper can rear his hooded head much closer to home. My former South African *Cosmopolitan* colleague Cynthia, for example, is as cosmopolitan as they come, and yet she ate the meal that was nearly her last supper, not in some far-flung place but in a posh restaurant in the Kruger National Park, just a five-hour drive from her Johannesburg home. But for the timely intervention of a honeymooning Californian doctor, she would have choked to death, her throat convulsing, blood oozing from her eyes. When holding Cynthia upside down off the edge of a table and shaking her to dislodge the meat didn't work, the doctor had inserted her entire, mercifully tiny hand down Cynthia's throat to wrench out the obstructive piece of ostrich steak. When she regained consciousness Cynthia joked, through stifled sobs, that she should have stuck to the soup.

And just 18 months after the end of our year of almost dying dangerously, we got another reminder that death takes staycations too. On 7 July 2005, Graham's birthday, four separate suicide attacks took place in London, not far from where we both worked. Fifty-two innocent people lost their lives in the worst single terrorist atrocity on British soil.

Graham and I knew by now that there was nothing to

prevent death, like a faithful puppy, following us home. And in October 2017 it did. The spectre of death moved in permanently, like an unwelcome house guest who burns cigarette holes in your furniture, walks their muddy feet all over your cream carpets and leaves a scummy tidemark in your bath. Graham's lung cancer diagnosis turned our entire world upside down.

Life would never be the same. But that was October 2017, 14 years in the future. First, we both had to survive 2003, and *that* wasn't going to be easy.

Popping frogs
Burma

Sign on arrival at Rangoon Airport: 'The following are illegal: guns, drugs, pornography and playing cards.' Sign on leaving Rangoon Airport: 'It is illegal to export taped music and videos.' A strange country it is that won't permit playing cards to enter and recorded music to leave.

Burma in 2003 was making international headlines because of the continued house arrest of opposition leader Aung San Suu Kyi, who'd urged tourists to stay away because visiting would serve to legitimise and prop up the military junta. We decided to go there anyway. We could salve our consciences by not putting money into the coffers of the repressive government by staying in guesthouses rather than hotels and using privately owned transport. The many Burmese who spontaneously thanked us for visiting reassured us that we'd made the right decision.

In the airport arrivals hall we were approached by Mr Min, a representative of Golden Trip tour agency.

'*Mingalaba.* Welcome to Burma. From where have you come? Ah, England. Very lovely. I have tours of Burma I wish to show you.'

After a decade of backpacking, we'd lost our fear of touts

and listened with interest to what Mr Min had to offer. It became immediately clear that his proposed two-week itinerary included twice as many destinations than we'd have been able to see if we'd used buses to get around. What's more, even though it was a tailor-made private tour and included a driver and a guide it only cost US$500. For all three of us, not per person.

'What's to discuss?' asked Lisa's sister Loren, who'd flown in from South Africa to join us.

We signed on the dotted line and told Mr Min that we'd like to be collected first thing in two days' time as we didn't need transport or a guide while in Rangoon. With our tour arranged, Mr Min dropped us off at our guesthouse where we showered before hailing a taxi to take us to Shwedagon, Burma's most sacred Buddhist pagoda. Like so many vehicles on the capital's roads the taxi was a wreck without interior door panels and had a lengthy crack across the windscreen in front of the driver, who therefore drove with his head displaced several inches to the right in order to see better.

'I bet his chiropractor sees a lot of him,' I quipped.

Alighting from the taxi, Loren was accosted by a man holding out three small wood-and-wire cages of trapped birds to buy and release.

'For good luck,' he said. 'Cheap.'

'Is he saying "cheap" as in price, or "cheep" as in the sound birds make?' asked Loren, already taken with the idea of buying and freeing a small bird. 'Okay, one,' she said, searching through her money belt and pulling out a couple of 1,000 *kyat* notes before pointing to the cage holding his more colourfully plumed stock.

He held out the other cage: Loren had paid enough to choose one of its tiny mousey-brown prisoners. Reaching in with both hands and cupping the nearest chirruping occupant, she drew it out and, after peering more closely at it through the space between her thumbs, opened her hands.

'Good karma, good karma,' the seller intoned as the bird,

without a moment's hesitation, flitted skywards and darted over the roof of the nearest building.

'Yeah, good karma for you, Loren,' I said. 'Never mind that the vendor is going to be reincarnated as a crap-covered cockroach for trapping and caging that bird in the first place. When he runs low on birds to sell, he'll go and capture more and the whole cycle of "karma" will be repeated.'

Sited atop a hill, Shwedagon Pagoda dominates Rangoon's skyline. No wonder Rudyard Kipling, visiting in 1889, described his first glimpse of the giant pagoda as 'a golden mystery upheaved… on the horizon, a beautiful winking wonder that blazed in the sun'. Up close, Shwedagon disappeared from view the moment you entered one of the covered stairways leading up to the central terrace. Stepping out from the shade into its open plaza was like walking into a sunbeam-suffused religious poster: the intense sunshine reflected off the 99m-tall gold stupa and white marble was dazzling and migraine inducing.

Surrounding the immense bell-shaped stupa, built to house four sacred Buddhist relics, were dozens of ornate golden temples and sentry box-like shrines congregated around its base like supplicating worshippers. The plaza thronged with barefoot visitors leaving offerings of fruit and cigarettes at the feet of Buddha statues as red-robed monks holding scarlet bamboo parasols padded quietly by. One devotee, his face prune-wrinkled and nut-brown, was on his knees, fingering his prayer beads, staring directly into the sun. We didn't know if he was blind from looking at the sun or could look at the sun because he was blind. Either way, he was blind.

What we found most compelling about the sacred space, however, was the way the Burmese, though always respectful, used it as a place for courtship, a venue to socialise or simply somewhere to have a snooze. In no way stuffy or serious, Shwedagon was sublime.

When Golden Trip's van arrived to pick us up it was driven

by Nanda, who sported knock-off Ray-Ban Aviator sunglasses and a very fetching gold incisor. He was accompanied by Tonton, an unassuming man who nonetheless proved to be a very able guide with a deep affection for his country's history and culture. Lisa instructed Tonton to tell Nanda, who couldn't speak English, that he should drive 'safely and slowly', leading Nanda to mime driving safely and slowly… before miming crashing. Oh, how we love mime, the lingua franca of travellers and clowns the world over. Every time Nanda stopped the van, he found a woman to flirt with. Even at traffic lights he would roll down his window, flash a very flashy smile and deploy his smoothest chat-up lines on passing female pedestrians. 'Do you believe in love at first sight, or should I drive by again?' we imagined him crooning.

The first stop on our tour involved driving 200km to Kyaiktiyo Pagoda, Burma's third most important Buddhist shrine. The last few kilometres of road were too steep for our minivan, so once Nanda had dropped us off we had to endure a bouncy, bone-breaking trip aboard a rickety truck driven by a driver who seemed dead set on getting us there in record time. It was stiflingly humid and the uncomfortable wooden benches were set too close together so our knees slammed into the back of the bench in front each time the truck hit a pothole or bounced over a rock.

'One really bad bump and both of my legs will be broken,' griped Lisa who begged to be given the money to sit upfront in the cab with the driver. That cost twice as much, so I refused. The elderly, one-eyed man beside me kept intoning 'Brake, brake,' squeezing my knee in emphasis, as if I had access to the pedal or that this would somehow make the vehicle slow down.

The road ended at the bottom of a hill. Loren instantly caved in to the blandishments of the palanquin touts and was ceremoniously carried, reclining on cushions like the Queen of Sheba, up towards the hilltop pagoda. Lisa and I are made of tougher stuff, so we proceeded to walk up. It turned out to be a long, hot, sticky and sweaty trudge in the company of a gaggle of palanquin bearers who wanted to be our 'ambulance bus'. Repeatedly saying 'Very hot, sir, you tired, sit, sit down madam, very hot,' they persisted almost to the top, where Loren waited for us, sitting smugly in the shade.

'What took you guys so long?' she teased.

'Loren, we did it the hard way, so we'd appreciate it all the more,' I replied.

'Piss off, Loren,' was all Lisa could muster by way of retort.

The shrine was spectacular, positioned on the top of a golden boulder perched precariously on a gigantic granite rock. A helpful pilgrim told us that men were allowed to approach the boulder, but not women, as 'men have power, ladies don't have power'. He obviously hadn't heard of the Spice Girls. Male pilgrims were rubbing fresh gold leaf onto the boulder and, as we walked around the base below it, the discarded pink and yellow backing papers were lifted by the wind and fluttered down on us like confetti.

As we walked back down we passed a stall that in South Africa would be called a *muti* or traditional medicine shop. On a low table was heaped a mound of centipedes, bear paws, snakeskin and monkey skulls. At the base of the grisly pile was a trough of evil-smelling scum that had emanated from, and filtered through the pyramid of animal parts. We deduced that the *muti* must work like this: the cure is worse than the complaint, so people don't get sick so they don't have to drink the noxious concoction. No one was buying this miracle medicine-with-no-name, so it must work.

By the time we arrived at Inle Lake, Loren had come over all peculiar and retired to her room. She had a rough night, vomiting, aching all over and with her joints feeling as though they'd been cracked open. 'Bone break disease,' diagnosed Tonton. It seemed an apt description. Skipping breakfast, we took Loren to see the nearest doctor. He spoke no English, and in his dispensary – a room that was both untidy and filthy

– were open bottles of pills and a basket of syringes and medical waste. Minutes later Loren clambered back into the van, the aches in her bones having miraculously disappeared. Frightened by what the remedy might involve, Loren's body had obviously taken the decision to heal itself. The placebo effect works in mysterious ways.

Nga Phe Kyaung Monastery aka Jumping Cat Monastery, built on stilts above Inle Lake, looked dilapidated, its dark woodenness giving the impression that it had seen much better days. Its interior, however, was pristine, and looked like the inside of an ornate wooden jewellery box decorated with gold. My stomach was also a bit iffy that day, so I asked for directions to the loo: a Burmese teak seat over a hole six feet above the water. What the lake's fishermen, renowned for powering their shallow canoes standing up using one leg to row, must have thought every time they heard it flush, I didn't know. Hopefully, it was 'Oh goody, more food for the fish' and not 'Oh no, another bloody visitor to Jumping Cat Monastery polluting our workplace.'

The monks served us tea and nuts as we sat cross-legged on the teak floor. A dozen or so cats and kittens prowled around and lay curled up asleep among the donation boxes and Buddhas in decorative glass cases.

'This is the Jumping Cat Monastery?' asked Lisa.

The monk nodded. We sipped our tea and waited.

'So there are cats who jump here?'

The monk nodded slowly again. We waited.

'*When* will the cats be jumping?'

'Any time,' the monk replied.

We waited some more.

'Can we see the cats jumping, please?' Lisa plucked up the courage to ask.

Finally taking the hint, the monk rounded up a black cat, bribed it with cat snacks and it jumped up and through the plastic hoop he held out. The cat repeated the trick three times before sauntering off in that disdainful manner cats have perfected. Show over.

Back on the road, passing through a nondescript town, Nanda suddenly pulled into a driveway and turned off the engine. Turning in his seat to face us, Tonton asked: 'Would you like to go to a Burmese wedding?'

'What, *now*?' I asked, looking quizzically at Lisa and Loren.

'Yes, now. There is a wedding going on here and you can see it if you like.'

'But I haven't done my hair,' I protested.

We weren't dressed in our finest glad rags, but Tonton assured us that our attire would not be an issue. Nor the fact that we hadn't been invited. Gate-crashing is completely socially acceptable in Burma, he told us.

The bride, radiant in pink, and the groom, handsome in white, welcomed us effusively and pressed plates loaded high with chicken biryani and green rice into our hands. As we ate, we chatted to the wedding planner, a camp gentleman sporting two large diamond earrings.

'It was me who organised all the decoration and beauty,' he said proudly.

'Well, you've done a wonderful job,' complimented Loren.

'So kind. Now, please come and be photographed with the wedding couple.'

To thank the bride and groom for their hospitality we presented them with a box of Scottish shortbread and a bottle of Guerlain perfume, Lisa's gifts to Loren hastily repurposed. I also slipped a few dollars to the assorted musicians who had gamely hacked and scraped at their instruments to produce an atonal layered screech.

A day later we arrived in Mandalay and asked Tonton to book tickets for us to attend the Mandalay Marionettes Theatre. Lisa suggested all three of us should have a pampering session before going out so, against my better judgement, the sisters cajoled me into smearing my feet with various girly products, such as mint toe-jam remover, wart varnish and bunion elixir. I partook reluctantly. And it wasn't too much longer before I was wishing I'd stuck to my guns rather than tempting fate.

Leaving for the theatre in a blacked-out city, we'd got one block from the guesthouse and crossed one road before I stepped into an open stormwater channel. I was covered in filth up to my knees, my right shin was scraped to the bone and my big toe was sliced open. A nearby traffic policeman who'd seen me fall rushed unbidden from his sentry box, torch in hand, to assist me, washing my wounded toe with his drinking water, after which I limped back to our guesthouse trailing blood.

Lisa couldn't cope with the sight of my wounds, so Loren had to lift the flesh flap on my toe to disinfect it with vodka, the only antiseptic we had to hand. The rest of the bottle we drank mixed with cream soda.

We went to see the puppets the next night, my big toe now held together with a plaster. The show programme proclaimed: 'Our desire is to give you a memorable glimpse into a dying art, which we hope will once again find its popular place in the entertaining world.'

Performed by five puppet masters to music from a five-piece orchestra, the show was outstanding, but we were saddened to see that we were three of only five paying patrons. It must be psychologically hard to perform before such a small audience and the performers deserved better. The tourist boycott of Burma was taking a heavy toll.

After the show we stopped at a beer station where we ate grilled pork and drank beer until Lisa's face turned as ruddy as a red-arsed monkey's arse. At that moment she became a tipsy embarrassment and we led her back to our hotel.

We departed Mandalay by ferry at 5.30am for the nine-hour journey to Bagan, leaving Nanda and Tonton to make their way there by road. Sleeping Burmese were sprawled across the deck; it was too early for them, too. Sitting on the bare deck boards because the few chairs were taken, we watched people going about their business on the riverbank. A young mother laboriously laundering by hand at the river's edge waved to us while her naked child, covered head to foot in suds, squinted through the lather clinging to his face. Mid-afternoon a middle-aged hawker in a ruby-red sarong-like *longyi* came aboard with a bamboo basket of chicken samosas on her head. After selling us some, she persuaded Loren to have a massage, leading her by the hand inside. Loren reappeared 30 minutes later, beaming.

'That was wonderful,' she said to Lisa. 'You must have a massage. I'll treat you.'

Lisa assented, and on her return joined Loren in trying to persuade me to have one too. Something was not right. After the foot-pampering fiasco, and being no fool, I resisted. Eventually, Lisa divulged that she'd lain face down on the hard, dirty floor and laughed hysterically through clenched teeth as the woman went to work on her, chatting in Burmese all the while.

'It was agonising. Like being repeatedly pinched by a spiteful monkey. But not wanting to embarrass myself, or offend her, I didn't scream even though I dearly wanted to.'

Nanda and Tonton were waiting for us at Bagan pier to take us to May Kha Lar Guest House. Outside, tears rolling down her dust-encrusted face, sat Miriam. A young French solo traveller, she told us she was utterly exhausted. Due to a lack of transport she'd been stuck in the countryside, had hitched rides with goods vehicles and had been refused passage on a local ferry. She'd travel one day, rest the next day to recover from the punishing journey and, if she was lucky, go sightseeing on the third day. Miriam related a very touching story of how, in a rural town, a woman had taken pity on her. She'd given her a sunhat, applied *thanaka* paste to her face to protect it against sunburn and had escorted her around town so that Miriam would be seen to have a friend. In Miriam's 28 days in Burma she was going to see much less than we would in our 12. There but for the grace of Mr Min and

US$500 went we.

Lisa invited Miriam to join us in touring the Bagan plain by bicycle, but she said she was too tired and needed to sleep. We pedalled off on our own, riding three hired Chinese clunkers. On the way my bike's rear tyre burst with an audible pop and had to be abandoned, so I hid it out of sight behind a wall. Reduced to two bikes between three people, Loren uncomplainingly rode side-saddle on the metal parcel rack on her bike as I pedalled and we reached the plain in the late afternoon, just as a group of shaven-headed monks walked by, as if on cue for a photo shoot.

Climbing to the top of one of the pagodas, we sat in contemplative silence as Bagan's 2,200 Buddhist temples, stupas and pagodas glowed pink and orange while tendrils of mist rose from the Irrawaddy River to slowly envelop them. Nothing stirred as the huge orb of the sun slashed streaks of saffron across the sky before sinking out of view across the ancient landscape.

Dramatic sunset over, we hastened back to our bikes to start cycling back. Retrieving my crock bike from where I'd left it, I held onto its handlebar with one hand and steered Loren's with the other, pedalling like crazy to maintain momentum so that Loren and I wouldn't topple over. It was hardly elegant, but it beat walking. Cycling in what was now the moonless dark, Lisa continually trilled her bell to indicate our presence to pedestrians and hoped that any oncoming cars would be using their headlights.

Pop!

'Aw, shit Loren. We've had another bloody puncture. It sounded like it came from the front tyre.'

I stopped, reached over the handlebars and pinched the tyre. The pressure was good. I asked Loren to get off the rack so that I could check the rear tyre. It was fine.

'Oh, well. No damage seems to have been done. Let's go.'

Five metres later there was another clear popping sound. Again, it came from the front wheel.

'I heard it that time,' confirmed Loren.

I repeated the procedure, pinching first the front and then the rear tyre.

'Nope, nothing. Both tyres are good. It's a mystery what's causing the sound.'

'Mystery indeed,' echoed Loren. 'If we hear it again let's just keep going. If we do get a flat tyre we won't get far anyway.'

'True that, Lol.'

I stood on the pedals, using my body weight to shift us as quickly as possible from a stationary start to something approximating a stable speed.

'There! I heard it again!' exclaimed Loren.

I'd heard it too and pedalled on.

Pop!

'And there!'

There were two more pops in quick succession, one from the front and one from under Loren. I wasn't going to stop because the bike was handling just dandy.

'We're getting close to town,' I informed Loren. 'I can see streetlights ahead.'

In less than a minute – a minute punctuated by several more distinct pops – the better-lit road revealed the grim truth: we'd been riding through hundreds of coat-button-sized frogs crossing the tarmac, and those unfortunates we'd ridden over had burst under the weight of our wheels with the sound of invisible sommeliers pulling corks.

Back in Bagan the streets were clogged with cyclists and, not far from our guesthouse, a stranger rode up alongside Lisa, who'd gone on ahead, and began quizzing her.

'You come from Mandalay?'

'Yes,' said Lisa politely, barely looking at the man as she concentrated on steering through the melee.

'You stay in Sabai Phyu Guesthouse?'

'Yes. At least I think so. I can't remember.'

'You two English and one South African?'

'Yes…' replied Lisa, now mildly alarmed that he seemed to

know so much about us.

'In Mandalay, you pay two nights, stay three.'

'No we didn't,' said Lisa defensively.

The man pulled away and disappeared into the throng. Back at May Kha Lar, Lisa related the disconcerting conversation. I assured her that we'd paid, and Loren and I retired upstairs to our room while Lisa stayed at reception to report the puncture. As she was talking to the manager, the stranger – a young man dressed, as all Burmese men seemed to be, in an ankle-length *longyi*, short-sleeved shirt and flip-flops – reappeared and repeated his allegation that we'd failed to pay for all of our accommodation in Mandalay. Lisa now knew full well we'd paid, but as we hadn't been issued with a receipt couldn't prove it.

'I need to fetch my husband. He'll be able to sort this out.'

When Lisa came to the room, I refused to go down.

'We've done nothing wrong, and if he needs to speak to me then he can jolly well come up here.'

'Graham, you can be a stubborn so-and-so when you want to be. I don't want to be here when that man comes knocking on our door. I'm going to have a shower.'

'Lisa, you can be such a nervous ninny,' taunted Loren.

When the knock on the door came, I accompanied the stranger downstairs.

'Please call the Mandalay guesthouse,' I asked the manager, 'and tell the owner there that I paid the money to the night watchman who let us in when we returned late from the puppet show.'

A lengthy phone conversation in Burmese ensued. I was starting to lose hope that we'd be able to amicably resolve the disagreement when the manager put the phone in its cradle and informed the stranger that our story checked out.

I went up to our room. Lisa and Loren looked pale and anxious. I had on my most sombre face.

'Do you think he's from the secret police?' asked a nervous Lisa. 'I don't fancy rotting in a Burmese jail.'

Loren joined in. 'How did he track us down? That's really scary. The regime must have been following our every move: it must have spies *everywhere*.'

Sensing the opportunity for a bit of fun at their expense, I told them that our presence was required at the police station.

'No!' they groaned in unison. 'Seriously?'

'He said we should bring some clean clothes.'

Anticipating a long and uncomfortable night in a cell, the girls hurriedly packed their daypacks. As Lisa opened the door to go downstairs, I burst out laughing.

'I was joking,' I confessed. 'I've managed to sort it all out.'

Lisa threw a curse at me and Loren a pair of socks.

'And I wouldn't worry too much about that man being a member of the secret police. We've only encountered 10 other tourists during this entire trip, so it couldn't have been *that* hard to find us.'

I'd never seen a dead body before, so to come across eight a few miles outside Rangoon sent me into shock: my thoughts slowed to the same crawling pace as our minivan as it carefully edged past the harrowing scene. I looked into a dead boy's eyes – but he wasn't looking back; he was staring through me at the cloudless sky beyond, spreadeagled on the tarmac, naked from the waist down. I suppressed the urge to rush from our van and cover him. Fifteen feet away, a man hugged the steering wheel of his truck, as if cradling a child, his broken face dripping blood into the footwell. Six other people, in grotesque poses, lay scattered in the road. I felt guilty for looking but couldn't bring myself to turn away. None of the bystanders were moving, paralysed by the tragedy they'd just been witness to.

'Oh no, that's terrible, I feel awful, I can't believe it,' said Loren sympathetically, her hands held to her mouth.

'I think the truck was trying to do a U-turn and got hit by that car,' said Tonton quietly. 'I'd ask Nanda to stop, but I don't think there's anything we can do to help – it looks like there's a policeman already here – and if we don't get back to Rangoon you'll miss your flight.'

I nodded, too upset to say anything. It was a sight I wanted to unsee. And the reason I'd insisted on a van with seatbelts. Only I'd relented when Mr Min told me his tour company didn't have any vehicles with seatbelts in the back, saying I could sit next to Nanda if I really wanted to strap myself in. Lisa and I have always thought of the front passenger seat as the 'suicide seat' in countries where we don't trust the driving, so we'd taken our chances in the back.

Had our minivan's air filter not developed the fault that forced us to limp the last miles back to Rangoon, I thought grimly, it could have been Lisa, Loren and me lying lifeless on that crossroad.

The Jesus nut
Kashmir

'The most dangerous place on earth,' US President Clinton called it three years before I went there. Bill was referring to the 740km-long Line of Control in Kashmir separating two hostile nations, armed to the teeth, squaring off over divided territory they both believe to be exclusively theirs. Since 1947 India and Pakistan have gone to war three times over Kashmir. Like Michael Douglas and Kathleen Turner in *The War of the Roses*, Pakistan and India are a (nuclear-armed) warring couple each trying desperately and sometimes violently to evict the other from the family home. Tourists are not welcome, so not many people go there, or even want to.

On the Pakistan side, permission to visit can only be granted by the Pakistan Army and one needs to have a good reason, or be a VIP, to get it. I'm no VIP, but in 2003 I was invited to travel there as the Pakistan analyst and 'bag carrier' for the UK's Chief of Defence Intelligence (CDI). At the time, the Line of Control was pretty 'hot' – a term that, in typical civil service understatement, was more appropriate to describing chutney than what was actually happening on the ground, where the Indian and Pakistani armies were shooting and shelling and killing one another's soldiers on a daily basis. They had been doing so for several years. I'd kept a concerned eye on it from the safety of London for quite some time; now I was going to see this war zone up close.

There are two ways to get to the Line of Control. By road from Islamabad or by air. There was no way that the CDI's gracious Pakistani hosts were going to subject him to three-and-a-half hours of chunder-inducing, winding roads in a Land Rover. He would fly in President Pervez Musharraf's private helicopter, his version of Marine One which whisks POTUS (the US President) and FLOTUS (the First Lady) around Washington and the world.

Because I'm a very nervous flyer I would have preferred to take the road route, even if I'd had to quietly barf into my briefcase. When a plane flies straight and smooth, like oil on glass, I'm calm, but if it encounters even the slightest turbulence then I transmogrify into an agitated, irrational wreck desperate to clutch the nearest hand for reassurance. Even if said hand belongs to a stranger, a member of cabin crew or God forbid the Chief of Defence Intelligence.

I'd never flown in a helicopter before, so this added a new dimension of fear to the flying experience. It also didn't help when Lisa, whom I hoped would put my mind at rest as she's a fearless flyer and is oblivious to turbulence, tactlessly agreed I was right to dread the prospect. 'I hated the five-minute helicopter ride I took over Manhattan so much that I pleaded with the pilot to let me off,' she reminded me. 'It was like being in the saddle of a bucking bronco, and I gripped my sister's leg so hard the whole time that I left five yellow-green bruises on her thigh.'

Our small entourage pulled into the helicopter base outside Islamabad. Nestled in the lee of the beautiful Margalla Hills,

Pakistan's modern capital looked to me deceptively like the sort of sleepy, leafy, low-rise city where nothing much happens and where excitement is measured in units of torpor. In fact, it is a heaving hotbed of divisive politics, religious enmities and occasionally spectacular violence. In 2015 the city's Capital Development Authority voted Islamabad the second most beautiful capital in the world, after London and ahead of Berlin. The CDA chose the criteria. It's not a 'crapital' but by any *objective* criteria Islamabad would *not* rank in the top 50.

The Super Puma was parked on one of the concrete helipads. It gleamed bright green in the morning sunshine. It wasn't new, but it looked it. Knowing that it was the President's personal transport took the fear factor down a notch. 'They're not going to polish the President's private chopper but forget to service it,' I told myself. As we walked up to it, I sized it up. It was larger in all dimensions than I'd imagined. Could four slim rotors really keep all that heavy metal airborne?

CDI climbed the steps, sat back in one of the sumptuous leather seats, buckled in and placed the headset hanging from a hook above him over his ears. He knew what he was doing. My palms were clammy as I imitated him. If this bird was going to spiral from the sky then I was going to die in style – albeit quite without dignity as I would scream and wail the whole way down. I looked around in vain for the flight safety instructions and wondered whether I was supposed to adopt the same brace position I would in a crashing plane. I didn't know any helicopter survival tips of the 'count the number of seats to the emergency exit' kind that airlines recommend, or the 'clamber over the seats and heads of passengers in front to get the hell out' sort the airlines don't go public with.

The engine started with a low whine and the rotors, indolently at first, began to turn. The whine picked up in pitch until it became a deafening howl. Now the headphones made sense. The helicopter rose slowly and unsteadily a few feet above the helipad before moving forward as it ascended. The sense of movement was disconcerting, as though we were swinging like a plumb line from an unfixed point.

No doubt noticing how tense I was, CDI came on the intercom: 'Have you flown in a helicopter before, Graham?'

Not looking at him, I shook my head.

'Don't worry. If the engine fails, the helicopter is designed to descend under control. The rotors will keep turning and provide some lift.'

Yeah, right. *Some* lift, but not enough to prevent about five tonnes of helicopter and us coming down hard, which would really spoil everyone's day.

And what if, catastrophically, the rotors came off? My mind turned to the hexagonal nut holding them to the body of the helicopter. Known as the 'Jesus nut', if this small component failed then the overhead rotor blades would detach, the chopper would drop like a stone and the next person the occupants would meet would be Jesus. I prayed the mechanics had tightened it.

Or re-attached it. Apparently, sometime, somewhere, a pilot and his mechanic took their helicopter for a test flight after servicing it and, 200m above ground, the rotor flew off. Air-crash investigators found the Jesus nut on the lid of the mechanic's toolbox. It's probably apocryphal, but for those of us with a flying phobia it's a morbidly compelling story.

Twenty-five tense minutes later the chopper swooped into Muzaffarabad, passing over the horseshoe-shaped bend in the Jhelum River that's a dead ringer for the Thames's Isle of Dogs in the opening credits of *EastEnders*, and landed in a military base. I'd have been thrilled had Pat Butcher, decked out in overlarge parrot-perch earrings and bottle tan, greeted us and led us to the Queen Vic for a nerve-steadying lager, but we were met instead by a crisply turned-out brigadier. His unlined face suggested that front-line command came naturally to, and agreed with, him. He struck me as an officer who'd done well and was destined to go far. He vigorously shook our hands and ushered us to his vehicle, where his driver and two armed soldiers waited to take us to the Line.

As we drove the 50km to the border village of Chakothi, the brigadier, a man tuned to 'transmit' rather than 'receive', related in an unbroken monologue the Pakistani version of the history of Kashmir. His was a dark tale of Indian perfidy, contrasted with the nobility of Pakistan's cause and the valiant role of the Army in seeking justice for the oppressed Muslims on the Indian side. All in all, it was rather tiresome, but I reasoned that had we been on the other side in the company of an Indian brigadier, then we'd have heard similarly unsubtle anti-Pakistan propaganda.

At the army base just beyond Chakothi, we were invited into a large tent, seated on fold-away chairs and served lukewarm Lipton's tea and teeth-dissolving sweetmeats by an imposing, bearded sergeant. In England, such delicacies are the dentist's friend; in South Asia they are considered one of the food groups. The brigadier, quite unselfconsciously, repeated his well-rehearsed narrative of Kashmir, now illustrated by innumerable pie charts and bar graphs of statistics as a silent major dutifully turned the flipchart on cue like a well-rehearsed magician's assistant. Again, his polished spiel majored on the illegality of India's occupation of Kashmir and the Indian Army's history of human rights abuses. It was always the Indians who started the shooting and the shelling, and it was always the Indians who deliberately targeted civilians.

Knowing better than to comment in a way that might endorse Pakistan's position, CDI instead asked diplomatically anodyne questions such as how many soldiers served on the Line and how long their tours of duty were.

'Thank you for listening to this brief,' concluded the brigadier. 'If you do not have any more questions – or are not in need of more refreshments – please, if you will follow me, we will proceed to the front line.'

We rose to our feet and the brigadier led us from the tent,

followed by his two guards who'd waited outside. We walked down a dozen wood-propped steps into a trench and zig-zagged our way to a frankly insubstantial bunker where we peered through the firing slit. By calling it the 'front line' the brigadier had given the impression there would be a visible, demarcated boundary separating the two sides. There was nothing of the sort. No fence, no barbed wire, no cleared ground. The Berlin Wall this was not. All I could see was thick greenery running riot up the steeply sloped hills ahead. I certainly couldn't see any Indian soldiers, not even when I peered attentively through binoculars. I asked where the Indians were.

'They are ahead of us and above us,' the brigadier replied, sweeping his right arm from right to left in an expansive arc.

Behind each and every tree and bush there could be an Indian soldier. I imagined Birnam Wood marching on Macbeth's army in Dunsinane.

'Here, they can see us better than we are able to see them. From their vantage point on the opposite heights they can shoot down at anything that moves on this side.' I took that to include us.

Without notice the brigadier exited the bunker, climbed out of the trench and stood nonchalantly, hands on hips, facing the enemy. He presented a clear target, and it would have been so easy for an Indian sniper to take the shot or a machine gun to cut him down. He swivelled about and motioned for CDI and me to follow his example. I could see how it would end: CDI would get a laudatory obituary in *The Times*, the brigadier would be venerated as a *shaheed* (martyr) and Lisa would have to pay for my body to be brought home and wait 20 years to get half my insubstantial pension.

No one was shooting, so after hesitating for a moment, CDI stepped from the trench. That forced my hand and, drawing a breath – not, I hoped, my last – I summoned the courage to join him. It was perfectly quiet. Nothing stirred. We could have been three ornithologists hoping to catch sight of a pair of long-legged buzzards as we stood on the forward edge of a 'hot' Line of Control, in plain view of I-don't-know-how-many concealed Indian soldiers.

As we gazed across no man's land – one high-ranking Pakistan Army officer, one top-ranking British officer and me, a very junior civil servant with the lingering taste of sickly sweetmeats in his mouth – a hand suddenly shot up and waved from an invisible trench not more than 30 yards away, and a disembodied voice called out, 'Hello! Welcome!'

The Indians were *that* close. We hello-ed and waved back and two helmet-topped faces, each flashing a broad smile, popped up from the trench.

'We radioed the Indians you were coming and that they mustn't shoot,' explained our host. 'You are not their enemy.'

It was all perfectly, misleadingly normal, a moment of bonhomie in an otherwise unpredictable, violence-wracked landscape. The 'holiday' from the business of choreographed violence that our visit delivered to that small sector of the Line of Control may have lasted only until we were out of earshot, but I'm sure that the soldiers on both sides were grateful for even an hour when they were safe.

The peasants are revolting
Bolivia

'At 13,300ft, the air at El Alto International Airport in La Paz is so thin that planes have to land at a much higher speed because they'd fall out of the sky otherwise,' reported our guidebook, causing me to spend the entire landing willing the plane to stay airborne. Probably not the most logical thing to do when an aircraft's trying to land. This is something I usually reserve for take-offs, when I use the sheer force of my will to levitate the plane into the sky. Though the science of lift has been explained to me many times, when it comes to getting something as weighty as an Airbus airborne I still think a bit of positive thinking on the part of its passengers can't hurt. I was a little disappointed, then, to find that the landing was like any other, except that the lack of air pressure caused my deodorant's rollerball to pop out and cover the contents of my rucksack in sweet-smelling slime.

Graham and I spent our first two days in La Paz eating llama steaks and drinking coca tea. Llamas look nicer than they taste, the opposite of monkfish which taste better than they look. We learned three things about coca tea: it's legal in Bolivia, it can ease the symptoms of altitude sickness and it tastes absolutely foul. Our other activity, when not eating and drinking, was trying not to die in the Posada del Angel's dodgy 'electric chair' shower, the wires of which dangled into the stream of water giving us a short but unnerving shock each time we touched the tap.

After acclimatising, it was time to hit the sights. At the Museo de la Coca, whose 'message' was a dissonant blend of anti-drug rhetoric and pro-coca-leaf propaganda, we learned that it takes up to 600kg of coca leaves to make 1kg of cocaine and that, allegedly, coca-leaf extract is still used to flavour Coca-Cola. Even if it's true – and the company denies that it is – drinking Coca-Cola will turn you into a 110kg Type 2 diabetic long before it induces a narcotic high. The museum also informed us that none other than Sigmund Freud was the first cocaine user. Only he wasn't, though he did conduct a lot of research into the use of cocaine to, of all things, cure his morphine addiction. It was while returning from the museum that someone – in a portent of what was to come – threw a pebble at me. Far from being alarmed, I was slightly flattered. In Bolivia it's a sign of flirtation: at harvest time, young women dress up in their finery and men throw small stones at them to attract their attention.

'I'm looking rather rugged today,' teased Graham. 'How can you be sure it wasn't aimed at me?'

A stone's throw from our hotel was one of La Paz's top tourist sites: *Mercado de Hechicería*, the Witches' Market, run by women in small black bowler hats rather than big pointy ones. Here the modern occultist could purchase anything they'd need for potions and spells, including coca leaves, dried frogs and animal skins. We stopped at a stall piled high with the dried llama foetuses that Bolivians bury in the foundations of new buildings as a way of asking Mother Earth for protection. As a pretext for taking photos we bought a travel talisman, a small glass bottle filled with a clear liquid, strips of coloured plastic and two metal amulets in the shape of a bus and a couple copulating. As she painstakingly wound a piece of pink llama wool around the bottle's neck the witch, a fresh-faced Aymara woman with jet-black, centre-parted hair, explained that it would keep us safe on our journeys. Or that's what we thought she was saying – we can't speak Spanish, so she may well have been putting a curse on us. At that moment, only vaguely aware of the increasingly tense political situation in Bolivia, and thinking only of how best to capture our spooky souvenir on film, we had no idea how much we'd be needing that lucky charm.

Early next morning we caught a bus to Uyuni, a small town in southwest Bolivia, where we wandered around the nearby steam-locomotive graveyard before grabbing an outdoor table on the village square and ordering bowls of taste-free quinoa gruel. Uyuni is the jumping-off point for four-wheel-drive tours of the Salar de Uyuni, a vast salt lake. Driving across its sun-cracked surface was like speeding into Narnia, except it wasn't snowy and the 'trees' were 1,200-year-old cacti clustered atop low hillocks peppered like islands in a perfectly flat 'sea' of blinding white salt.

Our driver Juan didn't think that being personable was part of his job description. He made it very clear that he had three things, and only three things, to do each day: drive the Toyota – the potholed, boulder-strewn road did require a fair bit of concentration; exhort us to hurry up – Juan said '*vamos*' as often as Graham says I say 'basically'; and point out the wildlife – which, on a salt flat and surrounding barren mountains, was hardly abundant. In effect, Juan alerted us to the one animal to be seen. Every half hour or so he'd slam on the brakes to bring the Toyota to a juddering stop, point through the windscreen with a gnarled index finger and solemnly announce 'vicuna'.

Looking at the long-necked woolly animals he was referring to, we'd ask in unison, 'Llama?'

'Vicuna,' he'd repeat.

Only later did we learn that llamas are common, but vicunas, believed to be the wild ancestor of domesticated alpacas, really are rare. They produce an extremely fine wool that commands top prices as they can only be shorn every three years, and have to be chased through the scrub and caught first. Juan could have told us this at the time, but that would've been a fourth item on his 'to do' list.

Over the four days of our tour we saw stratified mountains that looked as if they'd been crafted from layers of multicoloured bath salts, volcanoes blowing smoke rings into the clear blue sky, gushing geysers and pits farting sulphurous mud. We also saw two otherworldly lakes, each nestled at the foot of a volcano. Laguna Colorada, the reddish colour of a rusty oil drum shot through with lilac streaks, was home to podgy flamingos who, buffeted by the cold gale-force winds, performed a weird aerobics-style sidestep while feeding in the shallows. Laguna Verde was a Caribbean-turquoise colour, an effect created by wind whipping up sediment from the lake bottom. We were high when we saw them – 14,000 feet above sea level to be precise – but neither of us had been chomping coca leaves or snorting Bolivian marching powder.

After a disappointing dinner of stringy chicken and chips, we caught the night bus from Uyuni back to La Paz, intending to travel on from there to Lake Titicaca, where we planned to end our trip. About two hours beyond Oruro, the driver's erratic swerving woke us from our fitful slumbers. Dawn had broken so we could see he was coursing the bus around piles of rubble in the road. Shortly after, he pulled into a field, turned off the engine and instructed everyone to disembark.

We didn't need to speak Spanish to know that this was the end of the road and that the bus had stopped for good. It wasn't hard to see why: buses with smashed windows and shattered windscreens surrounded ours, and the highway ahead was liberally strewn with chunks of concrete, hacked-down advertising hoardings, tyres, burned tyre remains, ceramic sinks and toilets and a few odd shoes for good measure. It was like a plane crash scene, without the bodies.

The rumours of insurrection we'd been hearing over the past few days had been true. The *campesinos* (peasant farmers) had been so angered by plans to sell natural gas to the US that they were making good on their vow to bring the capital to a standstill by blocking all access roads. Two things had angered them. The first was that a meagre 18 per cent of profits would accrue to Bolivia, yet another example of foreign exploitation that had started with 16th-century Spaniards looting its silver and gold. The second was the government's choice of Chile as the country through which the gas would be exported. Bolivia had never forgiven Chile for the 1884 land grab that resulted in the loss of 400km of coastline and turned it into a landlocked nation. This loss, following the War of the Pacific, was so keenly felt that, 119 years after the event, Bolivians still celebrated a Day of the Sea on 23 March every year to mark their country's continued determination to reclaim what it sees as its rightful access to the ocean. The present government's decision, therefore, was the political equivalent of allowing a malicious neighbour who'd appropriated your entire front garden to charge you a hefty toll for the privilege of accessing the pavement.

We had no idea where we were, but everyone we asked told us that La Paz was either *cinco*, or at most *diez, kilómetros* away. I'd recently run the Berlin Marathon so 5km or 10km was easily doable, even though my backpack was weighed down by the A3 manuscript of my first running book and a stash of warm clothing for the Uyuni desert.

Retrieving our rucksacks from the belly of the coach, we swung them onto our shoulders and began walking towards the capital in the company of Steve, a 30-something English backpacker who spoke fluent Spanish. He'd be able to confirm the answers to any questions Graham or I asked of Bolivians. If 'No, madam, I don't know how to peel a porcupine' was the answer in quickfire native Spanish to the question clumsily mistranslated from English, 'Please, sir, is there a toilet here?' then Steve would put us right. Come to think of it, Steve could ask the question for us! I was reassured to have him along.

A couple of kilometres down the road we came across a one-room breezeblock shop where we purchased the elderly shopkeeper's last two litres of Pomelo soft drink to bring our total supply of fluid to… two litres of Pomelo soft drink. To lighten my load I gifted the woman two fleeces and the book proofs. The fleeces pleased her; her response to 104 draft pages of *Running Made Easy* was more inscrutable, but most likely bemusement.

As the hours ticked by we plodded on, increasingly alarmed when every person we asked how far La Paz was unfailingly replied, '*Cinco kilómetros*' or '*Diez kilómetros*'. Were they keeping us hopeful enough to continue walking? Surviving on sips of Pomelo and a tube of Love Heart sweets I'd dug out of my hand luggage, we came to the first roadblock manned by a group of whistling and waving *campesinos*. When one of them picked up a rock, my heart froze. If he threw that at me, I knew for sure he wouldn't be flirting.

'If anyone asks you, tell them that you're South African,' whispered Graham urgently. 'They may have a grudge against Americans, and possibly the British too, but I doubt South Africa has done anything to them.'

That lie would hold for as long as the *campesinos* didn't demand to see my passport.

Cinco kilómetros down the road, still believing that La Paz would appear around the next bend, a middle-aged Bolivian supporting a heavy vinyl suitcase on his head with one arm approached us. He urgently explained to Steve that we needed to head inland to avoid the next roadblock, and offered to accompany us. I could understand very little of what he said, but I did learn a new Spanish word I'd never heard before: *molestada.*

He was warning us that we'd be molested if we didn't take evasive action. So, with the stranger leading the way, we left the highway and entered the outskirts of El Alto, the sprawling city built on the plain above La Paz. Footsore, hungry and thirsty, and with the early afternoon sun hammering down, the man led us to a shack-like house and asked the owner if we could fill our bottles from her tap. As we popped Puritabs into our water the woman took fright and ducked into her walled backyard. Hiding behind the door, she peered fearfully out into the street as several trucks with singing *campesinos* brandishing broomsticks with black rubbish bags tied to them screeched by.

Looking very concerned, the woman said something to Steve in Spanish.

'Those are people commemorating the demonstrators who've been shot dead up here today,' Steve translated.

'Shot *dead*?' I gasped in alarm.

'Yes. She says that the army and the police have been shooting at protestors and there have been dozens of deaths all over the city.'

My mind went into meltdown. All I wanted to do was beg the water woman to take me into her house and hide me under her bed until it was all over. I didn't care how long for. I could stay for weeks if I had to. I was poised to ask Steve to translate this request when our guide moved off down the road. I had no choice but to follow, suddenly struck by how incredibly kind and brave this stranger was to have gone out of his way to help us. While carrying a suitcase on his head.

Eight hours after leaving the bus we reached the rim of a

deep canyon and hoped we'd be able to look down into La Paz, but it was at least one more escarpment away. We needed another plan. Wary of the approaching dusk, Steve suggested we try to reach the airport before dark.

Graham agreed: 'I think if there's one place in El Alto that the government will want to retain control of, and which can be quite easily secured, it's the airport.'

I felt strongly that going to the airport was unwise. I was sure a firefight between the government and the *campesinos* would ensue there, but after a brief discussion I was outvoted and we started back to the highway, where we encountered a small crowd at a crossroad. One of the *campesinos*, a squat, middle-aged man with a weather-scored face topped by a worn leather hat, motioned us to stop. Handing Graham, Steve and our guide a pickaxe each, he indicated that they should start digging.

'God, no! They're being asked to dig their own graves!' I thought. 'And then mine!' Paralysed with fear I watched in dumb silence, terrified that anything I did or said would make matters worse. Already I'd entered the state of dissociation I often use when running marathons to distance myself from discomfort. I pretended I wasn't there, and that I was simply an invisible witness to a scene I wasn't part of. I didn't allow myself to think what would happen once the hole was dug, nor did I speculate on what I would do if they asked us to jump down into it.

After a few minutes of chipping inconsequentially at the unyielding road, Graham threw down his pickaxe as casually as if he'd finished a spot of Sunday gardening, wiped his brow, picked up his rucksack and started walking away. No one tried to stop him, so Steve and I grabbed up our bags and followed him as a crowd of *campesinos*, drawn by our presence, advanced towards us, one of them making slashing motions across his throat while calling out '*Muerte a los gringos!*' ('Death to the gringos!').

'Smile and wave, smile and wave,' muttered Graham to me

through gritted teeth. 'We need to show them we support their cause.'

With a few cheers of '*Viva campesinos! Viva Bolivia!*' and fake-grinning as if our lives depended on it – which I truly thought they did – we passed through unscathed.

'Graham, I really did think they were asking you to dig your own grave,' I whispered.

'Don't be ridiculous, Lisa. That ground was so hard that it would have taken us a week to dig a hole six feet deep. And besides, if I'd thought for a single moment that they were going to kill us, I'd have run away. I'd never have obliged my executioners by digging my own grave.'

An hour later we reached our guide's house and, as helicopters circled noisily overhead and tall plumes of black smoke from burning barricades melded with the darkening sky, hugged and thanked him before taking our leave. We didn't ask how far we still had to go. We already knew the answer would be *cinco* or *diez kilómetros.*

As we reconnected with the stone-strewn highway, stumbling along it as night fell, it began to drizzle and we knew we could go no further. It was 10 hours since we'd set out and we were dog-tired, so we hobbled into the first hotel we found.

In our room, Graham and I sat on the beds drinking Coke and *Singani* (Bolivian grape brandy) and stuffing down handfuls of chilli cashews, the only sustenance the hotel could provide, as we compared our tortured feet. Mine were in relatively good nick as they'd been toughened up by my marathon running, but one of the blisters on the side of Graham's foot was the size of a grape and when he lanced it, liquid squirted against the wall. Exhausted after what we think was a 50km trek, at altitude, we fell asleep.

At 3am we were woken by loud banging on the front door. 'Shit! They know we're here and they've come to get us!' I thought, trying to banish from my mind images of being dragged outside by a baying lynch mob. The insistent banging continued. It wasn't polite 'I forgot my keys, can you let me in' type banging but forceful 'We know you're in there, and you'd better come out' banging. And then it stopped. Within a minute I went from being primed to fight for my life to fast asleep, I was that done in.

'Tanks! There are bloody tanks in the street!' yelled Steve from the hotel corridor at 7am.

Rushing to the window, we watched as several rolled by. We hurriedly showered and on tender feet set off again, but not before buying a newspaper that, we were shocked to see, featured on its front page photos of dead *campesinos* from El Alto in open caskets surrounded by grieving relatives. We knew what the headlines said without needing Steve to translate them.

Eager to get off the streets and into the airport as quickly as possible, we hitched a ride in the back of a passing police van. Naturally, there was chaos at departures, with stranded passengers camped out on every available yard of floor. It was like a varsity sit-in protest. Steve left on his 11am flight to Rurrenabaque, and we were alone. Propped up against a marble pillar while Graham went to see if we could escape by air, I burst into great heaving sobs. I didn't want to be at the airport where I was convinced every tank in town was now heading for an apocalyptic showdown. I wanted to be hiding out of harm's way under the water woman's bed.

With news that only one more flight was scheduled to leave that day, and not for a destination helpful to us, we knew we weren't going anywhere so we decamped to Burger King, where we bought lunch and went to sit with three travellers.

'Do you mind if we join you?' asked Graham. The trio moved to make space for us.

'Where have you come from?' asked Henri, a pale French 20-something with eyes red-rimmed and puffy – probably from crying.

'We were coming back from Uyuni after visiting the salt

lake, but our bus was stopped by the barricades. We had to trek about 50km to get here. How about you?'

'I came from La Paz. You know the really steep road? The one from La Paz up to the airport?' Henri asked, pausing between each sentence as if shell shocked. We nodded. 'I walked up it to get here. There were no taxis. I had to run and hide behind parked cars to dodge the stones thrown at me. It was all very scary.'

'We had a few tense moments, too,' I said. 'One of the *campesinos* shouted "Death to gringos" at us. And we were in El Alto when the police shot all those protestors.'

I turned to the English couple seated next to me, who looked barely old enough to be travelling without their parents: 'And you, how did you land up here?'

'We've just flown in from Brazil,' said Dave, hungrily tucking into his burger. 'We're students and we saved up for months for this trip. Our first stop was Colombia, but we felt too unsafe to leave our Bogotá hostel so we flew on to Brazil. Three hours after landing, Sarah was mugged by a guy on a motorbike. Her daypack contained her diabetes medication so she hung on to it and nearly dislocated her shoulder in the ensuing struggle.'

As if providing evidence, Dave held up a bag with the shoulder strap half torn off. Sarah looked like she was elsewhere.

'Then I got appendicitis. The hospital in Rio refused to operate until they were guaranteed payment, but my health insurers didn't answer the phone so my parents promised to pay. I don't know why, but no matter how hard my parents and Sarah begged, the hospital said they'd only accept payment from the insurers. I was in a lot of pain and started to think I was going to die.'

Thankfully, Sarah eventually managed to get through to the insurers and Dave's appendectomy went ahead. They'd spent their remaining time in Rio waiting for him to recuperate.

'We were determined not to leave Brazil without seeing a

single sight, so on our final day we climbed up to the statue of Christ the Redeemer. My appendix wound was oozing plasma and I found it painful to walk, but we eventually made it to the top.'

'Wow, it must have been incredible to look down on Rio and Copacabana Beach,' I said.

'I wouldn't know. We never got to see anything,' said Dave glumly. 'By the time we got near the summit a thick mist had descended. All we saw was fog. And then, today, we flew here. No one bothered to tell us it was a fucking war zone.'

Throughout Dave's tale, Sarah hadn't spoken a word. Even during the 'best bits'. I don't think I've ever let Graham tell a story without interrupting him to elaborate.

'Perhaps she can't speak English,' I thought, 'or is mute.' When Sarah went to the loo I asked Dave whether the former was the case, thinking it rude to enquire about the latter.

'No, she speaks English, but she's so furious I brought her to South America that she hasn't spoken to me since we landed here and learned about what's going on in Bolivia.'

As Dave and I chatted, a voice came over the public address system in Spanish, and afterwards in broken but comprehensible English, announcing that Burger King was about to close and would not re-open until Tuesday. It was Sunday and, not knowing how long we'd have to hunker down in the airport, we hastened to stock up on food: a stack of boxed salads and two family-size buckets of deep-fried chicken, which we thought would stay edible longer than burgers. Great minds think alike, and the passenger run on Burger King cleaned the franchise out.

After finishing our lunch, we moved downstairs to be near the check-in desks and flight information boards and tuned in to 'radio rumour'. What we heard was very alarming, and we had no way of verifying whether or not any of it was true: the cash machines at the airport had been emptied by armed guards; the soldiers protecting the airport had abandoned their posts; all Bolivian nationals had been surreptitiously evacuated; everyone should be ready to leave in five minutes, carrying only what was on their body, and we'd have to fly in a military aircraft as the *campesinos* had threatened to shoot down civilian aircraft.

'What with?' snorted Graham when I told him about the final rumour. 'David slew Goliath with a single stone, but I can't see the *campesinos* bringing down a plane by chucking a few bricks at it.'

Graham soon tired of the rumours and got some shut eye. I stayed up to witness giant military planes landing and disgorging streams of ant-like troops from their lowered rear ramps onto the runway. I wanted to shake Graham awake and howl 'Why, why, why did you insist on coming to the airport? I *knew* this was a dumb and dangerous idea.' I was angry with him but even angrier with myself for having listened to him. I let him sleep because I didn't want to have the 100-decibel row that was brewing inside me at 4am in front of an airport full of strangers. And then, exhausted from walking, watching, waiting, sobbing and raging in my head at Graham, I ate a piece of cold chicken and fell asleep.

We woke to find there were no flights listed on the information boards. Not a single one. I mentally adopted the brace position for the fight between the military and the *campesinos* I was sure was coming, and slumped miserably in the departures lounge, wondering why I couldn't see a single Bolivian. Graham, who'd gone off to the loo, bounded up.

'A taxi has just pulled up outside,' he said excitedly. 'Grab your stuff. I'm sick of sitting around here doing nothing and I want to go back to our old hotel. Besides, there's no beer in the airport.'

I was astounded that he was basing at least part of his decision on the availability of alcohol, but at the same time hugely relieved that he wanted to leave. We dashed outside and, after a garbled negotiation, managed to persuade the driver and his radio operator to take us to Posada del Angel for twice the going rate. As the vehicle dipped off El Alto and began the twisting descent into La Paz we saw a burnt-out car, heaps of rubble, the odd burning tyre and clusters of protesters. One, a brawny *chola* woman wearing a multi-layered skirt and rainbow-coloured shawl, abruptly swung round and with all her might threw a fistful of gravel at our taxi. It rattled noisily off the side of the car. We hadn't seen *that* coming. That got me worried, and when the driver of an approaching vehicle gesticulated urgently for us to turn back, my chest tightened with fear. Our driver, too, took fright and, leaving the highway, sped up the first exit into the side streets of the slums that cling tenaciously to the sides of the La Paz crater like ticks to a cow's udder. Just three blocks later our path was blocked by a barricade and he ordered us out using a mixture of hand gestures and Spanish, assuring us that we would not be '*molestados*' but that he and his vehicle most definitely would be if he took us any further.

'Please, please take us back to the airport,' I pleaded, before remembering he didn't speak more than a few words of English. '*Aeropuerto, por favor? Aeropuerto?*'

The driver shook his head. He wasn't prepared to risk it. Acrid smoke was billowing from flaming tyres at each end of the barricade and I could hear the demonstrators arguing with each other. I didn't want to leave the safety of the taxi, but we had no choice. I looked down at my hands: like 10 dripping taps, beads of sweat were falling from my trembling fingertips. 'So this is what extreme fear looks like,' I thought, my mind darting back to the harrowing footage I'd seen of 'necklacings' in the 1980s, South African township 'justice' where suspected collaborators with the apartheid regime were executed by placing tyres filled with petrol round their necks and setting them alight.

As we cautiously climbed out and manhandled our rucksacks onto our backs I faced a dilemma: what to do with the buckets of chicken and boxes of salad I was carrying. If we had to make a run for it they'd hamper my progress, but if I threw them away now that would betray how panic-stricken I felt.

Graham took charge.

'Walk behind that old couple,' he said, pointing to a man in a dark green suit who was trudging slowly downhill toward the city with a woman we took to be his wife.

I glanced at the people gathering stones in the grass at the side of the road.

'We can't use them as a human shield,' I protested.

'Act normal,' Graham replied, already sauntering past the small group of arguing protesters.

Pressing my chin firmly into the top of the pile of Burger King boxes, I took a deep breath and followed Graham downhill. I kept walking and insincerely smiling, expecting at any moment to feel the pain of a rock striking the back of my head. I didn't dare look back.

On reaching the Posada del Angel on Avenida Illampu, where we'd stayed when we first arrived in La Paz as it was round the corner from Calle Sagarnaga, La Paz's main tourist street, and Plaza San Francisco, one of the city's liveliest squares, we buzzed insistently until Fanny, the owner, came to the open first-floor window.

'You are back?!' she half questioned, half exclaimed before hurrying downstairs to raise the metal roller blind covering the entrance and ushering us inside.

The hotel had one guest, a blue-eyed young American. He was sitting on the sofa in the lounge reading a Gabriel García Márquez novel.

'Hi folks, I'm Jonathan. Where have you guys come from?'

We told him we'd just arrived from the airport.

'The airport? Seems that most folks are trying to get to the airport, not escape it.'

Too tired for small talk, I told Graham I was going to bed, suspecting that I was in the early stages of a chest infection brought on by all the stress, but not before warning him to keep a low profile.

'Under no circumstances let anyone see that gringos are staying here. I'm worried they'll set the place on fire.'

'You're overreacting, Lisa. No one's setting fire to anything. Fanny says the *campesinos* are marching to Plaza San Francisco so I'm going up to the rooftop to take some photos.'

'I'm begging you Graham, please don't endanger Fanny by letting the protesters know we're here.'

I retired to bed and fell asleep, only to be woken by the sound of a gunshot.

'Get dressed right now!' ordered Graham, bursting into our room. 'We need to be ready to leave at any moment. I've just seen a policeman nearly get killed. He was on a motorbike and some *campesinos* dragged him off it. It was only by firing his pistol into the air that he managed to escape. The *campesinos* are building barricades and digging up street cobbles to throw at the police, and the cops are firing teargas and rubber bullets at the crowd to get them to disperse.'

Pulling some clothes on over my pyjamas I hurried down to the lounge to be closer to the exit should we need to make a hasty getaway. Faint wafts of teargas – enough to sting my nostrils but not so heavy as to make my eyes stream – were seeping unseen into Posada del Angel through the closed but poorly sealed windows. Fanny was pacing back and forth, clutching the crucifix around her neck and praying quietly. We sat down on the sofa to watch the events live on TV, piecing together the action from the Spanish news captions and what we could see and hear on the street outside, where demonstrators carrying staves and waving flags streamed by on their way to Plaza San Francisco. It was rioting in stereo.

After a few hours of violent confrontation, silence descended on the surrounding streets: the *campesinos* were rioted-out for the day and it was starting to get dark. None of us ventured outside that evening, staying in to eat warmed-through Burger King chicken with Jonathan, Fanny and her husband Rudy. At least I hadn't braved the burning barricade clutching fast food in vain.

The next morning Graham and Jonathan wandered out to look at the legacy of what the television news was now calling The Battle of Sagarnaga, trying not to gag on the stench of teargas that still hung in the air. They came back to tell me that the Doryan Shopping Centre around the corner had been torched. The rioters had targeted the adjacent Tourist Police Bureau and once that was ablaze the shopping centre couldn't be saved. I was incandescent, enraged that Graham hadn't taken my fears seriously.

'You see, I told you they were going to target tourists,' I raged. 'Why don't you ever listen to me?'

'They weren't targeting tourists, Lisa. They were targeting the police.'

'Frankly Graham, I don't care who they're targeting, it's dangerous out there and it's all turning ugly. I don't want you putting our lives, or those of Fanny and Rudy, at risk.'

The *campesinos* returned around midday and there was another bout of marches and demonstrations but none of the violence of the day before. After hearing a rumour that protesters had blockaded all entrance roads to La Paz to prevent food reaching the city, Graham sortied out to register with the British Embassy and procure some provisions. He returned with tinned pilchards, pasta, chorizo and a few onions and tomatoes.

'The women I bought them from were really nervous,' he related, unpacking the groceries onto Fanny's dining room table. 'I think they were worried about being beaten up by the protesters for breaking the boycott, so they wrapped up their produce in shawls to conceal it and smuggled it into the city on skateboards.'

On the Wednesday I made a very apologetic call to my boss Kate at *Zest* magazine.

'We're hiding in a hotel in La Paz and there's a lot of rioting right now so I'm not sure when I'll be able to come back to work,' I told her.

Judging by what was going on in the streets outside I was

hoping it would be before Christmas, two months hence, but didn't dare tell her that.

'We've been in touch with the Foreign Office and they say there's not much they can do. Why on earth do you insist on holidaying in dangerous countries? Couldn't you have gone to Bognor Regis?'

I acknowledged she had a point, pleaded a bad line, and hung up.

That evening the British Embassy phoned to tell us that the *campesinos* might try to cut off the city's water and electricity supply, so we filled every empty container and pot we could find with water as if in preparation for a siege. Even empty beer bottles were pressed into service. Not knowing when we'd next be able to, we risked the dodgy electrics and took a shower.

On Thursday, the fourth day we'd been holed up in Posada del Angel, we were woken by reverberating explosions. The miners had come to town, and were announcing their arrival in Plaza San Francisco by throwing sticks of dynamite around. As I lay nursing my chest infection in our room, I became even more paranoid that we were going to die, but nothing further of note happened until the evening when Fanny cooked up pilchard pasta. Jonathan swore blind that 'nothing, absolutely nothing' could make tinned pilchards in tomato sauce palatable, but when Fanny's delicious dish was served he ate humble pie – and lots of pilchard pasta.

The next day Jonathan walked to the Radisson Hotel to hear the US Ambassador brief American nationals. They were told there were no plans to get anyone out anytime soon, prompting some chump to ask for the keys to a diplomatic Humvee so he could drive himself to the airport.

By nightfall, after almost a week of cowering indoors, I'd had enough of hiding so didn't argue when Graham proposed dinner at a nearby Lebanese restaurant.

'Please excuse the baklava,' apologised the owner Yussef at the end of the meal as he poured us freshly brewed coffee. 'I managed to buy most of the ingredients I needed to cook this meal from the *chola* ladies with the skateboards, but I couldn't find the honey I needed to make a new batch.'

After we'd eaten, Yussef sat with us, sharing wine, grappa and stories. Gentle and gracious, he had the demeanour of someone who'd seen it all before. As indeed he had. He'd survived far worse during the Lebanese civil war, he told us, spending 16 years hiding out in a Beirut bunker playing poker while being regularly bombed. Yussef carried a hint of sad regret about him, which was understandable given that he was living in exile.

'I'd love to start a Lebanese restaurant in London,' he told us. 'Let me know if you hear of anyone who wants to set one up. I'm tired of all the problems in this country. Now I just want a quiet life.'

I thought of Yussef as a piece of human driftwood, tossed about by the waves of war, who'd washed up in the Andes. Now he was hoping the tide would come in and carry him somewhere else. Somewhere less turbulent, where he could get honey whenever he needed it.

We returned to the posada in time to see dramatic TV footage of President Gonzalo Sánchez de Lozada waving farewell from the steps of a plane taking him into exile in Miami. The Gas War was finally over. The protesting *campesinos* and the dynamite-chucking miners had won. Rudy sang the Bolivian national anthem and we all drank gin and ginger ale to toast the end of the siege of Sagarnaga.

By the next morning, Saturday, the scars of battle notwithstanding, La Paz had almost returned to normal. Already the roads were being repaired and the rubbish collected. There was now the prospect of getting out of Bolivia, so we went to a travel agency and bought tickets for a flight departing that evening. Curious to see the key 'battleground' for myself, we wandered down Calle Sagarnaga which was covered in scorch marks, past the fire-gutted

Doryan Shopping Centre and into Plaza San Francisco. It was mostly deserted and strewn with the detritus of protest – stones, rubble and broken glass – but in the near corner, below the church, was a knot of *campesinos* in thick, handknitted jumpers and heavy ponchos. Their job done, they were preparing to go home. One of them spoke enough English to tell us they'd walked 70km to get to the capital to make sure their voices got heard.

'We walked to La Paz too,' we told them. 'But it wasn't 70km, more like 50km.'

As we chatted and posed together for pictures they shared cheese with us and in return we bought them biscuits to sustain them on their long journey. It felt strange talking so amicably with people who, only the day before, I'd viewed as a threat. But then, their quarrel had not been with us.

Fanny rang for a taxi to take us to the airport. In that intense week, when she and Rudy had sheltered us, it felt as if we'd become family so we were all a bit choked up when it was time to hug farewell.

'We'll send you the photos we took the night of the pilchard pasta dinner,' Graham said. Fanny nodded, like me, too tearful to speak.

Though most of the obstacles on the airport highway had been cleared away, the road was still partially obstructed by a train carriage that had, somehow, been pushed off a 30ft-high bridge. The rioting had been worse than we'd thought.

As Graham and I sank into our plane seats we exhaled an enormous sigh of relief. We'd survived the Gas War, which turned out to be one of the bloodiest events in Bolivia's modern history. We left with mixed emotions: sadness for the 60 *campesinos* who'd lost their lives and admiration for their compatriots who'd suffered and prevailed; immense gratitude to Fanny and Rudy who'd so generously taken us in and, despite the risk to themselves, kept us safe.

'Well, that was a trip we'll never forget,' said Graham,

pouring himself a cup of airline red wine.

'Yes, I didn't see that coming,' I replied, thumbing through the inflight magazine and chancing upon an article promoting Bolivia's tourist draws. It featured all the country's sights we hadn't been able to see. 'You'll never guess how La Paz got its name.'

'No idea.'

'Have a guess.'

'Was it named after a *conquistador*?'

'No. In Spanish La Paz means peace.'

Yellow snow at sub-zero
America

What a fine start to the day: Lisa and Loren buckled into their seats, with thumping hangovers, Lisa feeling very fragile and Loren quite broken after we'd spent our first night reunited in Los Angeles in a seedy motel on Sepulveda Boulevard, drinking cabernet sauvignon and Van Der Hum, a tangerine-flavoured South African liqueur. Now they had to endure the 500-mile drive to the Grand Canyon, and I had to endure the two of them enduring the drive.

After a late breakfast of horrible 99¢ Taco Bell bean and cheese burritos we were keen to purchase more substantial camping provisions, so we popped into a mom-and-pop store en route to discover that they sold mostly junk food such as nachos, Twinkies and Hershey chocolate bars. We bought a packet of frankfurters, some spongy white bread rolls and a single, sad onion, the only one they had, resisting the temptation to splash out US$4 on a jumbo jar of pickled pig feet.

'If I buy them, and either of you eat one, then I'll give you 100 dollars,' Loren challenged us.

Lisa and I peered into the jar. The trotters were puffy, a deeply unappetising beige-grey colour, and the grotesque toenails loomed unnaturally large through the distorting curvature of the glass. Nope, that wasn't going to happen.

'Who the heck eats pickled pig feet?' I wondered. 'People who like the taste of pickled pig feet, I suppose.'

Mid-afternoon we reached Pahrump, a one-horse town in Nevada. We saw the town's one horse: it had an unsightly sore on one leg, suggesting that Pahrump would soon be a no-horse town.

'Do you think "pahrump" is a verb for a socially unacceptable bodily function as well as a noun?' I asked.

The girls groaned in unison. They really were in need of hair of the dog. A little apprehensively we pulled into the parking lot outside Our Bar, the kind of shady, sketchy joint featured in Tarantino's vampire movie *From Dusk Till Dawn*. In the parking lot, a solitary pick-up truck bled oil into a quart-sized Coke cup. On the wall behind the dimly lit bar we could make out a hangman's noose, a red pressed-steel tricycle and a collection of rusted number plates; various random objects – old cowboy boots, strips of tyre and beer mats – had been artlessly nailed to the low wooden ceiling.

Our Bar's barkeeper, whose florid cheeks publicised the fact that she dipped into her own liquor supply more often than she should, sported a T-shirt emblazoned with a pointed message: 'Arguing with a bar lady is like wrestling a pig – you'll get dirty and sooner or later you'll realize the pig likes it.' While we sipped our Michelobs, she stubbed out a cigarette to take a call from her irate boyfriend. It was a short conversation. Slamming down the phone, she ran her hand through hair that had been exposed to more bleach than a hospital floor and indignantly complained to all and no one in particular, 'I only drank the last two shots from his schnapps bottle, goddammit, and now he's telling me not to bother coming home. What a jerk!'

In the hard-drinking town of Pahrump it was clearly a grave transgression to polish off the last of a man's alcohol. As we left, we pocketed a couple of booklets of matches advertising

Cherry Patch Ranch, 'The best little whorehouse in Nevada'. The matches were to light our camping stove, not for directions.

As we closed on the Canyon, patches of white appeared at the side of the road.

'Is that salt?' asked Loren.

I had no idea, but it did remind me of how, on a hot summer's day in June 1993, we'd sat behind an American student on a ferry crossing to England. Despite them being famous and immortalised in song, he'd obviously never heard of the White Cliffs of Dover. As the imposing chalk headland came into view, he'd let out a whistle and exclaimed, 'Sweet Jesus, is that *snow*?'

Chalk? Salt? Snow? We weren't sure. We could have answered Loren's question by stopping, but we didn't need to because within a few miles we were motoring through a winter wonderland of snow-dusted trees. Though it was December, coming from a warm and sunny Los Angeles this was totally unexpected.

At Mather Campground, on the South Rim of the Canyon, we paid the US$12 entrance and camping fee, pitched our flimsy three-person, two-season tent in the one snowless patch of ground under a tree, and threw in our sleeping mats and summer-weight sleeping bags. We had no neighbours and had passed only two other occupied pitches in the entire park, and they had mains-connected heated motorhomes parked on them, not tents. Then we drove to the nearest supermarket for provisions and bought some diced lamb and vegetables for a one-pot stew, plus a bundle of firewood and a slab of Milwaukee beer. We set about making a fire and cooking the stew on our propane stove, chilling the beer in the bank of snow near the fire. The latter worked a treat but, once the sun set at about 5:30pm, the temperature dropped precipitously and keeping our food on the boil became a losing battle.

'This isn't ever going to cook,' observed Loren, peering

gloomily into the pot as we sat on the table, our cold feet on the bench seat to keep them out of the snow.

'Give it time,' advised Lisa. 'It's lamb, my favourite, so it'll be worth it once it's ready.'

By 8pm we'd consumed our half-cooked stew and several snow-chilled beers and it was bloody freezing. It was time for bed. Lisa and Loren spent an unusually long time in the shower and laundry block and on their return told me that they'd been fascinated by a programme on the laundry-room television they'd dubbed *Sue 'em and See*, about a man who'd accidentally swallowed a two-inch-long metal bristle from the brush he'd used to clean his BBQ grill. This being America, he was suing for millions of dollars after the bristle became lodged in his chest. The real reason they'd stayed in the block for nearly an hour wasn't their fascination with reality TV, it was their desire to get warm.

'I'd quite happily have spent the night there,' said Loren, wistfully. 'It would've been cosy and, if we needed to, we could have sat up and waved our hands under the hand dryers to warm us through.'

Sadly, the toilet block was locked up at night – why does anyone lock public toilets? Are they afraid someone will clean them? Us tent-dwellers had to urinate al fresco. This was probably a good thing as I'm not sure what Loren's high-powered corporate lawyer colleagues would've thought of her sleeping on the pee-spattered floor of a public restroom.

'Let's make ourselves hot water bottles,' Lisa proposed as we got ready for bed, her hands blue with cold.

Already my mug of water had frozen solid.

'Good idea,' said Loren, her teeth chattering.

We heated some water, poured it into our metal water bottles and, after Loren and Lisa had donned every single item of clothing they possessed, rushed headlong into the tent and our sleeping bags, forgetting to douse the fire – just six feet from our tent – which hissed and popped angrily, casting flames and sparks into the black night sky.

Inside my down sleeping bag, silk sleep sheet and cotton mummy liner, wearing my Lycra leggings, socks, T-shirt and fleece, I was toasty warm.

'I'll lie awake for 30 minutes and keep an eye on the fire,' I promised, and promptly fell fast asleep.

It took Lisa an hour to nod off because her feet and backside stubbornly refused to thaw out, and in the end she had to wake me up and beg for my hot water bottle which she stuffed under her pyjamas, leggings, tracksuit pants and wool skirt. At 3.30am she was woken by the pain in her achingly cold feet. Shivering uncontrollably, she realised with horror that neither I nor Loren had moved from the positions in which we'd fallen asleep. Not only that, but she also couldn't hear us breathing and so, as she afterwards told us, had nightmare visions of trying to breathe life into our stiff corpses. The thought that a motel room would have cost a miserly US$30 also preyed on her mind. When she'd booked the camping pitch online, Lisa had been pleased that there had been so many available but had not thought to question why. This reckless, ill-informed decision was going to be very hard to explain. She lay there for 20 minutes, paralysed with fear, wondering how she was going to break the news of Loren's demise to their mother.

'Graham, Loren, wake up!' she barked, at last resolved to try to rouse us.

'What's the matter?' I said groggily.

'You've woken me up,' said Loren grumpily.

'Thank God you're both alive! I was beginning to think you'd frozen to death. I can't sleep. My feet are so cold, they're burning: it feels as if they've been doused with petrol and set on fire. I'm going to have to go outside and make myself a hot water bottle. Do either of you want one?'

'No thanks, I'm toasty warm,' I declined.

Loren gratefully accepted, so Lisa slipped and stumbled out into the cold, leaving the tent flap open.

'Zip up the bloody door!' Loren and I chorused, 'you're

letting all the warm air escape!'

But Lisa failed to return to close it, so within seconds all the carefully conserved heat was gone, stolen by the dark night. She was so bitterly cold that she couldn't think straight. We heard her have a quick pee. I looked across to Loren.

'Never eat yellow snow.'

'What? Why not?'

'Just think about it.'

She thought about it.

'That's disgusting.'

We heard fumbling as Lisa struggled to light the stove with the damp Cherry Patch Ranch matches.

'If we survive this,' she later told us she'd been thinking, 'it'll make a good story. But I'm not sure we're going to.'

It took Lisa several minutes to get the stove going and 20 more to warm the water; bringing it to the boil was impossible. By this time the temperature had plummeted so far that the water that spilled from the kettle turned into icicles that hung from the stove. Almost hysterical with cold, Lisa staggered back into the tent with her lukewarm hot water bottle and, pulling her sleeping bag tight over her head, spent the rest of the night miserably trying to breathe warm air onto her legs and feet.

Loren and I also shivered until 8.30am when, our faces red-raw from cold, we all made for the warmth of the re-opened toilet block.

'I just want to get the hell out of here,' I said when we regrouped at the tent.

'I do, too, but I think a cooked breakfast will cheer us up,' said Loren. Our eggs and bacon were frozen solid. As was our milk, which had been attacked at dawn by squawking ravens who'd punctured the carton to feast on the milk lolly inside. Puzzlingly, they'd also pecked lumps out of the bar of soap we'd left overnight on the campsite table. Undaunted, with numb, chapped hands we cooked the best breakfast we'd ever tasted.

To preserve precious body heat, Lisa ate hers with her brown beanie pulled all the way down over her head to her neck, only raising it to take mouthfuls of food. She looked for all the world like Chewbacca's severed head atop a pile of jumble sale clothes.

We bundled our tent and possessions into the car, leaving our washing-up sponge frozen to the park's table, and departed for the South Rim Trail. As we exited the campground, the uniformed ranger, her hair tightly bound up under her broad-brimmed, high-crowned hat – a hairstyle we know disparagingly as a 'Croydon facelift' but which looked amazing on her – expressed surprise that we'd camped.

'You folks camped out in the snow? The mercury last night fell below 16 degrees Fahrenheit.'

'What's that in Celsius?' Lisa asked.

'That'll be minus nine, ma'am.'

'Minus nine degrees? No wonder I was in so much pain,' Lisa blurted out.

'You'd think someone could have told us how bleeding frigid it was going to be *before* we pitched our tent,' I muttered indignantly, driving off.

After almost becoming the *last* item on our bucket list we'd ever get to tick off, the Grand Canyon fortunately lived up to its name. At least I thought so. Loren and Lisa deemed it 'not as interesting as Kimberley's Big Hole in South Africa' and hot-footed it back to the warmth of the car after just 10 minutes. Though not the grandest canyon in the world – that title belongs to the Yarlung Tsangpo Grand Canyon in Tibet, which is two miles deeper and 30 miles longer – I still thought it pretty damn grand, and couldn't quite get my head round the fact that mere water, and not a fire-trailing meteor or nuclear explosion, had created this enormous gaping wound in the landscape. Back in the car, the park leaflet informed me that the Colorado River had carved out the Canyon at a rate of a tenth of a millimetre a year, the thickness of a piece of paper.

'Can you please stop reading that and find us a motel?' begged Lisa.

'I didn't nearly freeze to death to take five photos and leave,' I griped. 'I can't believe you two philistines have taken precisely 10 minutes to appreciate the wonder of six million years of geology.'

'I know, I feel bad about that,' said Lisa. 'Next time we'll come back in summer and hire mules and get them to take us down to Phantom Ranch. But right now I need a hot bath and a proper bed!'

It was a two-hour drive south to Sedona, and when we got there our first priority was to find a motel. Wind-burned, dirty and thoroughly duffed up, we made for a sorry sight. We must have looked like three walking sacks of manure.

'My goodness, what happened to you? Where have you been?' asked the kindly owner, looking quizzically at our red, frost-nipped faces. We told him of our ordeal.

'Why on earth didn't you stay in a motel?'

Embarrassed by our stinginess and ignorance, we admitted that we could and should have done that.

'Well, you're here now, and you should all go and have a hot shower and get some rest.'

In the room I headed straight to the shower and, once I'd dressed, collapsed onto the bed. Loren picked up the Grand Canyon leaflet.

'It says here that hikers should watch out for the four "umbles": grumble, fumble, mumble and stumble,' she read out. 'If you start doing any or all of these when it's cold, then you very probably have hypothermia, which can be life-threatening.'

'Alternatively, if it's a pleasantly warm day, then you are very probably pissed. Which can be life-affirming,' I joked.

Lisa, we now realised, in her grumbling, fumbling, mumbling and stumbling attempt to boil water in the wee hours, had indeed come perilously close to hypothermia. And it could have been Loren and me who'd have had to explain her demise to their Mum.

The moment we ventured out after a lengthy nap I discovered why Lisa had seemed to be avoiding answering my questions when I quizzed her about Sedona's charms. Yes, it was set among stunning red cliffs and deeply shaded gorges – all very *National Geographic* – but I soon discovered it was Lisa's idea of heaven, as it was also a 'spiritual energy centre' famed for its 'vortexes', mysterious energy whirlpools that supposedly made trees grow in strange shapes. My alternative explanation, that perhaps this wood-distorting phenomenon was down to something a little less 'out there', like the wind, was met with a stony silence from Lisa. Sedona was, I was soon to find out, the Roswell of Arizona without the aliens.

Entering the tourist office, situated a few doors down from a candy store that innocently advertised staff vacancies with a window sign reading 'Fudge packers wanted', was like walking into the Wacky World of Woo. Instead of the usual stacks of maps and rotating brochure stands we were faced with an entire wall of business cards. But these cards weren't offering the services of babysitters or a man-with-van, they were advertising all manner of hippy-dippy, new-age kooks: psychics, mystics, clairvoyants, energy healers, chakra tuners and their ilk. While I sat glumly in the corner studying a map of the quickest way to get out of town, Lisa and Loren spent a happy hour finding reasons to stay. And spend money. Judging by the prices quoted on the business cards, spiritual reconditioning didn't come cheap.

'Should I go and see a Soul Scribe or a Quantum Healer?' Lisa asked me eagerly as she shuffled through the handful of cards she'd picked out.

'Neither,' I grumped.

'Oh, come on, Graham,' she implored. 'We'll only ever be in Sedona once and we should at least give something a go.'

'In that case, why don't you have a shamanic colonic?'

'What?'

'You heard me,' I said, handing Lisa a business card offering her the chance to 'cut the crap' and give her energy field a 'total clean out'.

The next afternoon, after spending the morning visiting several gnarled trees, the supposed proof of the existence of vortexes – as though clouds shaped vaguely like Donald Duck are proof that Walt Disney controls the weather – we headed to one of Sedona's leafy suburbs so Lisa could keep her appointment with her chosen practitioner. Lisa was in a bit of a mood because, despite doing a yoga session and meditating at Boynton Canyon, supposedly one of Sedona's most powerful vortexes, she hadn't felt anything. And she'd been disgusted to find that, instead of being a pristine wilderness, developers had somehow wrangled permission to build a vast strip mall at the base of one of the mountains that totally ruined the view.

'It's a bit like hiking down the Grand Canyon and finding a tacky casino full of slot machines at the bottom,' ranted Lisa. 'Or plonking a golf course at the base of Uluru. They've totally ruined a really spiritual place.'

Here, it seemed, big bucks had won out over natural beauty. Red rocks? Mountains? Who needs those when you've got Whole Foods Market and a McDonald's?

We pulled up outside a sprawling house with dreamcatchers hanging from the eaves.

'I'll wait in the car with Loren,' I said, resigning myself to spending the next 90 minutes of my holiday searching for something on the radio that wasn't Country & Western or the rantings of a shock jock or evangelist.

When she returned, Lisa was much happier. She'd chosen to consult a Holistic Intuitive and the woman had obviously impressed her. The practitioner was also a Holistic Master Pedicurist and Master Toe Reader but Lisa, being a marathon runner, is deeply ashamed of her pork-scratching toenails – her words, not mine – and so refused to bare her feet.

Instead, she bared her soul and opted for a light sage smudging and palm-reading session that was so illuminating that Lisa said it encouraged her to start researching an alternative career to journalism.

The cynic in me said it was common sense, and not the sage, that had prompted this decision. She had, after all, been with the company for a long time and was growing increasingly restless. But at the time I didn't dare tell Lisa that.

Escaping the pull of Sedona's vortexes, two days later we motored down the Strip to our budget motel at the 'original', shabby Stratosphere-end of America's 'adult playground', Las Vegas, aka Sin City. If you Google it, Vegas is famed for almost all the vices known to man, namely (and I quote) 'gambling, bookmaking, easy marriage, easy divorce, organised crime, prostitution, strip clubs, cabarets, clubbing, 24-hour liquor sales and, in former days, organised crime and police and political corruption'. It's such a free-wheeling, gambling-whoring-hard-boozing town that it gave rise to the expression 'What happens in Vegas, stays in Vegas'.

We spent much of our time trudging from casino to casino to gawp at their free attractions. It's not every day you see a lava-spewing plastic volcano just along the street from a 300m-long dancing fountain – or a newly-wed in a bridal gown hitched up to show her garter, smoking a cigarette while yanking on the arm of a one-armed bandit, her groom nowhere to be seen.

All tramped out, we caught a taxi from our hotel to the Bellagio to attend a show that one of Lisa's colleagues had said was 'absolutely unmissable'. Thanks to the horrendous traffic, what should have been a very short ride took 30 minutes, so the show very nearly was missed. It was an interesting half hour as our driver, a New Yorker with a passing resemblance to Elvis, was happy to chat.

'Almost no one in New York owns a gun. That's why crime there is so bad,' he said in his unlost 'Noo Yoik' drawl. 'I much prefer living here in Vegas as everyone here has a gun and burglars know that if they break into somebody's home, the odds are they'll come face to face with a semi-automatic.'

The reason there had been so many shootings in American schools, he opined, wasn't because of the country's liberal gun laws but because the teachers weren't armed and couldn't shoot back.

'Arm the teachers,' he said with conviction, 'and I guarantee you, no more kids will get shot.'

Except by teachers who can't shoot straight, I thought.

With the worrying vision of vigilante teachers with a piece of chalk in one hand and an Uzi in the other – an idea many years later President Trump would seize on as the way to stop school massacres – our driver dropped us off.

What can I say about the show? It was expensively and cleverly produced but we'd been led to believe there would be a storyline. There wasn't. Or if there was, it seemed to be about a chaotic, dystopian world populated by clowns and contortionists and acrobats who acted but never interacted and who never uttered a single word of dialogue.

To us it was reducible to the following deal: 'We will give you 90 minutes of technical wizardry, loud music, slapstick action, jazzy lighting and an unfathomable plot and in return you'll buy into all the publicity we've pushed out, suffer a momentary lapse of reason and give us US$495. Thank you very much.'

Incensed at the consensual raid on our wallets that had just occurred and adamant that from this moment henceforth we would never, repeat never, commit to spending princely sums on entertainment without first reading at least some reviews, we shuffled leadenly back along The Strip to our insalubrious accommodation. At each traffic light, young men approached us and thrust fans of glossy business cards at us. Curious, I took one. It advertised a better than buy-one-get-one-free deal: *three* hookers for just US$99. That was three for the price of one show ticket, with US$66 left over to blow in a casino.

'If I went back to the theatre and asked for a refund do you think…'

Lisa cut me short.

'If *that* happens in Vegas, then *you* stay in Vegas!'

CHAPTER TWO

2010: The Grown-up Gap Year
America, Belize, Nicaragua, El Salvador

I didn't do it on purpose, I really didn't. I'm not that brave. When planning my five-country trip to Central America I had no idea that a United Nations survey had listed Belize, Guatemala, El Salvador and Honduras as four of the 20 countries with the highest rates of homicide in the world. It was like playing Russian roulette with countries rather than bullets: if Belize didn't blow my brains out then Guatemala might.

Had I known, I'm sure fear would have stopped me going. I'd initially intended to tour the whole of South America – some of it on my own or with my sister Loren, the rest with Graham – but when I realised how vast the continent was, I opted instead for a region that was a little more 'manageable', in my ignorance not knowing it was also a lot more 'murdery'. I chose 2010 as my grown-up gap year to celebrate the publication of my second book, *Adore Yourself Slim*, and successfully establishing my hypnotherapy practice after leaving *Zest* magazine two years before.

I also wanted space to grieve my mother, who'd been tragically killed by a reckless motorist in Pretoria while training to run the Médoc Marathon in Bordeaux with me. Life had been so busy since she died that I felt I hadn't had time to process her death and thought a trip where I'd spend at least some time alone would be therapeutic. I'd certainly felt travel had helped me grieve when Graham and I took the difficult decision not to have children.

While we'd been on some wonderful trips since 2003 – Syria, Lebanon, Morocco, Namibia and South Africa – none of them had been for more than two weeks as I couldn't take more leave, and once I'd set up my hypnotherapy practice I was simply too caught up in writing content for my website, doing marketing and attending training courses to have much time off.

'Take good care of yourself, you're very precious to me,' said Graham as I boarded the X26 bus to Heathrow. 'And don't do anything foolish.'

We'd already gone through some rudimentary survival tips. I was to keep my wits about me by never having more than two beers, and when paying for things was to pass a calculator to taxi drivers and hostel staff so they could show me the prices they wanted to charge as my rudimentary Spanish wouldn't allow me to understand what they were saying. Handling money was a first for me: I usually dealt with the sightseeing itinerary, leaving all the negotiating and payment admin to Graham. I'm like the Queen when I travel: I never carry cash, not even enough for an ice cream, so I knew this aspect of the trip was going to prove tricky. I also have a horror of having to do mental arithmetic in public, a hangover from getting 32 per cent in my mock matriculation maths exam, so prefer to let Graham tax his brain with figuring out foreign exchange rates.

Suitably prepared, I made it all the way to Heathrow before I hit my first hurdle: an airline official demanding to see a return ticket from Belize.

'But I'm not flying back from Belize,' I explained. 'I'm going to Belize via Miami and I'm flying out of El Salvador.'

'I can't let you onto this plane unless you've got a return ticket.' My heart sank.

'But I can prove I've got a ticket home on a flight that leaves from El Salvador.'

'That's not enough, I'm afraid. You can buy a return ticket

from Belize at that counter over there and then go to one of our offices anywhere in Central America and get a refund,' said the official, trying to be helpful.

Almost in tears and fearing that buying a ticket was going to bankrupt me, I lined up at the counter and purchased the required ticket before making a heads-up call to Graham, who was due to join me in a week's time.

'I'm surprised to hear from you so soon,' he laughed. 'What's gone wrong?'

'Nothing,' I sniffed. 'I just wanted you to know that they've just forced me to buy a one-way ticket from Belize to London before they'll let me on the plane – and you're probably going to have to do the same next week when you fly out.'

In the event Graham wasn't asked to buy a second ticket, but we nonetheless had to take a detour during our trip in order to arrange a refund for the ticket I'd had to buy. The place we chose to do that was San Pedro Sula, Honduras's second-largest city, a modern metropolis full of car showrooms and mirrored high-rises. Three years later *The Guardian* described it as 'the most violent city in the most violent country in the world', reporting that it had a murder rate of 173 per 100,000 residents, compared with just 1.2 in the UK, the highest in the world outside a war zone. That unnecessary, unwanted and ridiculous ticket could well have proved a one-way ticket to heaven.

South Beach's slapdash psychic
Miami, America

A man I nicknamed 'Long Island Iced Tea' showed me where to get off the airport bus in Miami's South Beach. Like the cocktail, he informed me he was a mixture of pretty much everything: Colombian, Mexican, Spanish, Italian and 'probably Mayan'. Sixty-something, he was a tad dodgy looking, but it turned out he had a heart of gold to match his blingy gilt-framed sunglasses, and gave me lots of advice on staying safe as a lone female traveller.

'Watch out for South Beach's hustlers,' he cautioned. 'It's a magnet for them and you gotta be careful. And don't be tempted to buy drugs as it may be an undercover cop selling them to entrap you.'

I settled down to enjoy the view from the bus window of Miami's yachts, canals and billboards offering 'Buttock implants: only US$3,500' in nine-foot-high letters. Boy, did Graham get lucky when he married me: mine were free and already installed when we met.

After throwing down my backpack at the beachfront Deco Walk Hostel, I sat on the beach with a cold Coke watching a young woman in a thong bikini provocatively thrusting out her curvaceous posterior and insisting her friend take a snap of the life-size Jesus-face tattoo on her back. A caravan of skyscraper-tall cruise ships, some with huge tail-shaped funnels, as if a whale had nose-dived and crashed through their decks, processed out of Port Miami, taking their pampered passengers on luxury cruises to the islands of the Caribbean. 'The funnel never stop,' I imagined the advertising slogan saying.

A stroll along Ocean Drive further exposed me to the joyous insanity that is South Beach: a six-foot-ten drag queen belting out Tina Turner numbers on the pavement outside a bar while chaps in leather chaps and Stetsons performed synchronised line-dancing inside; a cyclist conversing with the tame, nappy-clad lemur perched in his bike's basket; and a muscle-bound man wearing a yellow albino boa constrictor as a scarf posing for photos with passers-by.

In a side street off Ocean Drive I thought I'd treat myself to a palm reading at Mystic Psychic. It wasn't the patterned pub-like carpet or ornate Rococo furnishings I could see through the floor-to-ceiling window that attracted me, it was the neon sign advertising readings for US$20. 'What have I got to lose,' I thought, 'except 20 dollars?'

Hesitantly, I pressed the buzzer and was let in by a dark-haired woman in a leopard-print crop top, frayed denim shorts and CD-sized gold hoop earrings. Parting the curtains of a gold-and-red velvet tent set up against one wall of the room, the psychic plonked herself onto a throne-like brocade chair and instructed me to take the seat opposite.

The reading lasted five minutes, two of which were spent trying to convince me to have my 'very scattered' aura rebalanced for US$125. I was told I was very intuitive and possibly psychic and that I had a strong lifeline and so would live a long life, although she foresaw that later on I'd have stomach and lower-back problems.

'Your scattered aura is causing sleep problems,' she went on, peering occasionally at my outstretched palm when not casting belligerent looks at her two-year-old who let out the occasional howl while clumsily riding a toy scooter back and forth across the carpet.

'I actually sleep very well,' I replied.

She frowned. 'Ah yes, but you wake feeling tired.'

This much was true, but I knew full well my tiredness resulted from going to bed too late, not my wonky aura.

A tattooed man in jeans and a Hawaiian shirt wandered casually through the room.

'Don't mind my boyfriend,' said the psychic, sounding bored. 'How many times have you been married, honey?'

'Hang on,' I thought, 'aren't *you* supposed to know that?'

And then she said the one thing in the entire reading that was spookily accurate: 'Your husband, you talk to him, but he doesn't listen to you.'

How *could* she have known? I wanted to rush from the room and make a transatlantic call to Graham to let him know that someone was onto him. His habit of pretending to listen to me – and then doing the exact opposite of what I'd told him to – had been exposed. He was well and truly busted. How many times had I sent him to the supermarket with strict instructions to buy something like sour cream only for him to return without it?

'Where the heck's the sour cream?' I'd ask, as I unpacked the groceries.

'I didn't get any,' he'd reply.

'Why not?' I'd ask, thinking that perhaps our local Co-op had sold out.

'It's unhealthy,' he'd say, cramming broccoli into the salad drawer of our fridge.

'I don't care what you think about its nutritional credentials – it's the single critical ingredient when you're making beef stroganoff besides the beef,' I'd fume. 'So it'll just have to be beef stew – thanks for nothing! Why the hell can't you just do what you're told – or at least tell me in advance that you have no intention of doing it?'

'Go shopping yourself then,' he'd sulk while stacking baked beans and tinned sardines in our store cupboard.

'You are just so bloody stubborn,' I'd rant. 'I never ask you to do anything dumb, so why can't you just do what I say?'

The psychic continued her reading.

'I really recommend that you get your aura rebalanced, it's so out of whack,' she insisted.

'I don't have time. I'm leaving for Belize first thing in the morning,' I fibbed, convinced the US$125 could be more wisely spent.

'I can do it remotely. Pay me now and give me your email address,' she said.

'I'll have a think about it and email you if I decide to go ahead,' I replied, wondering if psychics can tell if you're lying.

Getting to her feet the psychic unceremoniously ushered me to the door where I handed over my US$20 without so much as a 'thank you' or 'goodbye' in return.

When he joined me in Belize a week later and heard of my disappointing encounter, Graham said the psychic was wrong – it was *I* who should be listening to *him*, and that if I'd listened, he'd have told me… not to waste my money by going to a cut-price clairvoyant in South Beach.

Sharks suck
Belize

Belize was my first solo stop in Central America. And apart from magazine press trips and a few city breaks, it was also the first time I'd travelled without Graham. So far, so friendly, I thought as I chatted to my airport taxi driver about Belizean food. All restaurants serve rice and beans, a one-pot mix of the two foods – not to be confused, he warned me, with beans and rice, where they're served separately.

'What happens if they don't serve rice and beans?' I enquired as we hurtled towards the Belize Water Taxi Terminal in his rusty jalopy lashed together with wire.

'People walk out. They want their rice and beans, and if they don't get them, they walk.'

Exactly like Cuba then, I thought, recalling how every menu featured the same thing: chicken or pork or fish – with beans and rice. Obviously, in the Caribbean people know what they like, and they eat it. Every. Single. Day. I wondered how many locals died each day of diet tedium.

A short boat ride took me to Caye Caulker where, for a ridiculously affordable US$5 a night, I booked myself into the Mirador Hotel, a clapped-out clapboard guesthouse right on the beach. Eager to get my bearings, I went for a walk. About 1.5km offshore, a long line of waves broke white, disclosing the whereabouts of the world's second longest reef; 200m inland, along a sandy path, a collection of scrap metal, rusting supermarket trolleys and rotten-plywood-and-corrugated-iron shacks revealed the presence of a village, hidden from sight by a glade of palm trees.

A woman in a bikini top and overtight denim cut-offs emerged from one of the sorry-looking buildings, trailed by an equally mournful-looking dog. She introduced herself as Angelica and, without prompting, proceeded to tell me about her abusive – as in battering, strangling and womanising –

boyfriend. Massaging her chin, and staring down at her flip-flop-shod feet and thighs mottled by an assortment of unsightly bruises, she told me how she was going to go to jail for assaulting him unless she paid US$250, money she didn't have as she was sending her son to the 'Oshun Cademy'. Her tears seemed real and I felt bad for her.

I was just about to give her some cash, and an impromptu counselling session, when her friend arrived carrying a polystyrene container of food and spoke to her in Kriol. I struggled to follow the rest of the conversation. All I heard was 'Is not right, man. No, is not right.' The doleful dog followed me for a few paces as I made my way back to the beach but then even he lost interest and turned tail, leaving me to finish my walk in solitude.

That night I was woken twice by the amorous couple next door. Their second coming was followed by an industrial-volume post-coital argument that resulted in a bang so big it blew off the Band-Aid I'd stuck over the hole in the wooden wall separating our rooms. I briefly speculated that they were angry that I'd blocked their peephole, though I'm not sure anybody goes to a peep show to watch a woman sleep.

Caye Caulker is famed for its abundant sealife, so I signed up for a snorkelling trip led by Bo Derek (alright, it wasn't Bo herself but Ali, a blonde hair-braided lookalike) and Guy, a fourth-generation Belizean. He wasn't really called Guy, but he didn't introduce himself within earshot, so it's short for Boat Guy. The rest of my group were Spaniards, none of whom spoke English.

Our first anchorage was Hol Chan Marine Reserve, where we all hopped overboard and swam among purple fan seaweed that moved lazily back and forth in the current, as if waved by bored *señoritas* at a bullfight. Guy dived down to point at a fish before resurfacing to tell us what type it was.

'Four-eye angel fish,' he said, but the Spaniards ignored him and kept on chatting to each other in machine-gun-rapid Spanish. A disapproving-looking turtle paddled slowly by.

Guy had warned us not to get too close as turtles were very shy, but the Spaniards frantically swam after it to take underwater snaps, infuriating Guy who was no doubt thinking 'What part of "Don't harass the turtles" don't you understand?' To which I imagined them replying, 'None of it, stupid, we're Spanish.'

At Shark Ray Alley, a natural break in the reef, Bo ladled bloody chum into the water and within seconds the boat was surrounded by a churning mass of nurse sharks noisily feeding on it like ill-mannered teens slurping milkshakes.

'Who wants to be the first to dive in?' asked Guy, laughing, and, I suspect, mentally calculating which irksome Spaniard he'd toss overboard first, given the choice. Everyone giggled nervously and looked down at their flippers.

'They can suck your brain right out of your ear,' Bo helpfully informed us.

'You first,' I said, volunteering Bo. 'I'll take the photos.'

For most people on the boat I imagine the risk of being bitten by a shark was theoretical, something akin to being struck by lightning while juggling pots of tiramisu on a unicycle, or finding a zombie apocalypse in full swing when you opened your bedroom curtains. But to me, it wasn't. During childhood holidays in Amanzimtoti, near Durban, I'd watched the Natal Sharks Board haul their bright orange speedboats up onto the beach with hammerhead and great white sharks lying dead inside, their blood-stained, razor-toothed mouths agape as if silently screaming.

Not only that, but I knew two people who'd lost limbs to sharks. Damon Kendrick, the 14-year-old son of the woman who given my sister Loren, my cousins and I swimming lessons while we were on holiday, had lost his leg below the knee, and Bruce 'Sharky' Eldridge, a surfer friend of Loren's, had had his entire calf muscle bitten out by a three-metre great white. Damon had gone on to become a champion springboard diver, and Bruce ran the 56-mile Comrades ultramarathon with Loren, but they were the lucky ones: of the 143 unprovoked shark attacks off Kwa-Zulu Natal since 1900, almost a third of victims had died. And though I knew full well that sharks would order fish, seals, seabirds and even other sharks off the ocean menu long before they'd ever think of chowing down on people, I didn't much fancy becoming human sashimi.

A burly Spaniard entered the water and, when he was still alive and kicking a few minutes later, the rest of us followed, though I don't mind admitting that I was last off the boat. I'd eventually been convinced by Guy's assurance that nurse sharks very rarely bite and are so named because they suck up their food. By the time I entered the water, the feeding frenzy had abated and most of the sharks had zig-zagged off, though one or two were curious enough to give me a sandpaper-nosed nudge. I kept my hands balled into fists just in case they were in the mood for finger food.

Six coffee-table-sized stingrays swam by like underwater Jedi Starfighters, with the Spaniards in hot pursuit, trying to grab onto their wings and hitch a ride. Bo was furious.

'Leave the stingrays alone!' she shouted. 'That's the way Steve Irwin died.'

Now where had I heard that name before? As I bobbed about in the gentle swell it came to me: the fearless Aussie TV star who'd wrestled crocs for a living had been killed by a single stingray barb to his heart. A surge of adrenaline coursed through my body – I didn't want to be skewered any more than I wanted to be savaged – and I struck out for the boat, where I remained safely out of harm's way until we got to dry land.

That evening I nursed happy-hour cocktails and my severe sunburn at the Lazy Lizard, a lively pastel-coloured beach bar next to The Split, a narrow stretch of water created in 1961 when Hurricane Hattie allegedly karate-chopped Caye Caulker in two. It must've been one heck of a hurricane. The bar looked as if it had been built out of flotsam washed ashore by Hattie, and in the litter-strewn reeds stood the impotent sign 'This is Not a Dump'. A gaggle of tipsy Americans were swaying to the blaring reggae, while Rasta dudes loafed around trying to marry a Green Card by weaving palm-frond bikinis for women old enough to be their mothers. The bar was doing its best to live up to its inspirational slogan: 'A sunny place for shady people'.

It was after I'd ordered a truly revolting saccharin-laced strawberry daiquiri and pus-yellow pina colada, both poured, ready-made, as all cocktails were, from bucket-sized plastic bottles, that I was approached by a woman who offered to sell me a massage, manicure, pedicure or *ganja*. I declined all of the above, but half the daiquiri later a different local stroll-stumbled up, who'd clearly been taking full advantage of the same happy hour as I had.

'I've already had a massage today,' I fibbed, reluctant to let anyone near my sunburn. I hadn't realised how incredibly fierce the sun had been and my white, pink and brown back now looked like a block of Neapolitan ice cream.

'Why you telling me this?' she slurred in disgust, as if I'd over-shared, and wobbled off.

Barbara and Laura-Beth from Oregon asked if they could join me at my table.

'This trip is a present to Laura-Beth for taking care of me after my recent heart operation,' said Barbara, smiling gratefully at her granddaughter. We continued chatting and, as I neared the end of my now bathwater-warm pina colada, we were startled by two cigar-sized insects that alighted on a nearby palm and proceeded to writhe about and make some very odd sounds. On closer inspection we could see that they were energetically mating. When Barbara's cocktails arrived, she wasn't best pleased, but it wasn't their ready-mix nature or lurid colour that had given offence.

'Why did they stick two pieces of palm frond in them?' she asked with a look of intense distaste while carefully fishing them out. 'Don't they know that cicadas could have been having sex on them?'

Much as I enjoyed Barbara and Laura-Beth's company I couldn't stomach another cocktail, so I bade them farewell and made my way, a little unsteadily, to the Mirador, passing a broken-nosed man on a bicycle with a live racoon on his head, a Belizean take on a coonskin cap. I wasn't imagining things, but nonetheless told myself that I'd had quite enough alcohol for one evening.

My time in Belize did afford me the headspace I needed to finally properly grieve for my mother. I was standing staring out to sea one day when a little girl approached me.

'Why you so sad,' she asked, looking up at me.

'I'm thinking about my mother,' I replied.

'Your mother in heaven?'

I nodded a yes, and she turned and ran towards her own mother who was carrying some heavy bags of shopping and most likely on her way home. How that little girl knew to say that I'll never know, but our short conversation unleashed a torrent of tears that until then I'd been too busy to shed. I'd so dearly have loved to share this travel experience with my mum but realised that, in a strange way, she was there with me all along. Her DNA lived on in me, so in reality part of her really was still alive and was taking great pleasure in being able to stare out at the hypnotic beauty of the waves breaking on the offshore reef, a line of churning white against a multicoloured palette of blues, greens and aquamarine.

After a week my solo island sojourn ended and I boated back to Belize City, a city in name only: it was so compact that it was barely a town. A higgledy-piggledy mish-mash of decaying wood-and-cinderblock buildings, bisected by green, greasy-looking canals lazily belching methane, it should have looked quaint, but it ain't.

The guidebook had been alarmist about the ne'er-do-wells one was likely to encounter there, so once installed in my guesthouse it took me a very long time – the time it took to consume six mugs of tea and a whole pineapple – before I summoned up the courage to venture out to meet Graham, who was flying in from London. Belize City wasn't *quite* as scary as the book had made out, but I still felt vulnerable until I realised that the dreadlocked men lounging about in their overgrown front yards who cat-called as I passed all appeared to be stoned, reassuring me that I could outrun them if it came to it.

On the way I happened upon the tomb of the curiously named Baron Bliss, an Englishman who, despite never setting foot on the Belize mainland, nevertheless left all his money to the country off whose beautiful shores he spent the last weeks of his life, blissed out no doubt, aboard a yacht. The tomb was surrounded by shattered beer bottles, so the locals certainly weren't showing their gratitude by tending his grave.

All that pineapple eating and tea drinking had meant I'd left it rather late to rendezvous with Graham at the Tourism Bureau, and when I got there he was nowhere to be seen. It was Saturday, and the Bureau was closed. A battered Lincoln Town Car taxi drew up.

'You looking for your husband?' asked the driver.

Completely taken aback that my intentions had been so transparent, I denied it.

'I know where he is. Get in and I'll take you to him.'

Eyeing him suspiciously, I asked the driver what kind of luggage Graham had.

'A suitcase.'

I knew he was lying – Graham always travelled with his green rucksack. Heart hammering and preparing to run as fast as I could in the opposite direction, I shot back: 'If you think I'm getting in a car with a man I've never met before, then you're mad.'

'Lady,' said the driver, 'I'm not trying to cheat you. Your husband is waiting for you at the Water Taxi Terminal, so why don't you go there?'

Not knowing what else to do, and aware that the water taxi stop was a very busy, public place, I said I'd walk there. The taxi driver nodded and sped away.

There was no sign of Graham in the water taxi waiting room. I started to panic, alarmed that word had spread there was a lone foreign woman in town who might prove easy prey for muggers and murderers. The same taxi driver pulled up.

'Your husband's not here,' he said, 'but I know where he is, and I'm going to fetch him. You wait here.'

I decided I'd remain in the waiting room for 15 minutes as it was full of families and so felt safe, and then go back to my guesthouse to try to contact Graham by email. Neither of us had, as yet, succumbed to using a mobile phone. I hoped he'd have the good sense to go to an internet café. Our meet-up plans were falling apart more quickly than a dunked digestive.

And then, as if by magic, a grinning Graham appeared, sitting next to a grinning Gerald, his new best friend. Gerald went from would-be abductor to saviour in a heartbeat, and many handshakes, smiles and a substantial tip later we parted company. I'm still not sure how Gerald knew what I was doing, or why he mistook Graham's backpack for a suitcase, but I felt contrite for suspecting his motives.

'Belize isn't full of sleaze after all,' I said, happily.

But after I'd helped Graham settle into our guesthouse, I read the discarded newspaper I'd picked up in the waiting room. Every second story was about a murder. Or multiple shooting. Or stabbing. What made all this news supremely chilling was that I recognised the street names of almost every crime scene – Belize City really is that small. For pity's sake, one of the killings had happened in the hotel next to ours. Gerald had been one of the good guys, but there were plenty of bad ones about. I'd been right to be cautious.

Rather shaken, the next day Graham and I felt relieved to leave Belize City on a bus to Orange Walk Town. From there we struck out for the Mayan site of Lamanai aboard a motorised canoe. As we thundered downriver, Arlen, our guide and captain, a doppelgänger for a middle-aged Mowgli, though he was thankfully wearing more than a loincloth, pointed out two striped tiger herons side by side on a branch. They looked like birds who'd decided to slip into his 'n' her animal-print onesies for the day.

Cutting the engine a while later, Arlen allowed our canoe to drift into some tall reeds growing beneath a straggly tree. He clapped his hands and a black spider monkey swung down from the bough above us, graceful yet gawky at the same time, her long spindly limbs reminiscent of a stilt walker's. She tottered on her hind legs to the rear of the boat and casually rested her hand on Graham's knee to steady herself as she savoured the banana she'd snatched from Arlen's hand. A male monkey arrived shortly afterwards but didn't have the cojones to come aboard, instead grabbing a banana and fleeing back into the tree.

'Spider monkeys are matriarchal,' Arlen informed us. 'The females choose their mates and make all the decisions.'

I was loving the thought of these feminist primates calling all the shots, though I couldn't quite work out what decisions co-habiting spider monkeys would have to make. After all, they didn't need to choose curtains or agree on how often to visit the in-laws.

We pressed on and after another hour tied up at Lamanai wharf. A short stroll saw us standing on a jade-green lawn peppered with holes, in front of the multi-tiered Jaguar Temple. Arlen told us that the holes were burrows.

'Burrows?' I couldn't help blurting out. 'But they're tiny.'

'They're not rabbit burrows. Mexican red rump tarantulas live in them,' he laughed.

As holes for spiders they were bloody enormous. I glanced down at my flip-flop-shod feet and wished I'd worn wellies. Unsure if Arlen was joking, I stooped to peer into a hole.

'They're there all right,' he said. 'Imagine what it's like here at night when they all come out to feed.' With a shiver I envisaged the entire field crawling with hairy spiders, their glossy jet-black eyes glistening in the moonlight.

Arlen told us that female tarantulas can live up to 25 years, whereas the males last two or three, often because, much like some human couples enjoy a post-coital ciggie, the females often eat their mates as an after-sex snack.

As the barking of howler monkeys echoed through the vine-strangled trees, Arlen made what I considered to be an indecent-sounding proposal.

'Want to touch it?' he asked, pointing to a man holding a saucer-sized tarantula between his thumb and forefinger.

Everyone took an involuntary step back, anxiously eyeing the fearsome-looking beast.

'He won't bite,' Arlen reassured us. One by one our group allowed the man to gently put the creature on their outstretched hands and then, after Graham had taken his turn, I knew that it was now or never. Either I could face my fear and boast about my bravery for years, or I could let Graham always have the best travellers' tales. I couldn't allow that to happen, so I gingerly reached out my trembling arm, shuddering as the spider was placed on my hand. I'd never held anything that hairy – or scary – in my life and my face, as the photos confirm, was a mixture of fear and loathing. I was terrified the tarantula would scurry up my bare arm and bury its fangs in my neck, but the longer I held the unmoving spider, which was oddly heavy – the weight of a large egg – the more I came to view it as a furry animal that was strangely cuddly and non-threatening. In that moment I'd managed to achieve what it can take my hypnotherapy clients four or five sessions to accomplish: a lasting arachnophobia cure.

Lava palaver
Nicaragua

The *Lonely Planet* was pessimistic about our chances of escaping Central America unscathed. We found this surprising as it was usually a lot more gung-ho: it had advised tourists visiting Johannesburg, for example, not to venture into the crime-blighted inner-city neighbourhood of Hillbrow 'if they valued their possessions' whereas my sister Loren, a Joburg resident, felt very strongly that this should have been reworded to 'if they valued their *lives*'. Like a prophet of doom, the Central America edition was forever warning of the region's ever-present perils: if you weren't shaken down by highwaymen on the buses or smothered by mudslides or stung by scorpions you'd be attacked by armed bandits while climbing a volcano. The latter was why we chose to summit Masaya volcano by taking a taxi right up to the crater's edge – that way we could evade any bandits by skipping the hike. This safer alternative also suited my risk-averse sister who'd flown into Managua, Nicaragua's capital, the previous day. The reason we wanted to visit Masaya in the first place was that it's one of the country's most explosive volcanoes: if we were going to see one up close, we wanted it to be one so active it needed Ritalin, not one so tame you could toast marshmallows over it, as we'd heard you could do at Pacaya, just a stone's throw away down the road. Graham is under the impression that marshmallows are 'from outer space' because they 'just aren't natural' so I doubt I'd have been allowed to enjoy that particular activity anyway.

'Lisa, that's disgusting,' said Graham, wrinkling his nose as he disembarked from our taxi.

'What are you on about?' I said, before realising he was referring to the cloying rotten-egg smell that barged up my nostrils the moment I joined him in the car park where a handful of acid-rain corroded signs warned visitors of the dangers of flying debris and the effect of volcanic gasses on sensitive respiratory tracts.

Concrete slabs painted yellow instructed motorists to park facing the exit in case they needed to make a speedy getaway. When Masaya erupted in 2001, two people were injured and boulders the size of Swiss balls were hurled onto the car park, causing so much damage that it was three years before the site reopened. At the visitor centre we joined a group and were given gas masks that, despite being hard to breathe through, none of us refused: if sulphur dioxide could dissolve metal signs as if they were made of sugar we didn't want to find out what it could do to our less corrosion-resistant lungs.

'The parrots have adapted to be able to breathe the poisonous fumes,' said our guide Pedro, his voice muffled by his mask, as he pointed to a flock of green parrots swooping and somersaulting through the eggy air en route to the nests they'd made in the crater's walls. 'Most other animals can't survive here, so in a strange way it's safer for the parrots to live here than anywhere less toxic.'

In the gathering dusk we climbed aboard a truck that took us to a higher spot from where we could see the red glow of the lava under-lighting the smoke billowing from the crater.

'Sixteenth-century Spaniards called this place the Mouth of Hell,' Pedro informed us. 'Long ago the people who lived here tried to perform an exorcism by throwing children and virgins into the lava to placate the angry gods.'

Judging by the vigour of the volcano, we could see that it would take more than a correspondence course in exorcism to make any headway on the demon-expulsion front.

On our way back we were issued with hard hats and torches and Pedro encouraged us to enter a pitch-black cave where once ceremonies had been held to choose sacrificial victims for the volcano. I was petrified but went inside because I wanted even less to be left alone in the dark outside.

'Keep an eye out for snakes,' warned Pedro. 'One used to live here at the entrance, hoping to catch passing bats as they flew out to hunt.' I carefully lowered myself into the gloom, my eyes smarting at the acrid smell of the metre-deep, dark brown bat crap underfoot.

'Hold your arms close to your bodies so the bats don't nest in your armpits,' joked a tourist as the cave's 20,000 inhabitants whirled around us, their leathery wings occasionally brushing my ears. I thought bats were supposed to use sonar to prevent them bumping into things, but not these ones – they were literally as blind as bats. Snakes, bats, bat crap – forget the *conquistadors'* vision of hell, this was mine right here.

It was after we returned to England that a friend related the story of a colleague in South Africa who'd been bitten on the neck by a bat while watering his garden. He'd died an agonising death. Rabies infects the brain and, once symptoms appear, it's virtually 100 per cent fatal unless you've been vaccinated. It turns out that probably the most dangerous risk I took during my time in Central America wasn't my encounters with sharks, spiders or sleazeballs, or even our trip to get my plane ticket refunded in San Pedro Sula, it was that I didn't shell out for a rabies shot before I left home.

An uncivil war
El Salvador

The final country in my fear-busting tour of Central America was El Salvador, a nation that became a superpower pawn in the Cold War and was once ruled by fear and violence. For 12 years a civil war raged between the government and the Farabundo Martí National Liberation Front (FMLN) that resulted in the deaths of over 75,000 people. Fearful of 'Communist' expansion in its backyard, America decided to back the government, enabling it to carry out its 'scorched earth' policy. In practice it was a 'scorched people' policy, as death squads targeted anyone suspected of being sympathetic to the FMLN. The United Nations later estimated that FMLN guerrillas were responsible for only five per cent of the violence against civilians, while the armed forces and death squads accounted for about 85 per cent.

The civil war's most high-profile casualty was Archbishop Oscar Romero, an outspoken critic of the government, who was killed in 1980 by a single shot as he celebrated mass in San Salvador. Loren and I visited the small museum at the hospital where he was shot, where nuns had lovingly preserved his blood-stained vestments.

Museum exhibits are one thing, but to get under the skin of a country's history, you need to speak to someone who lived it. Loren and I were fortunate enough to do that when we signed up for a tour of the area around Suchitoto, a leafy lakeside colonial town an hour's drive north of the capital. Graham had flown back to the UK two days previously, so he missed what for me was the most memorable, and haunting, experience of my time in Central America.

'As the war escalated, fleeing into the jungle and joining the guerrillas was your best chance of survival,' our guide Rene told us as we toured the zig-zag trenches dug into the forest floor. Rene also disclosed something shocking about the road in Suchitoto we were staying on.

'Have you noticed the park at the top of it?' he asked. We had. 'One day the army came to town and set up camp there, and the townsfolk served them drugged tea. Then, when the soldiers were sleeping soundly, a group of guerrillas decapitated them and rolled their severed heads down your road before stealing all their weapons and ferrying them away across the lake.'

The horror of this scene took a while to sink in, and we continued our jungle tour in a more sombre mood.

When we arrived at the tiny village of Cinquera, Rene announced that we'd have lunch and then be taken to meet a remarkable man who'd survived the war. Outside the village's small bullet- and bomb-damaged church, the tail of a downed army helicopter had been mounted on a plinth, close to two five-foot-high bombshells that were used as bells to summon the faithful to prayer. Nearby murals depicted the 200 or so names, and some of the faces, of the villagers who'd been killed in the civil war.

During our meal of grilled chicken and rice, followed by strips of tasty mango dried in a dehydrator – the latest project designed to generate additional income for the community –

Rene showed us a calendar depicting all the villagers who'd died. Six of the faces, he said, belonged to the children of Don Pablo, the man we were about to meet.

Don Pablo was an elderly, soft-spoken, bespectacled man with a wonderfully warm smile, and Rene did an excellent job of translating his moving account of the conditions that led to the civil war.

'The people were very, very poor,' Don Pablo said, clasping and unclasping his wrinkled, work-calloused hands, 'so they came to the coffee farms to get work. Some were paid the minimum wage. They were the lucky ones. Others merely worked for food. And measly food it was too: tortillas and rice, infested with cockroaches. And they were given just one litre of water daily, so they often contracted urinary infections. The workers banded together and asked to be given one egg a day, but never got it.'

Don Pablo went on to relate how an army colonel had come to the village to warn against the dangers of Communism, worried that the ideology that had taken root in Cuba would spread to El Salvador. 'We told him, what is Communism? What is Cuba? We were poor uneducated peasants and we had no idea what he was talking about.'

When the civil war broke out in 1979, Don Pablo was forced to take to the hills with two of his brothers. They were soon killed by the army, leaving Don Pablo to fend for himself. He was arrested and tortured three times, but of this he did not speak. Instead, Don Pablo told us the terrible story of Aida, the village's first martyr. The Catholic Church was at the time staunchly pro-government and sent a bishop to Cinquera to order the villagers to cease their support of the guerrillas and abandon their attempts to build a clinic to improve their lot. It was God's will, said the bishop, for poor people to remain poor because the Bible said the poor would inherit the Kingdom of Heaven. Aida, 15 at the time, challenged the bishop and for her temerity she was kidnapped, put in a coffee sack and raped for three days, before having her nipples cut off and her eyes gouged out. Then she was shot, impaled on a stake, doused in oil and acid and left for her family to find. This part of Don Pablo's story upset me so much that I had to tilt my head up and look at the ceiling to stop tears streaming down my face and spilling onto my chest.

'Us villagers are no longer allowed to celebrate mass in the church,' said Don Pablo sorrowfully. 'The Catholic church kicked us out.'

Afterwards, Rene told us that the Catholic authorities had got fed up with Don Pablo pasting anti-church posters inside the building. He also mentioned that many Catholic priests had collaborated with the military by passing on information they'd heard in confession. To Loren and me it was unbelievable that Don Pablo hadn't lost his faith but perhaps, after losing so much, that was all he had left to hold on to.

'You remember that elderly woman Don Pablo waved to when he was saying goodbye to us as we left?' asked Rene as he drove us back to Suchitoto in his truck. We nodded. 'That was Aida's mother.'

CHAPTER THREE

2010-2016: The Multi-Marathon Years
Hong Kong, Jamaica, Latvia, Dorset, Czech Republic, Romania

It's just a blue T-shirt with yellow side panels that's not even made from a particularly all-singing, all-dancing fabric. And instead of a designer name or witty slogan printed on it there's just a three-digit number, two words and half a laurel wreath. But I simply had to have it. That 100 Marathon Club T-shirt, or rather the will to earn and own it, inspired countless heroic acts on my part, not least driving on motorways – which I hate – so I could get to far-afield marathons, and covering over 4,300km (the distance from London to Tehran as the crow flies) on my own two feet. As I revealed in my book *Your Pace or Mine?* I'm spectacularly unathletic, which meant that each and every one of those 100 marathons was an agonising slog, like ploughing through fondue with freshly hewn logs for legs. For the most part running, for me, is like banging my head against a brick wall: only enjoyable when it stops.

Graham, too, finds running a challenge. Much as he loathes it, though, he detested seconding me during races even more, so over the years he hasn't put up too much of a fight when I've entered him into marathons without his permission. As a result, he's racked up an impressive 29 marathons and ultras, entirely against his will. Or so he claims.

A binbag full of blingy medals – and in my case, the covetable T-shirt, which I eventually earned in April 2016 –

isn't all that running has given us. By twinning this more recently discovered reason for jumping out of bed in the morning with our passion for travel we've, quite literally, become globetrotters: we've quaffed fine French wine and slurped down oysters at the Médoc Marathon's famed unusual refreshment stations, accepted olive branches from spectators in the Athens Classic Marathon, and even shared several miles in Budapest with a *yoni* masseur (his rather unconventional line of work was familiar to me because I'd read an online discussion thread where a woman turned down a professional vaginal massage with the immortal line: 'My *yoni* says noni').

Along with these amazing memories have come an address book's worth of fantastic new friends, remarkable people Graham and I wouldn't have got to know if running hadn't brought us together. We met René Kujan, a pocket-rocket ultrarunner from Kralupy nad Vltavou near Prague, at the inaugural Jerusalem Marathon. On the press trip visit to the fortress of Masada beforehand, he brought the entire cable-car queue to a standstill by strolling in wearing a pair of close-fitting, New York-skyline patterned tights.

'Oh man, those pants!' gasped an American tourist, unable to suppress his astonishment that anyone would be brave enough to wear such budgie-smuggling apparel in public.

'What?' replied René innocently. 'A really good friend gave them to me. I like the pattern.'

'Er, are you sure he's a *good* friend?' teased Graham.

Over the five days we spent touring Israel with René we grew close and to this day he's the only runner who's managed to persuade me to go for a training run the day after a marathon. We were staying in a hotel on the shores of the Dead Sea and René suggested a sunset run: watching the miniature pillars of salt on the seashore turn rosacea-pink was an unforgettable sight. As was the number that popped up on my sports watch when we got back to the hotel.

'It says we've just run 6.66km,' I said to Graham and René.

'That's the number of the Antichrist! There is no way we can end a run in the Holy Land on that inauspicious, evil number. We'll just have to round it up to 7km. Seven is the number of God and perfection, and it's also my lucky number, so that'll be perfect.'

Always game for anything, René followed us round the car park as we did laps to reach the 'perfect' distance.

It was when visiting the UK to run the New Forest Marathon with us a couple of years later that René discovered his love of an unusual British beverage. In the bed and breakfast we stayed in the night before the race, Graham and I hosted a tasting session to introduce René to a few of Britain's best beers. We knew this would go down well because René comes from the country with the world's highest per capita beer consumption – a staggering 143 litres a year – one where beer is drunk for breakfast, as we knew from our visit to Prague back in 1993. We laid on a selection ranging from old faithfuls like Newcastle Brown Ale to curious craft newcomers like Stonehenge Ales Pigswill and Wychwood Brewery's Dog's Bollocks.

'To the metric system!' toasted René before each tasting, channelling Sheldon *Big Bang Theory* Cooper when he ordered his first Rosewater Rickey cocktail.

After studied deliberation, and once all the bottles had been drunk dry, René selected the unexpected winner, which wasn't really a real beer at all: Crabbie's Alcoholic Ginger Beer. Crabbie's isn't freely available in the Czech Republic, so each time we've run a marathon with René since, our luggage has been stuffed, not with sports drinks, but with bottles of his favourite 'beer'.

On a reciprocal visit to the Czech Republic to run the Prague Marathon we went illegal camping in the Bohemian woods with René and his girlfriend Bara, then eight months pregnant. After an evening under the stars toasting cheese and sausages on twigs over an open fire, we slept on the ground beneath an overhanging rock and woke to the glorious sound of birdsong chorusing from the acid-green canopy of spring foliage all around us.

It was during this visit that René let slip that he had once appeared in *Playboy*.

'Don't you mean *Playgirl*?' asked Graham, thinking of René's skintight tights and what lay beneath.

'No, I mean *Playboy*. They wrote a feature on me because of Run 30.'

Graham and I had sponsored René during this adventure, which had involved running 30 marathons in 30 days around the 1,300km-long Ring Road in Iceland, as we'd been moved by the cause for which he ran. René had wanted to raise money for wheelchair athletes, something close to his heart because, after almost dying in a car crash five years earlier, he'd been told he would never run again.

Our parting gift from René and Bara was a case of Staropramen, which we packed in our hold baggage. We smelled our suitcase on the carousel in Gatwick Airport before we spotted it. So did everyone else. Embarrassed to retrieve it, we waited till most of the other passengers had left before snatching it off the belt and making a hurried exit past Customs. Once home we were delighted to discover that, among the shards of glass and sodden beer labels, eight bottles had survived the flight intact. Our rucksack, however, wasn't so resilient. Once it had dried out we put it in the loft, and when we next came to use it were dismayed to discover it had been ruined by evil-smelling mould.

That's the funny thing about running and backpacking: they're great equalisers and break down barriers like nothing else. In 'real life', especially in London, you'd have to know someone for several years – or be paying them handsomely to fix your boiler or leaking tap – before inviting them round to your house, but throw people together in a race or a foreign country where their job title, the car they drive and their bank balance matter not a sausage, and new friendships spring up more quickly than mould on a beer-soaked backpack. In the decades we've been running and travelling, Graham and I now rate races and places according to the friendships forged and the memories made – rather than the standard criteria of race time achieved or number of tourist sights ticked off – meaning every single one of them has the potential to become a personal best.

Jogging our memories
2012 Hong Kong Marathon, China

Chungking Mansions was still as tatty as a student-digs sofa on the outside, and a haven of excellent-value accommodation on the inside, when Graham and I returned after a two-decade absence. The African traders were sadly gone, relocating to the Chinese mainland to buy mobile phones from source, and the lifts had been spruced up and the stairwells renovated. The middle-aged building, which opened in 1961, had scrubbed up well.

Hong Kong, however, had changed a lot since our last visit in 1992. This time we didn't ask to be dropped off at the Space Museum but disembarked right outside the Mansions, marched confidently up to the touts and asked to be shown what rooms were available. Minutes after viewing a handful of photos on mobile phones we were ensconced in a spotlessly clean, matchbox-sized double with en suite for £13 a night. Twenty years of travelling had taught us a lot.

'I'm going down to the ground-floor market to buy a samosa or three,' said Graham. 'I saw some when we came in. They look just like those fat-boy potato-and-pea samosas we used to buy here and I'm really hungry.'

'Please bring me back some,' I tasked him. 'If they're as good as they used to be, we can carbo-load on them for tomorrow's race.'

Graham bought six, with a small plastic bag of chilli sauce, and also returned with two litre bottles of San Miguel beer from a store around the corner.

'These are as good as I remembered them 20 years ago,' remarked Graham. 'They're crisp, plump with potato and peas and satisfyingly, if guiltily, oily. Just bloody delicious.'

The marathon started before dawn, pretty much on the doorstep of the Mansions. We'd only needed to set our alarm for 20 minutes before the starting pistol sounded.

'Ugh, it's too early.'

Pushing him in the small of his warm back I answered firmly, 'No way. Get up.'

It was a dawn like no other we'd witnessed, lit as it was by a forest of neon advertising signs. Nothing shouts 'Hong Kong!' more than its colourful billboards of bold Chinese calligraphy.

The race attracted about 5,000 runners, a handful of them, like me, in fancy dress: a shark, to highlight the plight of this endangered animal in a city where a bowl of soup made from its fin cost a paltry £1.50, and a rhino, similarly imperilled by AK-47-toting African poachers because of its role in traditional Chinese medicine – it's used to treat rectal bleeding, typhoid and boils full of pus, not impotence as most Westerners erroneously believe.

The marathon didn't turn out to be the sightseeing spectacular Graham and I had hoped it would be, taking in, as it did, three long tunnels and many miles of soulless freeways. The Hong Kongers I chatted to were thrilled by this, as it was their once-a-year opportunity to run on roads reserved for traffic. Stonecutters Bridge was the first major challenge: long and steep, the sole distraction was the container ships far below unloading cargoes from every corner of the globe. They looked tiny, like a scene from Legoland. The second bridge provided an unexpected highlight as the course turned back on itself halfway across it. Spotting Graham here was an enormous boost: we ran towards each other screaming greetings and encouragement but only managed a very clumsy high five before continuing our separate ways. Halfway came at a point on Ting Kau

Bridge, and as I anxiously looked at my stopwatch, which read 2h55, I was relieved to see I still had a chance of finishing before the six-hour cut-off.

As I entered the final tunnel that would take me under Victoria Harbour and onto Hong Kong Island I knew I was going to have to step on it. I imagined wild cheering would greet my emergence, but crowd support was sparse. I'd obviously been spoiled by the London and New York City marathons, where supporters line the entire course and jostle to get the best viewing spots at the finish. Judging by the armloads of designer carrier bags I saw pedestrians weighed down by, the residents were more interested in shopping than spectating. I focussed on getting to the finish line by pretending I was playing a game of Pacman and 'gobbling up' each runner I passed, eventually 'eating' over 100 before managing to sneak in with four minutes to spare. Graham, of course, had finished ages before.

The next day we had more time to note the ways Hong Kong had changed. When we'd first visited, our plane had flown in low and slow over the territory's forested mountains and high-rise tower blocks en route to Kai Tak Airport, causing the laundry hanging from lines suspended outside windows to flap crazily in its jet stream. The steep descent onto the runway jutting out into Victoria Harbour – nicknamed the 'Kai Tak Heart Attack' – had been a thrilling introduction to the Crown Colony. This time our descent to the new airport on the island of Chek Lap Kok had been sensibly sedate.

Hong Kong was still fascinating: the Star Ferry plied back and forth across the harbour; Hong Kong Island still had its Ding Ding double-decker trams, so called because of the double-bell rings their drivers gave to warn pedestrians to get out of the way or risk being separated from their legs; and the views from Victoria Peak of the Giant's Causeway-like cluster of waterfront skyscrapers, the harbour and Kowloon beyond were as jaw-dropping as ever.

But it seemed a lot more crowded, its once-green hills now encroached upon by a greyish forest of high-rises. Another 'new' addition was the Central-Mid-Levels Escalator, which opened in 1993, the year after we first visited. No longer did we have to struggle up flight upon flight of steps to reach the upper levels of Hong Kong Island, we could glide up the mountainside, stepping off whenever a restaurant, bar or shop took our fancy.

To ease the lactic acid out of our marathon-achy legs, we visited the ancient Ten Thousand Buddhas Monastery in Sha Tin where we climbed 430 steps – Graham refused to let me pay to use the funicular – to marvel at the preserved corpse of its founder Reverend Yuet Kai, on display in a glass case. After his death in 1965 he'd been buried in a box for eight months and when disinterred was found to be so miraculously well-preserved that he'd been plated in gold.

'Last time we were here and photographed the Reverend, he'd looked his 87 years,' observed Graham.

Now, 20 years later, his wispy moustache and bushy eyebrows were barely protruding from the gilding that his adoring worshippers had since applied to his embalmed body. The additional layers of gold leaf had smoothed out his wrinkles and chubbed up his formerly sunken cheeks.

'Yes, he's a bit like Benjamin Button – 20 years later he looks 50 years younger,' I said.

'He looks positively radiant.'

'More like "positively glittering".'

Back at the Mansions, we took the weight off our feet and read a copy of the *South China Morning Post*, where locusts were headline news. Not the six-legged, crop-chomping kind, but the derogatory term Hong Kongers used for visiting mainland Chinese who were resented for converging on the territory to stock up on everything from jewellery to baby-milk powder. Notwithstanding that they spent an average of US$650 on each visit, residents had long complained that mainlanders clogged up public transport, crowded out stores, devoured health resources and pushed up property prices. They were also regarded as uncouth because they spat everywhere, even in public swimming pools, and allowed their children to urinate on subway trains. The paper described mainlanders as though they were an invading horde of high-spending football hooligans.

That evening Graham and I went in search of the type of food markets and pavement restaurants we'd so enjoyed during our first visit. Back then we'd seen stalls where, alongside dried seahorses, shark fins and deer antlers, they sold fish, beheaded and slit open lengthwise, whose hearts were – don't ask us how – still beating to ensure the flesh stayed fresh. In Hong Kong, 'fresh' meant 'still alive'. And, in a neon-illuminated night market in Temple Street, we'd dined at an eight-table pavement café where the ingredients for our seafood meal (and our scribbled drinks order) were hoisted to the upstairs kitchen window in a wicker basket attached to a length of string. Twenty minutes later our food was carefully lowered back down, now steaming in a flavoursome broth. Sadly, 20 years on, Hong Kong was now awash with fast-food chains and search as we might, we couldn't find the stalls, the supper-on-a-string joint or any others like it.

Macau had changed even more than Hong Kong. Returned to China in 1999 after over four centuries of Portuguese administration, what had once been a low-rise and laidback colonial possession had been visibly transformed by Chinese tourism and gambling. Gambling is prohibited in China so mainlanders flocked to Macau to lose money: about US$600 billion was placed in bets in Macau every year, roughly the equivalent of all the cash withdrawn from American cash machines annually. In fact, in 2012 the enclave boasted gambling revenues five times that of Las Vegas. Old Macau, it seemed to us, had been crassly developed and disinfected along the Singapore model. Gone was the charming, sleepy backwater that had so delighted us when we'd cycled from island to island and seen the desiccated remains of Japanese Jesuit martyrs in a gloomily silent church.

'Macau has definitely not been sympathetically developed,' I commented while hunting for a coffee shop. 'Unless your sympathies are for high-rise Hacienda – in beige – meets Gulf bling crossed with Chinese cheap and functional.'

Macau now looked like the bastard offspring of Las Vegas' thrusting avarice and Shanghai's Pudong district's ugliest skyscrapers, its sense of intimacy usurped by neon and noise. The famous pineapple-like Hotel Lisboa, which starred in the Bond movie *The Man with the Golden Gun*, stood dwarfed by the new kids on the block, one of which looked as if the leaves of a humongous pineapple had been pasted onto its façade, no doubt in a (failed) homage to the iconic original.

One of our fondest memories from our first visit had been lying awake in the crumbling Hotel Ung Ieong while a ceiling fan lazily sliced through the still air to disturb the webs of dust that clung to the walls. We'd listened to the clinical clack of mahjong tiles being slapped down in the building opposite where pensioners played for peppercorn stakes. The new Macau was overrun with brash mega-casinos. We wagered and lost £5 in less than three minutes. Even had the one-armed bandit coughed up, the psychologically uplifting sound of coins cascading into a metal tray had been silenced and winners were instead issued with a slip of paper, like an ATM receipt, redeemable for cash. Where, we asked ourselves, was the fun in that?

Revisiting places like Macau where we had embedded so many happy memories is always risky. After an 11-year break we tracked down VS Guest House in Bangkok, where we'd stayed in 1993. The same friendly owner was there, letting the same stuffy rooms at knock-down prices. VS was just about hanging on, a relic of a different Khao San Road of authentic hostels, knock-about bars, good food carts and little hard sell.

Backpackers had been the pathfinders for Khao San Road's 'new generation', a displacing wave of undiscriminating young party animals, lured by *The Beach*, who arrived and still arrive in their legions in search of unrelenting loud music, abundant alcohol and free Wi-Fi. Once the road had been the epitome of boho, now it had crossed the line into trashy, though it probably still had a sizeable population of knucklehead dopers sitting up all night smoking and talking unadulterated shite. Now there were four-storey buildings, posh hotels, neon signs jutting out over the road and moneyed, middle-age tourists drinking and eating in the smarter restaurants and bars.

On the last day of our holiday, we caught a bus-boat to Wat Pho. It was a sausage machine. There was absolutely no chance at all of our reliving our last experience, where we'd arrived just after dawn and joined contemplative worshippers in circling the immense Buddha while dropping coins in a succession of metal bowls. Officious Thais instructed people to 'Take your shoes off here!', "Move along!', 'Buy your offering coins here!' There was lots of shoving and jostling to get the best pictures, won each time by a fat Russian with an intrusive video camera and a more intrusive wife. The atmosphere had been ruined by permitting so many people inside at one time. The offering coins couldn't tinkle in the bowls because they were full. It was a business first, and a contemplative religious site second.

Safari Tremaine's two-eyed snake
2015 Reggae Marathon, Jamaica

'Say no to drugs' has always made me laugh. I mean, if you're talking to your drugs, it's probably too late to say no to them.

It's an oldie, but a goody, and a joke that came in handy when trying to get Lisa to crack a smile when her sense of humour went AWOL at a beachside restaurant in the

Jamaican resort town of Negril.

'This oxtail stew is so tough it's as though it's been made from an ox that died of old age,' she griped. 'Either that or it's been cooked for about 20 minutes. I should've known that no-one makes better oxtail than my dad.'

Lisa's not a foodie, but when restaurants mess up dishes that she, or her father, know how to make – a short list of oxtail, steak, broccoli, scrambled eggs, avocado on toast and fruit salad – woe betide them for getting it wrong. She's of the opinion that as *professionals* they have no excuse.

When I heard Lisa ordering, I just knew it was going to end in tears. I'd told her that unless she'd be happy with 'Here's one I made earlier', boil-in-the-bag oxtail, what she was going to get was likely to be disappointing. You just can't keep diners waiting for the three hours it takes to cook perfect oxtail. Even in Negril, Jamaica's 'Capital of Casual', that would be taking casual dining too far. But Lisa is as stubborn as an ox, and when she sets her mind on something there's no dissuading her.

I followed up my 'say no to drugs' joke with a corking pun as a middle-aged American couple on the sand, exhaling billowing clouds of *ganja* smoke, gave their three children a group hug.

'That couple will have to take *joint* responsibility if their kids grow up to be stoners.' All I got from Lisa for my trouble was an eye roll and a dismissive groan.

Not being smokers ourselves, the news that marijuana had been decriminalised in Jamaica shortly before we flew there had failed to reach us. Hence one of the more unexpected memories we brought home, along with our Reggae Marathon medals, was refusing innumerable offers of marijuana from dreadlocked men who trawled the beach selling it. One even popped his head between the railings of our guesthouse's terrace as we breakfasted one morning and, with a cheeky, toothless grin asked: 'You ready for your smoking?'

By far the most goal-oriented event in Negril's calendar, the Reggae Marathon saw Lisa and me rising at 4am for the 5.15am start, rather than our more usual 10am. Even at that early hour, when the clip of a crescent moon was still visible, it was hot and muggy and someone had already started their 'smoking' for the day – or perhaps hadn't finished it from the night before.

When the start gun sounded we shot off southwards, running through an honour guard holding aloft flaming torches to a soundtrack of blaring reggae: pumped out from over-sized speakers on the roofs of parked cars and from a boombox on the back of a motorbike, it would accompany us all the way round the course. Reggae is laid-back and slow-tempo, and I blame my lacklustre performance entirely on the race pace it set and not on the training I hadn't done.

By the time I got to the halfway mark the sun had started to crisp my skin into crackling and the glimpses of ocean I could see between the seafront hotels looked more and more inviting. Even the wildly cheering marshals, who used Usain Bolt's trademark victory pose to point the way, and the countless renditions of Bob Marley's *Lively Up Yourself*, couldn't put a spring into this old dog's step.

'Go mon, go!' shouted a conch-blowing Rastafarian on my final lap. 'Me, I'm Dr Love and Dr Love 'tink all you runners is amazing!'

The final few miles passed in a blur: the shadeless route and radiating tarmac drained my batteries more quickly than Lisa inadvertently leaving the car headlights on. I perked up at the finish, however, when a medal and a chilled Red Stripe beer were pressed into my hand and I joined my fellow marathoners making the Caribbean a little saltier by cooling off in the sea.

Lisa joined me several hours later.

'It was so hot I thought I was going to collapse out there,' she said, flopping onto the sand under a tree. 'At one point I was feeling so faint that I wondered how much warning I'd have before I passed out. Thankfully, I managed to hitch up with a forensic scientist from Las Vegas who wasn't just a MENSA member but also a former paramedic. She gave me some of her salt tablets and I felt a lot better after that.'

'It sounds like you got her full life story,' I said smiling, by now used to the fact that Lisa seldom came home with a medal without a story attached.

'Oh, and she used her MENSA brain to enter some of America's most popular TV game shows. She won US$64,000 – and a Jacuzzi!'

Lisa's ability to turn every marathon into a marathon chat session never ceased to amaze me. I'm more of a 100m kind of talker: I'll talk for about 10 seconds and then shut up, meaning most of my in-race conversations go a bit like this…

Marathon runner: 'How're you doing?'

Me: 'Fine. You?'

Marathon runner: 'Great, thanks. I'm trying to keep my heart rate between 70 and 80 per cent of my maximum and I'm taking one gel every hour which seems to be working though my calf is killing me and I don't think I've got over my plantar fasciitis.'

Me: 'Nice,' and, slowing down or speeding up to shake him or her off, 'Good luck!'

I guess I'm someone who refuses to answer the mating call of the running bore. Lisa, on the other hand, has the patience to get past race-related small talk and winkle out fascinating gems of the 'she won a Jacuzzi' variety.

Negril asks only of visitors that they lie in the sun on the powdery white sand or walk the four miles of its justly famous, but inaccurately named, Seven Mile Beach. In need of more excitement than this after the marathon, and lured by a promotional flyer that promised 'the most exciting day of your vocation' [*sic*], we decided to go on a safari tour at an adventure park. The flyer featured – tellingly it turned out – a picture of a tortoise, hardly the poster animal for safaris.

The safari vehicle was a just-about-passable attempt to mimic its beefier African cousins in that it had four wheels, but not four-wheel drive, and though it was open at the sides it unhelpfully had inward-facing seats and a camouflage fabric roof which occluded our vision. Our guide stepped out from the vehicle. He was dressed for the part: khaki shorts, a short-sleeved safari shirt and an outsized pith helmet. All he needed to complete the look was an elephant gun.

'Good afternoon everybody, and welcome to your safari experience. My name is Safari Tremaine and I am your guide. Driving for us today is Woodrow.' In the cab, Woodrow put his head out of the window, raised one hand in salute and grinned. 'There is a lot to see and plenty for us to do, so if you are ready please climb into the truck and we will start our safari. Hold on tight as the road is bumpy.'

Safari gallantly helped the three women in our group climb the rear bumper into the vehicle.

'Do you think his mother really christened him Safari? That would've been a bit of a handicap if he'd wanted to become a dentist,' I joked.

Safari was friendly and enthusiastic and, I daresay, knowledgeable, but he was compromised by the lamentable material with which he had to work.

On the downside of the first hill we passed a small herd of skittish goats.

'What kind of goats are those? asked Kristen, the petite Canadian Hopscotch the Globe travel blogger seated next to Lisa.

'They're Anglo-Nubian goats,' said Safari. 'We Jamaicans breed them for their milk.'

'You don't eat them?'

'Well, yes, sometimes, some of the nicer restaurants round here serve them.'

Lisa and I gave each other a knowing glance, having enjoyed a goat curry only the night before.

'One Jamaican farmer in three owns goats,' Safari

continued, 'but many Jamaicans eat imported goat meat as it's cheaper. Foreign goats are not sweet and nice like our local ones.' That would explain the 'endangered' status of the goats seen scrabbling up the bank at the side of the road.

At the bottom of the hill, Woodrow pulled up in front of a locked gate to the beach where we were due to quad bike along the surf line. Only Safari had forgotten to bring the key to the gate, so scratch that.

'I thought that Woodrow had the key,' explained Safari. Woodrow gave him a look like thunder. 'And Woodrow thought that I had the key,' Safari hurriedly added. 'The key must be back in the office. This is too bad. Never mind, we will go on to the swamp.'

Woodrow swung the truck around and took the fork in the road signposted 'To the boardwalk 600m'. Dismounting the truck, we accessed the 200m-long boardwalk constructed above a mangrove swamp to view a modest menagerie of more 'endangered' animals in small wood and chicken wire cages. The unhappy-looking occupants were imprisoned, we suspected, more to prevent them from making their escape than for their own protection. There were two dozen quails, a one-eyed bird of prey – 'It wouldn't survive in the wild because it can't hunt,' Safari explained – and a pair of large tortoises in a bare concrete pen.

In the shallow waters of a pond lounged a trio of uncaged native crocodiles, sizeable enough to be made into purses but too small for handbags. In one of the cages was a solitary snake. Safari opened the latch and reached in to take it out. I was relieved to see that, unlike the bird of prey, it had two eyes, as being introduced to Safari's one-eyed snake would have required self-control I didn't at that point possess. The petting-zoo safari was starting to tickle my funny bone and I was finding it hard to keep a straight face.

'This is a Jamaican boa, fully grown and about five or six feet long. They are the longest snakes found on the island. They eat small birds and animals. This one is female. Anyone want to hold it?'

Danielle, an American who'd flown out to run the Reggae Marathon, put up her hand.

'I often get to handle snakes in my day job as an environmental scientist,' she said as Safari presented her with the boa as if it was a clean towel. Lisa shuddered.

Danielle casually handed the somnolent reptile back to Safari, who wound it round his neck. It urinated down the front of his shirt.

'Snakes do that when they're stressed,' he said, nonplussed.

I declined his offer to handle the poor creature. I thought it was agitated enough, and I didn't want my shirt pissed on by a python.

The final stop was the aviary, a netted enclosure the size of a tennis court. Our fast-rising sense of disappointment was now butting up hard against our residual hope that Safari would pull a rabbit from his pith helmet and amaze us with an impressive collection of hummingbirds. After all, the red-billed streamertail, a hummingbird with a tail like chopsticks, is Jamaica's national bird and the island is home to five of the world's 320 species.

'We have about 90 different bird types in the park,' the irrepressible Safari proudly declared. 'Help yourself to corn to feed them when you get inside.'

'I don't think hummingbirds eat corn,' remarked Lisa sceptically as she poured corn into a coconut shell half.

Inside the aviary were several breeds of bird, none of them humming. Except for two weird-looking silkie chickens so fluffy they looked as if they'd been freshly tumble-dried, the occupants were most definitely of the common-or-garden variety: chickens, ducks and doves and maybe a few pigeons chucked in to make up the numbers. Now I knew why the park's restaurant menu featured poultry so heavily. Of the 90 species in the park, two were imprisoned on the boardwalk and a handful lived beak-by-jowl in the aviary, leaving some 80-odd species unaccounted for.

Climbing back in the truck, we set off for base camp, and I shared the only bird joke I knew.

'Safari, why do hummingbirds fly south for the winter?'

He thought for a moment before shrugging his shoulders.

'Because it's too far to drive.'

'Good one, Graham. I'll use that joke with my next group of guests.'

The Grim Sweeper
2015 Riga Marathon, Latvia

'Yes, of course we fear a Russian invasion after what happened in Crimea last year,' said our taxi driver as he wended his way along Riga's cobbled streets to our apartment. 'Any country bordering Russia is always going to be nervous.'

This was our introduction to Latvia, a tiny country on the shores of the Baltic, a country with not only an uncertain future but also a haunted past. We'd come for the marathon, started in 1991, the same year that Latvia had thrown off the yoke of Communism and restored its independence.

Riga was a tale of two cities: it had a quaint Old Town where two streets boasted the finest collection of Art Nouveau buildings in Europe, and miles of bleak Soviet-era suburbs crammed with computer-chip-like apartment blocks. Riga Central Market – where impoverished-looking elderly women sold scoops of fruit and veg, flower posies and intricately patterned hand-woven socks in five repurposed First World War Zeppelin hangars – was just around the corner from Stockmann, a swish city-centre department store whose well-stocked aisles groaning with fine wines, caviar and posh produce almost put Selfridges Food Hall to shame. A fairy-tale city of Gothic church spires and glittering onion domes that spoke of its religious history, Riga was also a city scarred by its Soviet years when atheism was state policy.

Graham and I almost missed the start of the 25th Riga

Marathon. One moment we were lustily singing 'Happy Birthday' to the race and the next, 30 minutes ahead of schedule by my reckoning, we were told the start gun would go off in 60 seconds.

'Shit Graham! Quick, set my Garmin for me. I need to pop to the loo.'

'Ask me nicely,' said Graham, feigning hurt.

'*Please* set my Garmin, love of my life,' I said, thrusting the device into his hand. 'And wait here so I can get it from you after I've peed.'

The organisers hadn't got it wrong; it was my dislike of anything resembling a faff that meant I hadn't read the race instructions. Cheered on by dressing-gown clad passengers on the balconies of a gigantic cruise ship, Graham and I set off while I simultaneously tried to pin on my race number, strap on the Garmin and not trip over. Graham and the other runners soon vanished into the distance and it wasn't long before I was alone in the company of an unsmiling race official, wobbling on a bicycle, who'd been assigned to accompany the last runner.

'This is not going to be a fun race if I have to look at his grim face for 42km,' I thought.

Thankfully, my time with The Grim Sweeper lasted only until the 10km mark because there I caught up with and overtook the race's oldest entrant, 77-year-old Reinhold from Berlin, dressed in a pair of dazzling neon orange shorts and multicoloured trainers.

'You are amazing, an inspiration to us all,' I panted as I edged ahead of him.

Reinhold raised a hand and then dipped his head in acknowledgement. From here on, The Grim Sweeper was obliged to stick with him. Left to my own devices I tackled the two loops that took us past most of the leafy city's more impressive sights. I trotted by the House of the Blackheads – it wasn't a museum given over to a teenage skin condition but a 14th-century guild house with an intricate wedding-cake-like façade – enjoyed a lovely stretch on an idyllic island dotted with quaint wooden houses and, at the Freedom Monument, ran under an archway of folk dancers playing tinkling *trīdeksnis*, tambourine-like percussion instruments unique to Latvia.

The race wasn't without its moment of drama, however. On Vanšu Bridge fast runners came from behind and overtook me. I was ahead only of Reinhold, so how was this possible? Somehow, somewhere, I'd managed to 'cheat'. A runner I recognised from the Geneva Marathon confirmed as much.

'You didn't do the loop in Ķīpsala. You're cheating,' she called out as she loped past me.

Embarrassed, I approached a bearded race official.

'Will you be my witness that I've gone back to run the loop that I missed doing before?'

He shook his head.

'Do you speak English?'

He shook his head.

Reinhold, who hadn't made this mistake, was now ahead of me and it took me until I reached Vanšu Bridge again to catch up with him a second time. He was heading doggedly towards the finish in the company of a police car, its blue roof lights flashing. To deafening applause, we crossed the finish line together. Reinhold's police escort leapt from his vehicle and rushed over to shake our hands and pat us on our backs.

Post marathon, Graham and I and his mum, whom we'd invited to join us, started sightseeing in earnest, visiting the Museum of the Occupation of Latvia 1940-1991 which relates the harrowing history of Latvia's occupations, twice by the Soviets and once by the Nazis. During the Second World War an eighth of the population was killed, the highest percentage of any European nation bar Poland and Lithuania, and in the years after the war up to 42,000 Latvians were deported to Soviet gulags.

The innocent-sounding but chilling Corner House, once the headquarters of the KGB, left a deeper impression. Originally an apartment block for the city's elite, the ordinariness of the six-storey Art Nouveau building gave no clue to the horrors perpetrated within. The interior looked like a post office and, ironically, the door to the street had a small letterbox where concerned relatives could post requests for information about missing family members and where 'good citizens' could deposit tip-offs about those they suspected of being enemies of the state. The Cheka (secret police) and later the KGB used paranoia and suspicion as instruments of mass repression: anyone could be an informer, even your child or lover. Thousands of Latvians were imprisoned, interrogated, tortured and executed in the very heart of Riga right up until independence in 1991.

'That's not even that long ago – in fact, it's the year we got married,' I said to Graham.

We were led into wallpapered rooms that could have been the domestic front room of any European home circa 1960.

'This is the room where prisoners who'd been woken by a knock on their door in the middle of the night and brought here from their homes would be photographed and registered,' said our guide. 'Their belts and shoelaces would be confiscated, and their buttons and zips cut off, so they couldn't use them to commit suicide.'

Another room, with a one-way mirror on the jazzily papered wall, had only a table and two chairs. On the table, prominently but casually displayed, was a truncheon. My stomach lurched. The guide told us that the mere sight of the truncheon caused psychological terror and that beating was a common way to extract 'confessions' during interrogations that often lasted more than a week. Prisoners were presumed guilty so it was just a case of how long they could resist before admitting they'd had 'anti-Soviet conversations', or written 'subversive' poetry, or listened to the 'wrong' radio station or read a 'reactionary' book.

Between brutal interrogation sessions prisoners were housed in dank, musty basement cells meant for six but often crammed with as many as 36, all expected to use a single metal bucket as a toilet. Many prisoners were sent to Siberia, but some were executed on the premises in a room with padded walls. The engine of the truck used to take corpses away was left running to help muffle the sound of gunshots. The white-tiled floor had a central drain into which the blood of victims was sluiced.

As a runner, I found the interior exercise yard – the size of two squash courts – roofed with wire mesh but open to the sky, especially poignant. The only respite the half-starved prisoners had was to walk in circles with bowed heads for a few minutes once a week. The atmosphere was suffocating.

Lord of the ring
2015 Giant's Head Marathon, Dorset

Like much of our travelling, marathon running has provided us with some choice toilet tales, usually of the 'bogs of doom' persuasion. In 2015 we drove to Sydling St Nicholas, a village in Dorset, to run the Giant's Head Marathon. This hellishly hilly race had two main selling points: 'Love Stations', where fruit-flavoured vodka was doled out alongside sports drink; and a medal featuring a club-wielding nude figure with a huge erection, a copy of the 55m-high chalk one cut into a nearby grassy hillside.

We camped in a farmer's field the night before and, as we headed to the start, Graham availed himself of a Portaloo.

'What are you doing in there Graham?' I called through the door when he failed to come out after a good five minutes. 'The race is about to start.'

Graham's pale, worried face popped out from behind the blue plastic door.

'I've lost my wedding ring,' he said, abashed. 'I washed my hands and when I shook them dry it flew off.'

'It must be in there somewhere,' I said crossly, wondering how long it could possibly take to find a ring in a cubicle a metre square.

'You don't understand. It went *into* the toilet.'

Graham had already lost one wedding ring while water-skiing years before and I was determined that this shouldn't be his second. Barging impatiently past him I peered into the bowl, which had a shit-smeared flap hiding the chemical tank's contents from view. I examined the toilet and saw that the seat and the area around it could be hinged upwards.

'If you lift this up, you'll be able to see inside. Hurry up, I don't want to miss the start.'

I backed out of the loo and Graham stepped back inside. Outside, I heard a clunk, a retch, a second clunk and the sound of Graham vigorously pumping water into the sink.

'I found it!' he said triumphantly, exiting the loo with the gold ring held up between his thumb and forefinger. I almost expected him to start dancing like a mad thing, Gollum-like, crowing 'Precious, precious, precious! My Precious!'

'How did you manage to find it?' I asked, not really wanting to know the answer.

'Oh, it was wedged in a floater,' said Graham. 'Like a man in a canoe. If it hadn't been, I'd never have seen it among all the other grim stuff down there. This is going to make the best marathon story ever!'

'Yes, Graham, whatever floats your boat.'

Stinky cheese & a fugly building
2014 Olomouc & 2018 Karlovy Vary Half Marathons, Czech Republic

I'd never heard of Olomouc – a town whose name looks as though a hapless *Countdown* contestant had asked Rachel Riley for too many vowels – until Lisa insisted we go cobble-bashing there, promising me Pilsner-at-a-pound-a-pop post-race celebrations and the chance to see that there was more to the Czech Republic, a country we'd first visited in 1993, than the city of Prague.

I was told it's pronounced 'Olo-mowts', but that's of no real consequence as I only needed to say it once, when buying our train ticket to escape the tourist hordes traipsing through the Czech capital. Just over two hours later, Lisa and I stepped out of the railway station into what I am sure is rightly billed as the country's second most beautiful city, if architectural beauty pageants are your thing: a medieval mélange of pretty pastel-hued buildings, fantastical fountains and onion-domed and witch-hat-wearing churches. The city, it turned out, had been 'discovered' a good 200 years before the Lonely Planet called it one of 'Europe's top 10 hidden gems'. In its heyday, Mozart, Mahler and Nietzsche all beat a path to its door.

Unusually, the half marathon started at 7pm, which gave us plenty of time to get to know the city streets through which we'd soon be running 13.1 miles.

'I hope I finish before the pubs close,' said Lisa.

'You know what you need to do to make sure you do?' I teased.

'Yeah, yeah, run faster. You're so predictable.'

The main square, also the race start line, is dominated by two landmarks: the 300-year-old Holy Trinity Column, a towering thank-you in stone to God from inhabitants who'd survived a bout of plague, and the church-like Town Hall. All roads lead to the square so there's no getting lost. The Town Hall's original 16th-century astronomical clock was damaged by a grenade in 1945 and rebuilt along socialist-realist lines. The original saints were given their marching orders and replaced by a pair of muscular blacksmiths who hammer out the hours while sportspeople, happy proletarian workers, scientists and a heroic mother revolve slowly beneath them in a Communist-inspired conga. It tells the time like any other clock, but it also handily tells you when Lenin, Stalin and other important comrades were born. The locals clearly retain affection for their clock, if not for Communism. For foreign visitors it's a quirky throwback to another time.

At 7pm, the moment the soaring notes of the Czech composer Smetana's *Vltava* had faded away, the gun sounded and 4,500 of us set off down the cobbled street, its pavements thronged with cheering spectators. Like the city itself, the race was charmingly old school: spectating boys enthusiastically twirled wooden rattles of the kind last seen on English football terraces in the 1960s; a couple of stout sunburned gentlemen, bursting with beer and bonhomie, offered thirsty runners a swig of their lager; kindly grannies handed out orange quarters at halfway. And a beaming policeman hastily tucked his truncheon under his arm so that he could applaud me as I trotted by.

Starting towards the back of the pack, I caught the two-hour pacers but lost them twice when I had to retie my shoelaces, and once when I had to water a small patch of lawn in the Smetana Gardens. Thereafter, I stayed within panting distance of them and finished in just under two hours. Lisa, as is her wont, took her time, so I phoned her out on the course.

'I've finished. I'm not hanging about waiting for you. I want a beer. You'll find me at the meat market.'

'The *where*?'

'The meat market. A local guy I got talking to after the race recommended it.'

'I don't like the sound of that,' puffed Lisa, no doubt imagining a sleazy hook-up venue packed with horny people who'd swiped right on Tinder.

'It's not a figure of speech, Lisa, it's where the city's butchers' stalls used to be. It's a studenty pub and the best place to get beer. It's just around the corner from the finish. Just ask anyone where it is.'

I was well into my second Pilsner when Lisa hobbled in an hour later, struggling to reach me in the barrel-vaulted passage rammed with medal-wearing finishers.

'What took you so long?' I teased.

'Don't start!' she said. 'I wasn't going for a fast time and ran with the most amazing woman from Southend whose niece dressed up as her for Heroes Day at school by wearing a running vest and a replica London Marathon race number and medal. How cool is that?'

'Really cool. I suppose you want a beer?'

'Ask a stupid question,' Lisa nodded, now absorbed in admiring the medal I knew she'd wear to bed that night.

'What's that smell?'

I sniffed my sweaty armpit. 'Probably me – or you. You've been running for over three hours.'

'No Graham, I know what sweat smells like. I think it's that cheese.'

'Oh yes, I'd forgotten about that,' I said, pushing over a plate on which was a round of waxy yellowish cheese resembling a thick slice of votive candle. 'Try some, you'll like it. The guy who recommended coming here said it's a local speciality known as the "Guttery Breath of the Knight of Loštice". It's actually so strong it's served with breath mints.'

Ever eager to try local delicacies, Lisa wrinkled her nose as she popped a piece of Olomouc's *syrečky* cheese in her mouth. A second later she was searching frantically for a napkin.

'Where are the mints?' she demanded.

'I've already eaten all of them,' I smirked. 'I don't want *my* breath smelling like a gutter!'

Karlovy Vary, like Olomouc, was not a town I could pinpoint on a map until I realised I knew of it under its former name of Carlsbad. Bohemia, in north-western Czech Republic, has changed hands more times than I change my mind and Carlsbad was renamed Karlovy Vary in 1945 when its majority German population, Britain's own Princess Michael of Kent among them, was expelled.

Bizarrely, the town's founding was down to a dog. In 1349 the Holy Roman Emperor Charles IV was out stag hunting when one of his hounds discovered a natural hot spring – by falling into it. The hot dog's anguished yelping was the saving of the clumsy mutt and the making of a town: Charles established the first spa on the spot and the habitation that sprung up around it was named Carlsbad in his honour.

Like Olomouc, a who's who of classy European A-listers, from Marx to Bach and Goethe, descended here to take long pensive walks in the lushly wooded hills and partake of the 'Carlsbad cure'. The cure involved 'extreme bathing' – spending up to 10 hours a day immersed in hot mineral water – as well as 'extreme drinking' – imbibing up to nine litres of spa water daily, which often caused extreme diarrhoea. Nowadays most visitors prefer to settle for 'extreme sipping', wandering from spring to spring while taking sips of thermal water through the hollow handles of novelty porcelain cups, as if smoking small pipes.

There is only, it seems, one piece of music that signals the start of Czech races – *Vltava* – but as it sounds like a *Harry Potter* movie theme tune it makes for a fitting send-off. Cobbled streets; high-end shops; the Grandhotel Pupp, 'body double' for the Hotel Splendide in Bond movie *Casino Royale*; forest glades with grounded clouds of pink rhododendron blossoms; and a statue of Beethoven not moodily composing but seeming to run, were all a part of the Karlovy Vary Half Marathon course.

As was our Soviet-era 'brutalist' Spa Hotel Thermal, a concrete tower-block monstrosity better experienced from the inside looking out. French architect Le Corbusier described Karlovy Vary as 'a gathering of cakes' as the city is famed for its pastel-coloured Baroque and Art Nouveau gabled façades. The architectural crime committed by the hotel's deranged architects was the culinary equivalent of plonking a large turd upright in the midst of a plate of fondant fancies. The same Czech husband-and-wife team were also responsible for Prague's equally unlovely Kotva department store, from which Lisa and I fondly remember buying 'breakfast beer' in 1993 (at first we'd been shocked to see locals at the coach station imbibing lager at 9am, but it wasn't long before we started doing the same as the tap water tasted so terrible).

The race over – I didn't think my time of two hours and 46 minutes was too shabby for someone just a month post-chemo – I headed straight inside our hotel, not so that I could stop being offended by it – it really was a building so fugly I found myself cussing it and making the sign of the cross every time I so much as glimpsed it – but to avail myself of the 'endless beer' the organisers had laid on for finishers. Before I went inside, I took a selfie and sent it to my surgeon's wife Alexandra, a fellow runner who'd been incredibly supportive throughout my illness.

Lisa eventually joined me.

'I was asked to leave the course as I wasn't going to make the cut-off. That's the first time it's ever happened to me. But considering how slow I am, it's a miracle it hasn't happened before. By the way, Graham, when we're done here I'd like to go to that beer spa I saw advertised.'

'I don't want to do that.'

'Come on Graham, how many people do you know who've actually *bathed* in beer?' she pleaded, when I demurred.

'Lisa, it's not even really beer, it's just a barrel full of warm water with yeast and hops in it.'

'But Graham, you get to drink as much beer as you like,' Lisa continued. 'And you also get to eat beer bread. And recline on a bed of straw afterwards.'

'Lisa, you're not selling it to me. I'm not sure I actually want to go and lounge in a manger, and we can drink as much beer as we like for free here.'

'Graham, you are always such a stick in the mud. I really, really want to go.'

'All right, how much does it cost?'

'A hundred and twenty euros for an hour-long session.'

I spat out a mouthful of 'endless beer'.

'One hundred and twenty euros? Are you mad? We could drink 120 pints of Pilsner for that. No way, I haven't cut my own hair for 20 years to blow all the money I've saved at a beer spa.'

We settled on drinking some more 'endless beer'.

Bear baiting
2016 Transylvanian Bear Race, Romania

It's said that a bear's sense of smell is up to 3,000 times more acute than a human's, which was not exactly a comforting thought as I ran through a forest in Romania – a country home to 6,000 brown bears – with blood streaming down my forearm from a gash in my elbow. To compound my discomfort, the runner who'd seen me trip over a tree root could only offer me a dressing soaked in antiseptic Manuka honey. And who doesn't know that bears are crazy for honey?

Lisa and I were in Romania to run the Transylvanian Bear Race, which started in the village of Viscri and ended in Sighişoara, a hilltop town famed for being the birthplace of Vlad Dracul, or Vlad the Impaler, the inspiration for Bram Stoker's *Dracula*. Viscri's claim to fame is tamer: it's known for its colourful handmade woollen socks and felt slippers, which were strung up from fences and walls like rows of dead pheasants. Prince Charles, who owns one of the village's gaily painted houses and who has been instrumental in campaigning for their preservation, was rumoured to be in town. If he was, he didn't deign to get out of bed to cheer us off, though perhaps it was a bit naïve of me to think the heir to the throne would stand on a muddy street corner waving a giant foam hand or banging pot lids together when he could enjoy a lie-in spooning Camilla.

Though Viscri offered comfortable guesthouse options for those happy to pay extra, we chose to bed down on a barn floor with about 20 other runners. Here Lisa struck up a friendship with Melissa, a remarkable runner who'd survived a bone-marrow disorder that twice nearly claimed her life and who'd gone on to win no fewer than six gold medals at the World Transplant Games and set up Fehr Trade, her own successful activewear sewing-pattern business, while I got to know Jez, a video-game developer who intended to run the entire race in Vibram FiveFinger trainers, shoes so minimal I thought he might as well have shod his feet in clingwrap. As a very light and fussy sleeper, I was mightily pleased that I'd packed my luxury inflatable mattress: how anyone can get comfortable on a skinny, oversized mouse mat I don't know. I'd tried it, and the lack of shut-eye rendered me almost delirious overnight. I was lulled to sleep by the sound of distant howling, which I'd like to think was a pack of wolves but was probably a few of the village dogs crying out for some doggy-style action.

We set off after a hearty breakfast, following a gently undulating trail that traversed tranquil forest paths canopied in innumerable shades of green, emerging occasionally into sunlit, sheep-strewn pastures. I was careful to make a lot of noise, as the organisers had recommended, slapping my water bottle against the palm of my hand to ward off any curious or peckish bears. It wasn't a mass participant race, so other than two shepherds and five dogs I saw only a handful of other runners. We'd been warned that shepherds' dogs, used to fight or frighten off wolves, could be a bit of a menace – 'I'm thinking of wrapping my arms in newspaper for protection,' said one runner – but the five I encountered were of the contemptuously indifferent kind. In one clearing I spotted what looked like a bear paw-print in the mud... but it may just have been the imprint left by Jez's freaky FiveFinger shoes.

At about kilometre 16, I took the tumble that saw me faceplant on the forest floor.

'Are you okay?' asked Caroline, a former army reservist, who was running behind me and had seen me trip.

'I can't see,' I said, awkwardly twisting my arm in an attempt to assess the damage as blood dripped from my elbow.

The look on her face was one of horror.

'I know there's a lot of blood,' I reassured her, 'but it's actually not that painful.'

'Oh, when you said you couldn't see I thought you meant you'd been struck blind,' she said with relief as she carefully cleaned and dressed my wound. 'Perhaps a Manuka-honey dressing isn't the best idea in a forest full of bears, but it's antibacterial and anti-inflammatory so it'll stop your elbow getting infected.'

After 26 gruelling miles I entered Sighişoara to find that the race had a sting in its tail: an energy-sapping climb up the 175 steps of the colonnaded 17th-century Scholars' Stairs plus a further stretch of steep cobbles to the finish line next to the aptly named Church on the Hill.

At the summit Ben, the race organiser, presented me with a handmade pottery medal depicting the outline of a prowling bear, and then I trudged back down the hill to join the finishers who were drinking steins of lager at tables in the sunny central square. Hours passed. There was no sign of Lisa. She's slow, but never so slow that I worry about her. I'd told her that running in the ankle-length black *abaya* she'd purchased in Bahrain for our trip to Saudi Arabia wasn't a good idea – it was a trip hazard and would be uncomfortably hot – but Lisa will never pass up the chance to dress up and was absolutely determined to pay homage to Dracula. No one else felt it necessary to do so.

Ten-and-a-half hours after the start she still hadn't appeared. I knew how gnarly the route was underfoot, and had the bloody wound to prove it. Fearing that today was the day the bears had picnicked on Lisa, I stiffly got to my feet and went looking for her. Just beyond Sighişoara's fortified city walls, I came across a bedraggled, black-cloaked figure snivelling and weeping.

'Where the hell have you been?' demanded Lisa angrily.

'Drinking beer and waiting for you,' I snapped. 'Thanks to you we're late for the after-party.'

'For the past four hours I've been hoping you'd come to find me,' she moaned. 'I must've got lost and was all alone in the forest. It was bloody scary. This is over three hours longer than I've ever taken to finish a marathon.'

'Well, you've not got far to go. But be warned, there's still a steep hill to climb.'

'Graham, don't joke with me. I've had enough of this race and I'm *so* not in the mood.'

I walked along in silence, dreading her reaction when she turned the final corner and looked up.

'Shit!' she wailed when she spotted the Scholars' Stairs. 'I can't go on. I really can't.'

'Don't be silly Lisa. You've done dozens of marathons and you know you always finish them. You've come this far. What's one last little hill?'

Blinded by tears, Lisa took her first painful step up the Scholars' Stairs, nearly falling over as she tripped on her cloak. I grabbed her elbow and balanced her as she lugged her way upwards, and was mightily relieved when, at the finish, the medal miraculously dried her eyes, as I knew it would. Medals have that effect on Lisa: no matter how brutal a race has been, the moment the medal makes its appearance, amnesia descends, the smile returns, and all is forgiven.

After two nights in Sighişoara we were ready to go vampire hunting and drove to Vlad's castle. Unlike Bran Castle which, because it looks the Hollywood film part, is marketed as Dracula's eyrie even though he never set foot there, Poenari Castle was Vlad Dracul's *real* castle, from whose ramparts his first wife hurled herself rather than be captured by the besieging Turks. It's now mostly ruined and perches precariously atop a crag in steeply forested mountains with commanding views of the Arges River valley below. Poenari is only reachable on foot, by climbing 1,480 concrete steps.

Each and every stone used in the castle's construction was manhandled to the top by Vlad's enslaved enemies, who literally worked the shirts off their backs and may have been turned into human shish kebabs on its completion by way of thanks from Vlad. Below the crumbling walls two bloodied, life-size and truly ghastly fibreglass models depicted the grisly fate of so many.

Soon after reaching the summit a violent electrical storm struck and the heavens opened, like a scene from a classic vampire movie. We made a run for it, hurtling down the mountain steps as fast as the raindrops came pelting down. We'd hoped the leafy canopy would shelter us from the downpour, but within a minute we were both as wet as an otter's pocket.

As lightning slashed across the sky, I asked Lisa, 'Do you think my metal water bottle will act as a lightning conductor?'

'God, I hadn't thought of that Graham. Yes, I think it will,' she said, hanging onto the metal handrail to stop herself from slipping on the dripping wet steps.

Though I can wire a plug, I don't understand the mysterious magic of electricity so, cautioning Lisa not to grasp the conductive handrail, I lost my nerve and flung my bottle into the forest. It was *such* a nice bottle, one that I'd travelled with for years and I was sorry to be forsaking it. I reasoned, however, that a bottle in a bush is worth avoiding a bolt from the blue.

The next day we traversed the legendary Transfăgărăşan Highway, voted 'best road in the world' by the TV motoring programme *Top Gear*. Urban legend has it that Nicolae Ceauşescu, the last Communist leader of Romania, noting how the USSR had invaded Czechoslovakia in 1968, had it built to ensure his troops could get across the Carpathian Mountains in the event of a Soviet invasion. That seems an unlikely explanation: snow blocks the road for seven months of the year, so I figured the Soviets simply needed to invade Romania between December and June. Whatever the reason,

'Ceauşescu's Folly' was constructed and the winding road – resembling a strand of spaghetti stuck to the side of a green bowl – with its seriously tight hairpin turns, long S-curves and sharp climbs made for a spectacular drive, if not an exhilarating one in a hired 1.2 litre VW Polo. It's an impressive piece of engineering. The road, that is, not the car.

Bucharest, we'd imagined, would be Communist-era drab, but its Old Town, filled with vibrant bars and crowded cafés, was anything but. The old man wearing a brown crumpled suit who came to our table at an outdoor terrace and held out a small pile of Romanian-language hardbacks, gesturing with a liver-spotted, veiny hand that we should buy one, was the only reminder we had in the thriving city that Romania was one of the poorest countries in the European Union.

In the 1990s, orphans were Romania's most infamous 'export' as foreign couples rushed to adopt the starving, abused children tied to bed railings they'd seen on the TV news. What Lisa and I hadn't known was that many of these kids weren't orphans at all but children whose impoverished parents were forced to have them when a power-crazed Ceauşescu banned contraception and abortion in a bid to boost the declining birth rate. Ceauşescu also decreed that women should be given compulsory gynaecological exams at work several times a year to ensure pregnancies were detected and abortions prevented. As the population increased, so too did the rate of child abandonment, with as many as half a million minors ending up in state-run orphanages. Up to 20,000 children died of neglect.

Despite the £2.5 billion that Ceauşescu lavished on the monumental Palace of Parliament – where he and his wife Elena planned to retire – it resembled a four-tiered wedding cake, managing to look imposingly grand and vanilla bland simultaneously. Finished the year before its separated-at-birth, equally ugly younger sister, the Bellagio Hotel in Las Vegas, it combined a similar mish-mash of bunny-hopping Roman arches with Greek Corinthian columns. Ceauşescu no doubt hoped it would be considered the most beautiful building in the world but had to settle for it being the heaviest. The interior was no less unattractive.

'I wonder if Ceauşescu intended for it to look like a Victorian brothel,' I mused, surveying the Murano glass mirrors, kitsch paintings and bling-tastic furniture in one of the rooms.

'He was obviously the kind of man who knew the price of everything and the value of nothing,' whispered Lisa as Florin, our guide, led us up one of the opulent 'his 'n' her' marble staircases Nicolae had installed in the entrance hall so that he and Elena could make symmetrical, synchronised Cinderella-like entrances.

'It's amazing to me that there are 1,100 rooms here and yet this one is the only room that has any atmosphere whatsoever,' said Lisa, standing beneath the giant twinkling chandeliers that had illuminated the 1996 wedding of the Olympic gymnast Nadia Comăneci to a fellow Olympian, the American gymnast Bart Conner.

'Despite being Romania's most famous citizen, Nadia Comăneci could no longer bear living here and in 1989, when she was 28, she defected,' explained Florin. 'She crawled through freezing water and ice, knowing she'd be shot if she'd been discovered, and scaled seven barbed wire fences to walk to Austria in the dead of night, arriving bruised and bleeding at the American embassy where she claimed asylum. It's incredible to think that she needn't have bothered risking her life like that as the Romanian Revolution took place just a few weeks later.'

Florin led us out past floor-to-ceiling red velvet curtains onto the room's balcony which overlooked a large square and processional avenue lined with trees.

'This building was inspired by a visit Ceauşescu paid to North Korea in 1971,' he informed us. 'He flattened a fifth of Bucharest and displaced 40,000 people to build all of this, and probably hoped it would help encourage the same hero worship Kim Il-sung got from his people.'

It didn't. Ceauşescu ruled unchallenged for 20 years until, on Christmas Day 1989, the people he'd oppressed for so long rose up and rebelled, capturing the self-styled 'Genius of the Carpathians' – who also insisted on being called 'Hero of Heroes', 'Titan of Titans' and 'First Personage of the World' – and his wife. After an hour-long show trial, they were executed, by firing squad, against a toilet-block wall. Sometimes Santa brings good people what they ask for.

CHAPTER FOUR

2013-2017: The Avid Adventurer Years
Zimbabwe, Zambia, Colombia, Azerbaijan

Despite appearances to the contrary, Graham and I are not 'dark tourists': we don't deliberately seek out places where assassinations, disasters, wars, bombings, torture, massacres and other crimes against humanity have taken place. However, if you have an interest in history, as we both do, visiting these sites is inescapable and, we both feel, essential to understanding the world we live in. Going to them has filled in many of the gaps left by my school history lessons and balances out the stories tourist boards often prefer to tell. If we hadn't been to visit the 'killing fields' of Choeung Ek near Phnom Penh in Cambodia, for example, and seen clothing poking out of the dirt track we were walking along – clothing belonging to some of the almost 9,000 people who were summarily executed there by the Khmer Rouge – I may only associate Cambodia with our trip to the incredible tree-strangled Angkor Wat temples, used as a location for *Lara Croft: Tomb Raider*. Without visiting that chilling place I would never have read four books on the Khmer Rouge to discover that their four-year reign of terror resulted in the deaths of a quarter of the country's population, nor that its illiterate torturers made up crimes such as 'threading a needle incorrectly' to justify the executions that occurred in Tuol Sleng, a high school converted into a death camp.

Usually, like Cambodia, when we've visited a country, its

dark past has been just one element of the impression we came away with, part of a bigger picture. But there are some countries, like Zimbabwe, Bosnia and Armenia, whose names are synonymous with tragedy. In my early travelling days, I steadfastly refused to go to places like these as I feel things so keenly and suspected that the tragic stories their museums, memorials and graveyards would reveal would plunge me into a state of mental anguish bordering on depression.

Our visit to Zimbabwe in 2013 changed all this. It 'cured' me of my fear of going to places where many tourists fear to tread. Graham and I returned there two years later, driving through on our way to Zambia. And in 2017, it gave me the courage to travel to Colombia, once one of the most violent countries in the world and definitely one of its most interesting. Bosnia and Armenia also came off my no-go list, and the latter meant I got the chance to tour neighbouring Azerbaijan, where I shared a crude-oil bath with a former crocodile hunter. Zimbabwe taught us a very valuable lesson for which we'll be forever thankful: there is always more to a country than the bad headlines it makes.

Rocks 'n' Rhodes
Zimbabwe

We went to Zimbabwe almost by accident. I'd torn my calf muscle and so failed to qualify for the 56-mile Comrades Marathon. We'd already paid for our flights to South Africa and now unexpectedly had two weeks of holiday booked and no plans for what to do with them.

'How about spending a week with your dad in Pretoria and then travelling to Zimbabwe?' Graham suggested.

Despite the country being right next door to South Africa, I'd never once thought of going there as I'd been haunted by the stories I'd heard on the news about its brutal civil war.

One in particular had shocked me as a 10-year-old: the shooting down of a civilian Air Rhodesia flight in 1978 by the armed wing of Joshua Nkomo's Zimbabwe African People's Union party. Although 18 passengers had survived, 10 of them were robbed of their valuables by Nkomo's fighters and then brutally massacred.

At primary school we'd been given a sobering lecture by a white survivor of the war.

'My family used to sleep on the floor in the passage of our house,' she told us. 'Every night we would pretend to go to sleep in our beds and then, when the lights were off, we'd drag our mattresses to the passage and sleep there. In the morning we'd put the mattresses back really early and leave our beds unmade so our maid would think we'd slept in them. That way, if the terrorists caught her and asked where we slept, they'd be given the wrong information.'

My classmates and I sat wide-eyed in terror as the woman impressed upon us the need for civil preparedness.

'A civil war is coming to South Africa, too,' she said grimly, 'so you need to be ready. Water lasts a long time if you keep it in bottles in the dark. And you should tell your parents to stock up on Ryvitas and tinned food. What's happening in Rhodesia can happen here.'

But my reluctance to visit Zimbabwe didn't only stem from childhood horror stories; my fears were flamed by more recent ones.

'Robert Mugabe's thugs threw his Ndebele opponents down disused mineshafts,' my father told me. I was also aware that the land grabs of white-owned farms that Mugabe directed, which were supposed to have redistributed land to veterans of the independence struggle, had turned once-thriving enterprises into wastelands.

'No, I really don't think I can go there. I can't visit a country where all the people are oppressed and starving. I'd just cry all the time and that wouldn't be a very enjoyable holiday.'

'I'm going to do some research and see what it's really like there now,' said Graham.

The next day he emailed me an online article posing the question, 'Does this look like a failed state to you?' I read about the orderly cities, functioning hospitals and incredible sights like the Victoria Falls, the world's largest waterfall, and decided that it was worth taking a chance. To save on sky-high cross-border fees on a rented car we would borrow my dad's car, cross into Zimbabwe and, if we didn't feel comfortable there, return after a night or two.

I was full of trepidation as we crossed the border, fearful of being upset by what I saw. To my surprise and relief, Zimbabwe looked no different to large swathes of South Africa. And, as the article had reported, the roads were surprisingly good.

'Wow, these are better roads than many in the UK,' said Graham as we motored northwards towards Victoria Falls, handing out some of the marathon T-shirts we'd brought along to kids we saw playing at the side of the road.

Just then a policeman stepped out from behind a thorn tree and waved us to a stop.

'Uh-oh,' I said to Graham. 'I bet this is going to be an attempt to extort money from us on the pretext of some trumped-up traffic violation. I read about it on a travel blog.'

'Good morning sir, madam,' said the officer through our car's wound-down window. 'How are you today?'

'Fine thanks, and you?'

'Fine thank you. Please can I see your papers?'

My heart pounded in my throat. We'd been really careful to get our documentation in order and had spent hours waiting in a Pretoria police station to get the letter my dad had written authorising us to use his car notarised to prove we hadn't stolen it.

The policeman scrutinised the papers carefully.

'It's all in order, sir. Where are you going today?'

'We're heading to Victoria Falls via Bulawayo,' Graham

replied.

'Would you mind giving two of my colleagues a lift to the next town?' asked the officer.

'Not at all,' said Graham.

I let out a huge sigh of relief as I heaved my daypack off the back seat to make room for the officers. Sadly, our conversation never got past small talk, because a few minutes later we reached their HQ and set them down. After accepting their grateful thanks, we drove on.

Our next set of hitchhikers needed a longer lift, so we had more time to chat. Most travel guides advise against picking up hitchhikers, but in a country with no discernible public transport and where the distances between towns can be vast, we felt it would be incredibly selfish to drive past people thumbing a ride. It turned out that Doris and Able were two pastors eager to preach a sermon in a village 60km away. I wondered what would have happened if we hadn't picked them up. Could their congregations have held a service without them? Or would they have waited for them to arrive?

'Why don't Zimbabweans rise up and rebel against Robert Mugabe?' I asked them.

'Because we are peaceful people,' Able replied quietly. 'We are not violent people like you South Africans.'

I was taken aback that South Africans were viewed as violent by other Africans but had to acknowledge how incredibly safe I felt in Zimbabwe. Unlike in South Africa, there weren't electric fences everywhere and it seemed its citizens didn't live in constant fear of being carjacked or held up at gunpoint.

Shortly after making sure the pastors reached their preaching gigs in time – and declining their offers of payment for the lift – we were again flagged down by the police.

'This is *definitely* going to be shake-down time,' I said as Graham slowed the car to a halt.

I was wrong. Another polite interaction ensued during which it transpired that, again, a couple of policemen needed transport and would we be so kind as to oblige.

'I'm turning into a police taxi service,' laughed Graham as we dropped the officers off on the outskirts of Bulawayo. 'Can you imagine trying to fight crime in Zimbabwe when you don't even have your own wheels?'

The next hitchhiker we picked up, a 30-something called Jacob, was dressed in trousers and a smart shirt with a fraying collar. By now I'd realised that giving lifts to hitchhikers was the very best way to get the inside story on what was really going on in Zimbabwe.

'The country is a lot more stable these days,' said Jacob. 'But I had to flee to Botswana in 2007 as I feared for my life when the Mugabe regime began arresting not only his political opponents but ordinary citizens, too. I'm a tour guide at the ruins of Great Zimbabwe, but I had to become a salesman in Gaborone. Ndebele is my home language, but I had to learn Tswana very quickly in order to survive.'

In Victoria Falls we were surprised to find a thriving town thronged with tourists, and hawkers trying to sell them souvenir banknotes with a face value of trillions of Zim dollars due to the mind-curdling 90 sextillion – that's 90 followed by an almost unbelievable 21 zeros – per cent hyperinflation the country experienced in the late noughties. At Victoria Falls we made some incredible memories, such as getting drenched by the spray from 'the smoke that thunders' while Ewok-like tourists in ankle-length brown plastic raincoats watched the Falls' many rainbows. At sundown we sipped cocktails aboard a boat on the Zambezi River while feeding chicken wings to a three-metre-long crocodile as semi-submerged hippos snorted water into the air like four-legged riverine whales.

'You really shouldn't miss the vulture restaurant,' advised the manager of our backpacker lodge. Visions of a circle of seated people eating barbecued carrion birds sprang to mind.

He noticed my distasteful expression. 'No man, they don't

eat vultures there. It's a place where they *feed* vultures, which are actually now an endangered species. It's up at the Vic Falls Safari Lodge. Every day at 1pm they give them scraps from the lodge's restaurant. It's quite a sight.'

We drove to the lodge just before lunchtime. Pulling into the car park we disturbed a family of warthogs trimming the garden lawn; they trotted off into the scrub, holding their scrawny tails bolt upright like car aerials. The lodge was built from enormous tree trunks topped by a thatched roof that gave the bar and restaurant, open on three sides and overlooking a waterhole, a wonderful grassy smell. At the appointed hour, a trio of staff members ambled out with buckets of food and emptied them onto the ground. High above, the scrawny birds – and some opportunistic Marabou storks – flew huge circles before slowly closing in and dropping to earth like missiles. It was rather comical to watch dozens of vultures converging into a circle and tussling noisily over the tasty chunks, kicking up a flurry of dust and feathers as they surged back and forth like rugby players in a scrum, watched over by the referee-like storks who kept a disdainful distance.

That evening we returned to the lodge for dinner. As our car swung round a corner Graham hit the brakes: blocking the road was the grey flank of an elephant slowly yanking foliage from a roadside tree with its trunk and then munching on it contentedly. Graham turned off the engine but kept the headlights on.

'This elephant reminds me how, when I was young, my cousin Jeremy used to send holiday postcards to his friends back home in the UK reporting that in South Africa giraffes and lions shared the streets with pedestrians,' I said. 'We were sure his friends believed him and thought it so funny that people could have such an inaccurate view of what it was really like to live in South Africa. And now I've found a country where that really happens. I truly wouldn't have believed this unless I'd seen it with my own eyes.'

We enjoyed the free safari for a good 10 minutes before the elephant finished his dinner and ambled clumsily back into the bush, allowing us to continue on our way.

We'd chosen to dine at the lodge on the evening of the day I should've been running the Comrades Marathon.

'I thought I was going to be feeling really sad today, but it's turned out to be one of the best days of my life,' I said.

As I spoke those words, as if by magic Amazulu Zimbabwe, a group of a cappella singers, approached our table and serenaded us with, of all things, *Shosholoza,* one of the songs sung at the start of Comrades.

'I'm covered in goosebumps,' I said to Graham, showing him my forearms. 'In all my life I never imagined going on a helicopter ride in the morning, visiting a vulture restaurant for lunch, taking high tea in a posh place like the Victoria Falls Hotel in the afternoon and then eating dinner in a sensational place like this, surrounded by African wildlife. We've spent more money in one day than we ever have before when travelling, but it's been worth every penny.'

'This is just fantastic,' agreed Graham. 'I feel so privileged to be here and to be able to afford this. When I was cleaning an office and selling jewellery part time when we first arrived in England all those years ago, I never dreamed my life would turn out like this.'

But it wasn't Victoria Falls that utterly captivated us, it was a much less touristed sight – Matobo Hills National Park – home to caves decorated with rock paintings and the burial place of arch-imperialist Cecil John Rhodes. It was Rhodes who gave his name to Rhodesia (as Zimbabwe was formerly known) and who famously dreamt of colonising Africa for Britain 'from the Cape to Cairo'. The man was so egotistical that he even harboured *extra-terrestrial* imperialist ambitions. 'I would annex the planets if I could; I often think of that. It makes me sad to see them so clear and yet so far,' he wrote.

The park was almost deserted so we had the caves where 13,000-year-old San art was etched into the rock face, to ourselves. Marvelling at the simple figures of running men – one jubilantly holding his arms aloft as if crossing the finish line of a marathon – and friezes depicting rhinos, giraffes, elephants and baboons, all no doubt painted by flickering firelight many millennia ago, created an instant connection with people who, though long dead, had achieved a kind of immortality through their art.

Rhodes' grave is at World's View, a huge outcrop of exposed, bare granite scattered with large boulders.

'It looks as though giants abandoned a game of marbles,' remarked Graham as we climbed the blue, lime green and orange lichen-pocked granite along with a dozen rainbow-coloured lizards.

In Ndebele World's View is called *Malindidzimu*, the Hill of the Spirits. Like Montserrat Mountain near Barcelona and Luxor's Valley of the Kings, it had a stillness, a grandeur and a spiritual timelessness that took our breath away. We could see why Rhodes wanted to be buried in this perfect spot in a country that the BBC's former Africa correspondent Michael Buerk once said was 'the most beautiful country on the continent'.

'Zim is so beautiful,' mused Graham as we sat holding hands on the low summit of World's View, scanning the idyllic landscape. 'Its beauty is possibly the only thing that that bastard kleptomaniac Mugabe and his trough-gorging cronies haven't been able to steal from ordinary Zimbabweans.'

A school-desk scam
Zambia

Land borders in Africa are notoriously chaotic and hard to navigate. There always seems to be backed-up traffic, poor signposting, reams of paperwork, unhelpful officials, vehicle inspections, arcane Customs formalities, slow-moving queues and 'facilitators' hanging about offering unsolicited and maybe unnecessary to-be-paid-for services.

'Mister, hey mister. You are in the wrong queue. That queue is for vehicle tax, but you haven't got the green form you need to get the blue form you need to import your vehicle. I can get you the form. Come with me.'

And in 2015, when we crossed from Zimbabwe to Zambia to visit the birthplace of Lisa's father in Broken Hill (now Kabwe), there was an added complication: we had to be screened for Ebola. At that time, Africa was experiencing its worst-ever outbreak of the lethal virus that would tragically result in 11,000 deaths. Lisa had questioned the wisdom of exposing ourselves to the crush of people we knew from our previous trip to Zimbabwe two years before would be at the border, but I doubted we'd be at risk as the disease was mainly confined to Guinea, Liberia and Sierra Leone. As we waited for the white-coated medic to take our temperatures we read the alarming posters that warned Ebola caused uncontrollable bleeding from any and all orifices and could be spread through eating bushmeat – the flesh of wild animals like monkeys, zebras, hippos and lions – and kissing corpses. It's traditional in many parts of Africa to touch or kiss the deceased before burial, and with bodies remaining infectious for up to a week after death this custom was creating what aid agencies called 'viral bombs'.

In the end the Ebola check only added 20 minutes to the proceedings so, once we'd been given the medical all-clear, we set about completing sundry forms from assorted piles to gain entry to Zambia for ourselves and our car. But first we had to change money because, unlike Zimbabwe whose currency at the time was the US dollar, we had to pay for our Zambian visas in *kwacha*, and *kwacha* couldn't be bought abroad. Stepping outside, we were besieged by jostling *incutras*, informal money changers, who assured us that the Bank of Zambia money bureau 100 yards down the road was closed. It looked as though it was, but in Africa many places look closed when they're open. It wasn't closed, of course, and though the *incutras* offered an advantageous rate I wanted proof of exchange in case I was asked for it by Customs officials. So I changed US$200 at the bureau and returned to the byzantine formalities of border crossing, which involved taking pot luck – and invariably getting it wrong – with the 'correct' sequencing of windows we had to queue at to purchase visas, complete Customs declarations and buy vehicle road tax. We'd patiently wait in line only to get to the head of it and be told that we should have got a stamp or a signature or the form to get another form to get a stamp elsewhere first.

'Lisa, I have absolutely no effing idea what we're supposed to do,' I complained. 'This whole process is bewildering, arbitrary and infuriating.'

Once all was done – or at least I *thought* all was done – Lisa hopped into our car, now baked by the sun, on the slip road outside. She hurriedly wound down the window to vent some of the super-heated air. She was as eager as I was to reach the thatched bungalow we'd booked on the banks of the Zambezi River and relax with a glass of cold white wine. I was about to get in when a large, middle-aged woman wearing a knitted hat and sweater in the 30°C-plus heat called out: 'Mister, you need to have a Zambian Certificate of Motor Insurance. You get it from me, here.'

I rolled my eyes. Another bureaucratic hurdle to leap and more money to pay.

'Really? Motor insurance? I've paid for the car already.'

'Yes, but not motor insurance.'

I sensed a scam, but in our guidebook there was a passing reference to the legal requirement for additional insurance. She led me to an old wooden school desk with a hinged lid and a hole for a long-missing ceramic inkpot, that had been positioned in the shade. It was exactly the kind of desk I'd sat at each school day for four years in Maseru when my diplomat parents were posted there in the 1970s. But back then I'd been a mere slip of a lad. This woman tipped the scales at 100kg. Squeezing her appreciable frame sideways into the undersized seat she opened the desk, straining to lift it clear of her ample bosom, and took from within a biro, a pad of pre-printed certificates and a white metal cashbox. Holding them in one hand she tucked her forearm under her breasts and, straining, lifted them high enough to clear the edge of the closing lid.

I handed her my passport and driving licence and she proceeded to complete the duplicate paperwork, painfully laboriously, in slanting capital letters.

I stood beside the desk, watching irritably. She could have etched the asked-for details into granite in less time. Lisa sat in the stinking hot car, watching impatiently. At last the woman's pen paused over the section at the bottom of the certificate where 'fee payable' would be entered. She turned her head – the rest of her bulk was immobilised – and nodded at a sun-bleached list of tariffs posted on the wall behind. I was a British passport holder driving a South African-registered car. Her pen hovered over the tick box for 'commercial purposes including hiring', which would set us back a stinging 420 *kwacha* (US$70).

Before she could check the box, I pre-empted her: 'It's not a hired vehicle, it's my father-in-law's car,' indicating by pointing that she should instead tick the 'private and pleasure purposes' box, meaning we'd only have to pay 116 *kwacha* (US$20).

'It is *not* your car, so you are hiring it,' she replied slowly and emphatically as if I'd struggle to understand the complexity of what she was saying.

'But I am not hiring it,' I replied, equally slowly and emphatically. 'This car belongs to my wife's father.'

To buttress my case I showed her the ownership papers and Lisa's passport so she could cross-reference 'Jackson'. She spent a couple of minutes studying them before dismissively returning them to me. She'd done due diligence and had not been swayed.

'You need to pay for the hiring purposes insurance,' she insisted. 'It is 420 *kwacha*.'

'I'm not paying that,' I said, taking 120 *kwacha* from my wallet and placing it on the school desk. 'I'm paying 120 *kwacha*, and that's it.'

Exhaling as slowly as she wrote, the woman wearily declared, 'I am *not* happy.'

'I am the one who's not happy.'

'You are not happy, I am not happy, we are not happy,' she replied, carefully tucking the *kwacha* into the cashbox.

She signed and dated the certificate, resignedly tore off the top copy and gave it to me with a disapproving look.

'Thank you,' I said with a hint of smugness. Victory had been mine.

I added the certificate to the sheaf of forms in my hand and joined Lisa in the car. Driving through the *incutras* and past the money bureau we pulled up to the junction with the main road. A lone policeman in a khaki uniform from the 1960s held up his hand. I wound down the window.

'Your documents please, sir.'

I groaned audibly. Lisa smacked my leg with her fist. I don't think the policeman heard my groan over the noise of the engine and the aircon on full whack, but if he did he made nothing of it.

'Your Certificate of Motor Insurance expired yesterday. And in your passport it says your name is Graham, not "Grahama", as is written here,' the policeman said.

He showed me the two errors. Despite taking an eternity to fill in the certificate was indeed riddled with mistakes – our car registration number hadn't been entered accurately either, but I thought it best not to bring that to his attention. Had the woman come to a convenient arrangement with the cops? Was she selling insurance with deliberately incorrect details and the police would then fine drivers for failing to have valid documentation?

Dreading that we'd either be asked for a bribe or have to go back to the hot and hassly border post to sort everything out, I was hugely relieved when the policeman handed back the paperwork and broke into a huge grin.

'It's not your mistake. Welcome to Zambia. Drive safely.'

He'd obviously seen it all before. He was happy. We were *very* happy. It was just the woman back at the school desk who *most definitely* wasn't happy.

Cracking up in Medellín
Colombia

Guns and roses. Flesh and blood. Life and death. Back in the late 1980s, there was only one word that paired naturally with Medellín, and that word was 'cartel'. In 1987, there were over 3,000 homicides, a rate *five times* New York's, prompting *Time* magazine to call Medellín 'the most dangerous city in the world'. And with a huge percentage of Colombia's police force suspected to be in the pay of the cartel, it didn't look even vaguely likely that the 'coke capital of the world' was going to morph into the 'choirboy of South America' any time soon.

In the 30 years since then, however, Medellín had worked hard to rehabilitate itself. But as late as 2017, like someone convicted of multiple murders, its reputation for bloodshed and bombings proved hard to shake off. Even the very best PR can only go so far.

Our coach pulled in to the city's deserted main bus terminus at 2am. It was raining, we'd been travelling for 21 hours and I was dishevelled, hungry, weary and anxious enough to want to stay on the bus until daybreak. At this late hour the only way to get to our hostel was by taxi, so we located the exit signposted '*parada de taxis*' and stepped outside. Four yellow taxis were parked up, their drivers sheltering under the eaves, smoking and squabbling volubly, taking not the least notice of us. We had to interrupt their conversation to catch their attention. Grudgingly passing among themselves the scrap of paper onto which we'd scribbled the hostel's address, not one of them was interested in transporting us. A fifth driver pulled into the cab rank and one of the sour-faced quartet pointed to us and shouted out our destination.

The fifth driver looked at us: '*Sesenta mil pesos.*'

Sixty-thousand pesos seemed a bit steep, but he knew we weren't in a position to haggle. We got in.

The empty streets glistened with wetness and we saw no one until several young men bolted across the road a few feet in front of us. The driver's grip on the steering wheel visibly tightened.

'If he's scared,' I thought, 'then we should probably be scared, too.'

The further we journeyed into central Medellín the narrower, darker and more menacing the streets became, with people huddled in almost every doorway and sorry-looking bars advertising their presence with flickering neon. The taxi turned a corner and stopped on one side of a scrubby square. Several fires made from collected rubbish flamed desultorily in the drizzle. They were tended by huddles of barefoot men sheltering under the sheets of cardboard they held above their bowed heads. Clutches of ragged people, including children who looked as young as 10, were fiddling with lighters, trying to ignite what looked like test tubes in their hands, their faces illuminated for a second or two before the flame went out and they receded back into the darkness. The driver gestured to the heavy wooden doorway to our left.

'This can't be it.'

'*Sí, sí*, Hostal Central.'

'Stay in the car,' I instructed Graham, convinced we were in the wrong neighbourhood and determined not to be left stranded if I was right.

Exiting the taxi, my heart pounding, I could dimly make out the words 'Hostal Central' above the door and began insistently ringing the doorbell. Inside my head a voice was wailing 'Open the door! Open the bloody door!' but I resisted the urge to shout as I was terrified the people in the square would be drawn to see what all the commotion was about. Locks and bolts slid harshly on the other side, the door opened and I was welcomed inside by a smiling woman in white overalls and a hairnet. If the costume department in *Breaking Bad* had got it right then she was dressed to cook crystal meth. Two burly, black-clad armed policemen were in reception, sipping coffee. Muscle for the drug-makers, I thought. They dipped their heads by way of greeting. I beckoned Graham inside.

We checked into our room and the moment we closed the door Graham rushed to dig out the guidebook and began thumbing angrily through it to locate the section on downtown Medellín.

'Look,' he said, jabbing at the page while I searched for my toiletry bag. 'It says here that this is quite a seedy area with a lot of prostitution and drug dealing and that it's not a great place to be at night. Why the hell did you book *this* hostel?'

'I didn't have time to properly research every single option,' I snapped back. 'You had several weeks to organise this while I was busy seeing hypnotherapy clients in the evenings and you didn't bother doing it. You know full well that I had to book *all* the Colombia hostels late one night. If you think you could've done better, next time do it yourself!' I went to bed fuming, fearful of what morning would bring.

In the light of day, Hostal Central proved to be perfectly lovely: sunlight poured in through its glass ceiling illuminating its polished tiled floors and wood panelling decorated with a selection of framed botanical prints.

'It's how I imagine a gentleman's club on Pall Mall might look,' said Graham, astonished. I was still brooding about the previous night's blame-fest so stayed sulkily silent.

After breakfast we asked for directions to the main square. The genial receptionist drew us a crude map, and warned that we should be careful as the neighbourhood was '*feo*'.

'*Feo*?' I said. '*No comprendo*,' using some of the only Spanish words besides '*una cerveza, por favour*', '*baños*' and '*gracias*' I've ever managed to memorise.

She looked up the translation on the internet and pointed to the word 'ugly' on the reception computer screen.

Before stepping cautiously outside Graham slipped his wallet down the front of his trousers and concealed his camera in his daypack. We also took a moment to work out the route to Plaza Botero so we wouldn't have to stop to read the map, which might invite unwanted attention. Better to be a moving target. Out on the dirty streets a trio of prostitutes dressed in micro minis, boob tubes and fishnet stockings tottered by, the broken pavements threatening to throw them from their spiky stilettos. Desperately poor men and women lay sprawled across the pavements and gutters, many emaciated by hunger and the ravages of drug addiction, falling where they'd taken their last fix. They looked like crumpled bags of rubbish put out for collection. It was the most heart-wrenching, upsetting sight I'd ever seen.

Within five minutes we were in the Plaza, where we spent a happy hour admiring the 23 voluptuous – some would say 'big-boned' – bronze sculptures by Fernando Botero, the failed matador who became Colombia's most famous artist. *Perro*, a stocky dog, was the people's favourite: touched for good luck, his protruding tongue and whiskers had been polished to a brassy shine. In nearby Plaza de San Antonio there were two Boteros called *Bird of Peace*. The bird on the right was shiny brown and plump, its tail set at a jaunty angle and its thick, muscular legs sturdily perching it on its plinth. It was a replica of the original just to the left, whose chest and entire rear were blasted open by a bomb that, in 1995, killed 23 people at an outdoor concert. The leftist guerrilla group FARC was responsible, claiming the bombing was to punish Botero's son, then the Minister of Defence, for not engaging in peace talks. In defiance, Botero donated the second identical bronze bird and saw to it that the names of the victims of the bombing were carved into the original's base.

We didn't much fancy going out after nightfall, so we brought our supper – a roast chicken and some bread rolls – to the hostel at the end of a day's sightseeing. A small swarm of bees buzzed about the balcony so, wary of being stung, we ate in the kitchen, where we were joined by Thijs, who looked like a Colombian but had an unexpected Dutch accent.

'How do you like staying here?' he said, unpacking his dinner as he sipped from a tin of Club Colombia beer.

'We love this hostel but the area's a bit iffy,' I said.

'Yes,' said Thijs, 'I stay here every time I come to Medellín but I never go out after dark. It's very central and safe just as long as you don't walk the streets at night.'

The reason Thijs kept returning was to continue his search for his biological mother.

'This time I believe I may have found her. My younger brother and I were adopted from here by a Dutch couple when I was six and I now live in The Hague,' he told us. 'I'm waiting for the results of a DNA test to prove if she's my mother. When I first met her, she couldn't recall if she'd had eight or nine children. She couldn't remember me, and I couldn't remember her either.'

'Why don't you try regression hypnotherapy?' I suggested. 'It may be able to help you to recollect your childhood.'

'My girlfriend suggested that, too,' he replied, 'but quite frankly I'm scared of what I'll find out. A woman who may be my aunt told me that my mother had a child by her brother. I was a street child, so God knows what abuse I was subjected to. Maybe I've forgotten my early life for a reason.'

Whereas Botero is the good son of Medellín, Pablo Escobar, the notorious head of the Medellín cocaine cartel, was its bad one. When asked what he wanted to be when he grew up Escobar, precociously eschewing 'train driver' or 'fireman', replied 'a billionaire'. Starting as a petty criminal – he was expelled from school for selling stolen examination papers – he graduated to stealing gravestones for re-use (you have to admire his chutzpah, and his green credentials) before kidnapping a businessman for ransom. By the age of 26 he'd made his first million dollars by smuggling cocaine to the US. Escobar became so fabulously wealthy that each week he spent US$1,000 on elastic bands to keep his banknotes bound up and, because he always kept his money as cash, he lost an incredible 10 per cent of it each year to hungry rats.

Fascinated by *Killing Pablo*, a book we'd read as pre-Colombia 'homework', and by what we'd seen in the Netflix series *Narcos*, we signed up for an Escobar tour that took us to the extant sights: the fortress-like Monaco building he'd once lived in before a rival cartel's car bomb forced Escobar and his family to flee; the suburban house where, in 1993, he was tracked down and shot dead; and his well-tended grave, alongside Evita Perón's reportedly one of the most visited in South America.

The most chilling stop of the tour, however, was the Virgen Rosa Mystica shrine, set into a hillside grotto surrounded by flickering votive candles and protected by a canopy of canvas. Plaques bearing messages of gratitude to the Virgin for favours she'd granted paved the ground and were nailed, haphazardly, to several trees. A strange blend of Catholic piety and callous murder, it's where Escobar's *sicarios* would anoint their bullets with holy water and pray for their assassination attempts to be successful and for the cartel's cocaine shipments to arrive safely in America.

'One *sicario* who came here,' our tour guide related, 'overheard an elderly woman praying to the Virgin Mary for the money she needed to pay her rent. He got irritated by this and, after telling her "Stop worrying the Virgin with stupid stuff like that, old lady. She needs to concentrate on me," answered her prayers by giving the woman her rent money.'

It is said the Lord works in mysterious ways, but I bet my bottom dollar that grandma never thought that He'd choose a hired killer His wonders to perform.

While checking out of Hostal Central we noticed a pile of glass bottles stacked on pallets in the ground-floor courtyard. Again, the receptionist emerged from the back room attired like Walter White.

'What is it with this place?' I wondered. 'Could it be a front for something sinister?'

Then I noticed a row of bottles labelled *La Miel* on a shelf behind reception, and it dawned on me: Hostal Central was not a meth lab or a cocaine kitchen but a honey factory. And so our departing memory of Medellín would be a sweet one, not of its violent past.

Getting greasy with a croc hunter
Azerbaijan

'Leecy, we can't get our money back so you might as well go and enjoy yourself. But not *too* much,' joked Graham when he heard that his ongoing health problems meant that he couldn't accompany me on the 2017 trip to Abkhazia, Georgia, Armenia and Azerbaijan we'd planned to celebrate my 50th birthday. At that point we were still hoping his extreme breathlessness was something minor, or at least something easily treatable, so after much deliberation I flew out to Tbilisi, the capital of Georgia, very apprehensive about going on my first-ever organised tour alone. I needn't have worried as Lupine Travel, which specialises in tours to unusual and difficult-to-reach destinations – think Chernobyl, Chad and North Korea – has a reputation for catering to travel addicts, and every single person in the group had so many travel tales to tell that I fell asleep each night feeling I'd been on a round-the-world trip in a day. For some of the Azerbaijan part of the trip we were joined by Lupine's founder Dylan, a wonderfully laidback James Blunt lookalike who'd visited over 130 countries. Not surprisingly, his traveller's tale was the one to end all tales and had me hanging onto the edge of my bus seat throughout.

'I'm not even sure if I was ripped off or whether it was all above board but what I experienced in Uzbekistan, all because of a single packet of Boots painkillers costing £2.59, left me reeling,' said Dylan. 'I was crossing from Uzbekistan to Tajikistan when a border guard found a packet of Co-Codamol, a common painkiller containing codeine, in my luggage. "This is illegal and as bad as heroin," the official said, accusing me of being either a drug smuggler or addict.'

Dylan was questioned for six hours and then locked in a holding cell for 36 hours more. By then he was starving so begged to be given something to eat. Eventually, the guards relented and escorted him to the canteen where he was handed a bowl of fly-speckled stew that stank of rotten meat.

'I've been to some pretty squalid places in my 20 years of travelling,' he continued, 'but this was by far the most disgusting. In one corner was a big tub of stew with strips of flypaper hanging over it. The flies stuck on it wriggled to get free, dropping into the pot at frequent intervals. I was handed a bowl of the stew and told to tuck in. I took just one spoonful, which smelled of rotten meat, and started heaving. Just that one mouthful of food was enough to give me the worst food poisoning I've ever had. It lasted five days.'

Food poisoning, it turned out, was the least of Dylan's worries, as the next step in the legal process involved being taken off to hospital for a blood test to prove their theory that he was a drug addict.

'The blood test was absolutely terrifying as the nurse, who wasn't wearing gloves, wanted to stick an unsterilised needle in my arm. There was no sink in the room and there was a man rolling around on the ground covered in shit. I vigorously protested but in the end I had no choice but to let her take my blood, praying I wouldn't get hepatitis or HIV.'

When he appeared in court, the judge bluntly told Dylan that he faced a five-year jail term or a substantial fine. Eager for his ordeal to end, and knowing his fiancée would kill him if he didn't get home for their wedding in six weeks' time, Dylan paid the US$1,000 fine plus the same again for his drug test, prison 'accommodation' and the spoonful of bacteria stew he ate while he was there.

Oil is to Azerbaijan what princesses are to Disney: a huge money-spinner. Oil had helped boost GDP almost five-fold since 2004, our Azeri guide Nemet informed us as our tour bus came to a halt outside a swanky Ferrari showroom while navigating Baku's rush-hour traffic.

'Fire-worshipping Zoroastrians called Azerbaijan the Land of Fire because they didn't have to venture far to find oil to fuel their temple fires: it quite literally seeped up from the ground like plasma oozes from a wound,' said Nemet.

The eclectic architecture of Baku, Azerbaijan's capital, was like one of those children's books where you can mix and match body parts to create a bizarre Frankencreature with the head of a horse, the body of a baboon and the legs of a lizard. The ultra-modern Flame Towers, like three imperious penguins, stood sentinel over the weathered, honey-coloured buildings of the Old City; converted caravanserai and the ancient Maiden Tower cosied up with the space-age Heydar Aliyev Center, whose sinuous white roof resembled – depending on who you asked or which guidebook you read – either the President's signature (a staggering act of political egotism considering it cost US$250 million and was designed by the late megastar architect Zaha Hadid) or Marilyn Monroe's scandalous knicker-revealing skirt (a saucier and hence less likely explanation).

It was after a walking tour of Baku's cobbled Old City, which with the addition of many tons of tarmac is turned into a Formula 1 racetrack once a year when the Grand Prix roars into town, that our tour leader James asked if any of us would like to join him for a bath in crude oil.

'Yes, it's definitely a "thing",' he assured us when most of the group looked at him dumbstruck. 'I've seen the explorer

Levison Wood do it on TV.'

I've long had a toxic relationship with oil. I pitied my mother's decades-long losing battle with the oil that leaked from our car onto our driveway's paving. And I remember as a child being disgusted when, after beachcombing near my Gran's house, I found big gobs of black crude stuck to my feet that had leached from the tankers moored off Durban as they pumped their cargo to the nearby refinery. In both cases, it took a heck of a lot of painful scrubbing to get it off. So when offered the chance to bathe in the stuff I wasn't entirely sure I wanted to – or, for that matter, why *anyone* would want to – but the idea was so mind-boggling that I just had to give it a go.

'Do you have to be naked?' I enquired.

James wasn't sure, so Nemet called up the Naftalan Clinic and got the low-down. It was going to cost US$40 and, yes, nudity was most definitely involved. This immediately settled it for the rest of the group: they weren't coming. And it immediately settled it for me: I would go. Not only was I intrigued by the prospect of bathing in something so sticky and dirty but I'd recently bought a new swimming costume after losing mine in Colombia, so as long as the experience didn't involve the ritual sacrifice of a cossie, I was up for it. The only other person prepared to come along was Jake, a lean, rangy former crocodile hunter-turned-builder with a buzz cut. A man of few words, before moving to Brighton Jake had spent several months in Australia's Northern Territories hunting man-eaters. To prove his story he kept a photo on his mobile phone of a partially digested human arm and foot extracted from a dissected croc's stomach.

On our way to the clinic Nemet told us that Naftalan oil is renowned for treating nervous-system disorders, joint problems and skin diseases and should by rights be called 'cure oil' not 'crude oil'. At reception, a heavily made-up young woman looked surprised to see three non-Azeris waiting to pay. Nemet dealt with the formalities before we were escorted to the second floor of the dilapidated clinic where we were greeted by half a dozen taciturn staff in white smocks and green knock-off Crocs. I was the first to be examined. A doctor seated at an antiquated wooden desk took my blood pressure and asked me a few basic questions.

'Baby?' she said, pointing to my belly.

'No, I'm definitely not pregnant,' I said, sucking in my stomach.

'Heart?' she said, pointing to my chest.

'No, it's fine.'

My cursory medical over, I was ushered into a small, white-tiled room and told to undress and wrap myself in a threadbare towel that had been folded over the back of a chair. Squirming with embarrassment, I obliged. Tie up your hair, gestured the elderly woman who'd accompanied me. As I had nothing to do it with, she reached into a cupboard and brought out an old duvet cover stained with oil. It looked as if it had wiped a thousand arses. Tearing off a filthy strip, she stood on tiptoe and bound my hair into a ponytail. Smiling at her own ingenuity, she led me next door where a bath half-filled with oil stood against a wall. I'd expected a Durban-refinery stink, but the smell was much less intense, like a motor mechanic's overalls.

'Get in, get in,' said the woman, indicating that I should remove the towel.

I was unsure about stepping into someone else's bath 'water' but, as quickly as I could, dropped the towel and stepped gingerly into the bath, belatedly realising how slippery it was underfoot. I thudded down into a seated position, sending a bow-wave of oil towards the tap end.

'Lie back, lie back,' the attendant urged me.

This was easier said than done as it was a very capacious bath and my toes barely reached the end. Fearful of slipping beneath the surface of the brown sludge, I held tightly onto the sides of the tub. The oil had the texture and temperature of melted chocolate and was strangely sensuous. Turning on the tap on the wall, from which gushed a thick stream of crude, the woman topped up the bath and gestured that I should wash oil over whichever parts of my body were still exposed. I did so with one hand and soon resembled a pink marshmallow in a chocolate fountain.

'Ten minutes. Smell can make you sleepy. Call if need me,' she said, leaving me alone to contemplate my oil-slicked navel and the smears of oil on the tiled walls that made the room look like the previous occupant had staged a dirty protest. I also had time to ponder the purpose of the long-handled shoehorn hanging on a nail next to the bath. Try as I might, I couldn't imagine what it was for. Mindful that I didn't want to pass out and slip quietly under the suffocating liquid, I anxiously monitored my consciousness levels.

My 10 minutes over, the attendant reappeared and indicated that I should stand up. I rose unsteadily to my feet, whereupon she unhooked the shoehorn from the wall and began to deftly de-oil me, much as one would make curls of butter for a posh dinner party. Where was that shoehorn going *exactly*? It was 'access all areas' as she expertly swiped oil from my breasts and nether regions.

'Ooh,' I blurted out as she flicked a gob of goo from my left nipple. Satisfied that most of the oil was off me and back in the bath, she motioned me to step out and handed me a loaf-sized sponge soaked in liquid soap.

'You wash,' she said.

I began a gentle scrub that was not to her liking. Grabbing the sponge from me, she added another substantial squirt of soap and began vigorously lathering me up and down as if she was cleaning a car. Again, no part of me was too intimate for her attentions. Having covered me in suds, she handed back the sponge and started to hose me down, insisting that I continue my ablutions. I felt incredibly awkward standing stark naked in front of a stranger watching me wash. Only when she was satisfied that I was squeaky clean was I allowed to dry myself and get dressed.

Emerging from the therapy room, I saw Jake the croc catcher sitting on a chair in the corridor.

'How was it?' he asked eagerly.

'Interesting,' I said grinning, wondering whether he was going to be immersed in the oil I'd recently bathed in.

The attendant led me to another small room with a 'Massage' sign on the door and brought me a cup of hot mint tea on a brass tray. Unsure whether I'd paid for a massage as part of my treatment, I debated whether I should get undressed again but thought better of it. Instead, as a token gesture of willingness, I removed my shoes and socks. This was just as well as within five minutes, while I was sipping my tea, James entered, fully clothed, and not long after that Jake joined us.

'Bloody hell, that was terrifying,' said Jake. 'I didn't expect the medical examination to be quite so thorough.'

'Terrifying? Thorough?' I said. 'All they did was take my blood pressure and ask if I was pregnant.'

'You mean you didn't get an ECG?'

'An ECG? No, why, did you?'

'Yes,' said Jake, 'and when the doctor was looking at the printout of my cardiogram, the only thing he said was "Heart attack". I nearly had one on the spot when I heard that! "Oi mate," I told him, "I only came here for a bit of fun."'

It turned out the doctor was enquiring whether Jake had ever had a heart attack, *not* indicating that one was imminent.

When we rejoined our tour group everyone excitedly asked us about our experience. Jake took great delight in telling them that he and I had shared a bath, only later revealing that it hadn't been at the same time.

'Why didn't you come along?' I asked Martin from Scotland, who'd been particularly interested in hearing the tale we related.

'Och, no,' he said. 'I've seen it on TV, and it all looked a bit yuck.'

CHAPTER FIVE

2018: The Year of Going Back to My Roots
Ghana, Togo, Benin

Ghana was the country where I was born, and it was also the country where my father nearly died before I entered the world. Fresh off the boat on his first diplomatic posting, he'd donned his Speedos and gone for a swim in the sea off Labadi Beach, a spot popular among locals in Accra. My mother, then seven months pregnant with me, had stayed sitting under a scrubby tree supporting her baby bump. Within minutes Pa was in serious trouble. The beach dropped away very quickly and soon, caught unawares by a powerful riptide, he was in over his head, in every sense of the word. His frantic waving caught the attention of my mother.

'I knew Reg wasn't a strong swimmer,' she told me, 'and I could tell by his face that he was scared, so I ran over to some of his High Commission colleagues who were picnicking nearby and told them he was in trouble. They didn't believe me. One of them said that your dad wasn't even that far out and that he'd be fine. "Trust me," I pleaded, "I know he's drowning." I was absolutely frantic.

'Thankfully, one of them stood up and, when he saw how badly your father was being buffeted by the waves, he told the others that they needed to get Reg out. Five chaps leapt up and ran into the ocean where they formed a human chain, bracing themselves against the waves that threatened to knock them off their feet. The strongest swimmer went out to get your dad, who was utterly exhausted by then. Between them they managed to haul him ashore. I was so grateful to them. I've never been more scared in my life.'

The Labadi Beach story, and my parents' love of their first diplomatic posting, had been told countless times throughout my childhood, sparking a desire to visit the country of my birth. But other countries kept popping to the top of our to-see list, displacing Ghana as a priority. Either they were cheaper to get to, or the weather in Ghana wasn't good for the time we could visit – two weeks of incessant rain in Japan had made me an inconsolably miserable travel companion with a mild case of trench foot and I'd vowed to never again go anywhere out of season. Someday I would go to Ghana. It was a case of when, not if.

'You must visit Ghana,' urged Steve, a Ghanaian security guard stationed at *Zest* magazine's reception desk whom Lisa had befriended and stayed in touch with long after she'd left the company. 'Graham must see again the place where he was born. Once people know he is Ghanaian, he will be welcomed like a long-lost brother. Did you know that Accra has the biggest parade ground in Africa? Black Star Square. And that Akosombo Dam made the largest man-made lake in the world? Oh, yes.'

From Steve's tales, and the postcards he showed us, we knew that Ghana wasn't going to be chockful of tourist sights, but we also knew from chatting with Steve and several other Ghanaians that it was going to be full of warm, welcoming, friendly people.

'Of all six countries we were posted to, Ghana was my favourite,' Ma once said. 'You'd be hard-pressed to find friendlier, kinder people anywhere.'

The existential threat of my October 2017 cancer diagnosis put Ghana right back into contention: if I didn't go there soon then I may never get there at all. But six weeks to recuperate after surgery and then 15 weeks of chemotherapy meant it wasn't until May that I could travel. It also meant that I felt rinsed through, without the mental strength or the physical stamina for anything more taxing than three weeks in the Croatian sun. Ghana would have to wait a little while longer. It would have to wait until September.

A cursory look at a map of West Africa and a quick internet search decided us: we'd fly into Ghana, traverse neighbouring Togo and fly home from Benin. Our shockingly inadequate French would make Francophone Togo and Benin challenging and the short time I could take off work argued against travelling independently – and hence slowly – so we agreed we'd join an organised tour.

'This is going to be interesting,' said Lisa. 'Besides what Steve's told me, I know nothing about Ghana or West Africa. All I know is that it's likely to operate on Africa Time.'

Recalling how Steve and his wife Aurelia would invite us round for lunch at 1pm and only serve it at 4pm, by which time we'd be almost stocious from drinking wine on an empty stomach, I had to chuckle. Steve had explained that Ghanaians have a different concept of time – and happiness.

'Here in the UK people are much richer than we are in Ghana,' he said as Aurelia piled our plates high with rice, potatoes, plantain, carrots, chicken and lamb chops, 'but they are not happier.'

'Yes,' agreed Aurelia, 'that is why we are building a house in Accra. When Steve retires we are going to move back there to live.'

'In Ghana we may not be rich, but we are not stressed,' continued Steve. 'Part of the stress comes from worrying about being late all the time. We just don't do that in Ghana. In Ghana, we work on Africa Time. If you want to meet someone at 12 noon, you should say "Meet me at 10am". And that way they may arrive at noon, but maybe also at 1pm or even 2pm. In the end it doesn't really matter. You meet them and that is all that counts. Why get stressed about nothing?'

'We'll be sad to see you go,' said Lisa. 'And when we go to Ghana, we'll remember what you said about Africa Time.'

Ghana have a good time
Ghana

'You must pay 150 US dollars for the visa,' deadpanned the Ghanaian immigration official at Accra airport from behind a sheet of customer unfriendly glass. She swivelled in her chair to continue her conversation with the female official next to her, letting her belt out a notch or two to be more comfortable. She looked comfortable enough already, I thought. Too bloody comfortable.

'But the High Commission website in London said that citizens of certain countries, like South Africa, don't need a visa,' objected Lisa. 'I'm entering Ghana on a South African passport, so I don't see why I have to pay.'

The official swivelled lazily back to face Lisa.

'It is 150 dollars for the emergency visa. You should have got a visa in your home country. If you do not pay, then you will be sent back to England.'

Lisa changed tack and asked to speak to the woman's superior. Rolling her eyes, she leaned back and passed Lisa's passport over her right shoulder to the man standing behind her. He thumbed through Lisa's passport, confirmed that she needed to purchase an emergency visa and handed it back.

There was clearly no point in arguing any further. The official wasn't faceless – in fact, she was sour-faced – but she was playing the part of a faceless bureaucrat perfectly: passive, unhelpful, indifferent and immovable.

'We don't have any US dollars. How much is it in sterling?' I asked.

'In British pounds, you must pay 115.'

That was twice the price I'd paid for my visa in London. I told her that it was, and that they should post accurate information on their website. She couldn't have cared less. I handed over the money. It was just as well we'd brought a small stash of cash, almost all of which was now spent. As I paid dearly for her visa, Lisa surreptitiously disposed of the fruit we'd brought from London that she'd forgotten to leave on the plane, placing the plastic bag by her feet under the counter. There didn't seem to be CCTV to record her illicit act. We received a receipt for £115, Lisa had her passport stamped and an official demanded to see our yellow fever vaccination certificates. Welcome to Ghana.

In the car park outside, our pre-booked driver was waiting to take us to Somewhere Nice, a hostel we'd chosen partly for its nice-sounding name. It was pitch dark apart from the light that spilled from open doorways and curtainless windows, and the streets were almost empty of pedestrians. I guessed that a combination of rain and darkness had driven most people indoors.

Our driver turned off the main road and carefully navigated down a rutted and potholed side street and pulled up in front of a closed metal gate. He parped his horn and the gate swung open to let us in. Retrieving our rucksacks from the boot, we presented ourselves at reception. A young man in a patterned wax-print cloth shirt decorated in pink spirograph circles checked our names against a list of bookings and insisted – quite unreasonably, we thought – that we pay, in *cedis*, before he'd give us the key to our room.

'We've just come from the airport,' I protested. 'We don't have any Ghanaian currency. Please can we pay tomorrow? You can keep our passports until then, as security.'

'No, I'm afraid you must pay now, sir. We don't accept credit cards here. There is a cash machine nearby. You can leave your bags here.'

Lisa appealed to his better nature: 'We're very tired and it's dark and we have no idea where we are or where to go. Please can we pay you tomorrow?'

His response was to tell us where to go, literally.

'Turn left from the gate, go over the main road and then at the end of that road, turn left. You will walk until you see a Société Générale bank. There is a cash machine there. It is only five minutes' walk.'

As with the immigration official, we knew there was no point in arguing further. The hope of a friendly welcome had faded completely by now.

'I just can't believe that bloody receptionist,' said Lisa indignantly as we picked our way down the unlit dirt road, trying to avoid the puddles. 'We've stayed in hundreds of hostels and never once have they insisted that we pay in full before they'd let us into our room. I wouldn't even do this in the UK – walk down a street in a neighbourhood I don't know in the pitch black. I'm trying not to be scared, but I don't like this one little bit.'

'I can't say I'm thrilled either, but there's nobody around and I'm sure he wouldn't have sent us out if it was dangerous.'

'What's making it feel so scary is the fact that it's so deserted.'

We reached the bottom of our road and heard the faint melodious strains of gospel singing.

'That's making me feel a whole lot better,' said Lisa. 'I'd forgotten Ghana is a very religious country, so maybe we're more likely to be accosted by someone trying to persuade us to go to church with them than a mugger.'

'If someone mugged us now they wouldn't get anything. We were already mugged for all of our cash back at the airport,' I joked.

'Ha ha, very funny. I swear the website said I didn't need a visa. Didn't the receptionist say we had to cross a main road?'

'Yes, but I can't see one. Which way now?'

'Your guess is as good as mine. I can't see any lights to the left, but there are a few to the right, so my guess is that it's that way.'

As we drew closer to the lights we saw that they were naked lightbulbs illuminating a series of tiny plywood kiosks on either side of the road selling all manner of packet snacks and cellphone cards. The receptionist had assured us that the bank was easily locatable, but we'd walked for 20 minutes and there was still no sign of it.

'I think we have to conclude we're lost, Lisa. Let's retrace our steps back to Somewhere Nice.'

'No way, Graham. You always give up too easily. I didn't walk down this scary road for nothing. This is just so bloody typical of you and it drives me nuts. Why can't you just ask someone for directions? Is it a man-pride thing? They speak English in Ghana, you know. Even when we're just a few metres from our destination you always refuse to ask for directions. Like the time we spent two hours in the Delhi traffic looking for that graveyard of colonial statues. If it weren't for me asking that shopkeeper where it was, we'd have gone back to Ringo's Guesthouse without seeing them. And they were only round the next block.'

Before Lisa could get even more into her critical stride, I spotted the bank's illuminated sign at the top of the street, glowing brightly above the roofline.

'There's the bank!' I exclaimed, pointing. 'Now let's hope that my card works in the machine.' If it didn't, I'd hear more from Lisa about my reluctance to ask for directions and more about how ridiculously inflexible the receptionist had been.

'That's the sound I want to hear,' I said to Lisa as the whirring ATM counted out our *cedis*.

'Isn't that the road our driver turned down when he dropped us off?' asked Lisa. 'I think I recognise the "Correct Sexual Weakness Naturally" billboard.'

'I believe you may be right. I remember seeing "Do not urine here" painted on that wall over there.'

Five minutes later we were back at Somewhere Nice. Like Lisa, the receptionist obviously had difficulty telling his left from his right. Grumpily, we paid for and were shown to our spartan but spotlessly clean room.

'I could murder a beer. Let's head to the pool,' I said, dropping my rucksack on the floor.

'I want you to put on your anti-malaria clothing first,' insisted Lisa.

'What, *now*? No way, I'm putting my shorts on and going for a drink.'

'Graham, your mother will never forgive me if I let you contract malaria. You didn't go through surgery and chemo only to die in the country where you were born. I want you to put on that T-shirt I bought you and slather any exposed skin in Jungle Juice.'

While waiting to be issued with our anti-malaria pills, Lisa had read a brochure in our local chemist about the disease and discovered that it was one of the top five causes of death in sub-Saharan Africa. Two of the case studies it cited had been young Brits who'd contracted malaria in Ghana and subsequently died. Lisa was paranoid that I'd get malaria, and so had spent the three weeks leading up to our departure ordering an array of desperately unfashionable DEET-impregnated T-shirts and trousers, along with mosquito-killing coils, a mosquito net and two bush hats with drop-down gauze veils.

'I am not walking around West Africa looking like a complete plonker,' I told her when she proudly unwrapped the khaki headgear. 'I'll look like a beekeeper who's lost his bees. Or lost the plot.'

'I don't care how ridiculous we look, Graham. The only thing I care about is coming back from West Africa alive. I don't want either of us to end up as a case study in a pharmacy pamphlet.'

The £200 Lisa spent turned out to be £200 wasted. As we sat by the pool drinking Club beer we saw precisely one mosquito, and that one mosquito was the only mosquito we were to see during our entire 18-day trip.

In the morning, after breakfasting on tropical fruit, pancakes, eggs and delicious smoothies, and with *cedis* in our pocket, we took a taxi to the *tro tro* terminus in central Accra from where we could take one of these minibus shared taxis to Cape Coast. The *tro tro* rank was on the edge of chaotic, sprawling

Kaneshie Market which thronged with hawkers weaving through the narrow spaces between the stalls carrying artfully placed piles of fruit, bags of plantain chips and loaves of puffy white bread on their heads.

'Oh wow, look at that hawker,' said Lisa, pointing at a man dodging the heavy traffic wearing a tiered wedding cake-like crown made from toothbrushes and tubes of toothpaste. 'Perhaps he's the Crown Prince of Dental Care.'

Beneath posters for revivalist Christian meetings, salesmen portered racks of self-help books such as *Rich Dad, Poor Dad* and *Think Yourself Rich* creating a motivational combination of God and mammon, spiritual wholesomeness and temporal wealth. We needed sharp elbows to reach the beach umbrella-shaded rickety tables where *tro tro* tickets were being sold to clamorous would-be passengers. I waved a handful of cash and called out 'Cape Coast, two tickets' only to be waved away or ignored. Eventually, after an hour in the hot sun, Lisa and I twigged that we were standing in the wrong queue. Thirty minutes after relocating ourselves to the correct one and paying for three tickets, the third for luggage, we were ensconced in the back seat of an old Ford Transit minibus. Unless we were rear-ended by a lorry, these had to be the safest *tro tro* seats.

Once free of Accra's traffic, the fast road to Cape Coast was heralded by a road-safety billboard proclaiming, 'Drunk driving: choose one… jail, morgue, hospital'. During the four-hour journey we passed innumerable churches, not a few of them Mormon, and billowing camouflage car covers strung up from roadside trees and posts. It made me wonder if car theft was so rife that owners camouflaged their cars in the hope that thieves wouldn't find them. Not that I could imagine theft being a big problem in Ghana, considering that every *tro tro* we passed had a slogan painted on its rear window promoting Christian values: 'Trust God', 'Be Honest', 'Obey Your Parents' and 'Don't Envy'. Mind you, I never saw one saying 'Do Not Steal'.

'By the time we get to Cape Coast it's entirely possible I'll have re-read the entire Bible,' said Lisa. 'It looks like the church has outsourced its sermonising and evangelising to the *tro tro* trade.'

'And by the look of things, shop owners have got in on the act, too,' I remarked as we motored past God is Great Refrigeration and Air Conditioning Services, Christ the King Supermarket – perhaps specialising in bread and fish? – and Abundant Grace Hair Salon. Further down the road, for women who needed help 'lifting and separating', there was the Hand of God Brassiere Boutique. And on two sides of a crossroad, Goodness and Mercy Spare Parts competed with By His Grace Bicycle Repairs.

'What services do you suppose 30 Days Supernatural Repositioning offers?'

'I haven't the foggiest,' answered Lisa, 'but if we get hungry we can ask our driver to stop at No Yesterdays Pies.'

'I'd feel safer at No Weapon Food Joint.'

Two passengers in the seats in front of us struck up a conversation.

'Have you ever had the chance to visit Nigeria?' the middle-aged businessman asked the smartly dressed young woman next to him.

'No. I would like to go, but Nigeria has a reputation for being a bad place, very dangerous.'

'It *is* very dangerous,' he agreed. 'It is unbelievably corrupt. Even the police are bad. The best Nigerian policeman is worse than the worst Ghanaian policeman.'

Turning to me, Lisa whispered: 'I'm glad we're not going on to Lagos, even though I was tempted to as it's next door to Benin.'

The Transit put us down in the centre of Cape Coast, from where a taxi took us the last leg to Oasis Beach Resort.

'We have no room for you, sir,' said the overweight man in reception. He dabbed away the sweat that escaped the drying effect of his desk fan and waved an arm in front of his face to swat away a nuisance fly. 'There is a festival in town.'

'But we booked a room through Booking.com,' said Lisa, thrusting the printed-off confirmation at him. 'It was booked a long time ago, as you can see.'

'I am very angry with Booking.com,' he sighed lethargically, not deigning even to look at the A4 sheet held out to him. 'I told them they must not book any more rooms as we are full, but they keep booking people. You can stay in one of our dormitories. There is room there for you.'

'That's not good enough. We've booked a private room. Is there anywhere else we can stay round here?'

It was as much energy as he could muster to suggest that we try Orange Beach, the establishment next door. Orange Beach looked tired and to its rear was a row of offensively smelly cinderblock and tin-roofed toilets. The unseen dormitory had to be better.

'I'm so pleased I didn't lose my temper with that man in reception,' said Lisa rushing back across the beach to the Oasis Beach Resort before rather sheepishly re-presenting ourselves to him, paying for the last free beds in the ten-bed dorm and taking a table in the resort's open-air restaurant.

As we ate our lunch of fried chicken with red-red (stewed black-eyed peas) and two large Club beers, we marvelled at the courage – or, if he'd miscalculated, the stupidity – of a Westerner swimming in the violent, crashing surf in defiance of a large sign prohibiting bathing. He seemed to be having a whale of a time in the huge waves.

'I don't want to see that man drown, but I can't stop watching him. What will we do if he gets into trouble, Graham?' Lisa asked.

'If I go into that water, I'm a dead man. Remember how we nearly drowned in the Philippines? And what happened to Pa at Labadi Beach? As far as I'm concerned, he's on his own.'

Lisa tried her best to ignore him and enjoy her food and beer, but kept shooting worried glances seawards until he swam to shore, collected his towel and sauntered up the beach to Orange Beach.

'I think that swimmer was just desperate to rinse off the stink of those Orange Beach bogs,' remarked Lisa.

Cape Coast Castle, just up the beach beyond Orange Beach, was our first sobering encounter with the horrors of slavery. Set on a rocky cliff overlooking the wild Atlantic, its photogenic whitewashed ramparts studded with cannons mirrored by several toppled ones rusting on the rocks below belied its truly horrendous past. Slaves captured in the interior were brought here and 'stored' before being loaded onto the ships that would, if they survived the treacherous passage, take them to the Americas and the Caribbean.

'This is the male slave dungeon,' said our guide, leading us into a dank vaulted underground room. 'Each of these five rooms housed 200 slaves. Can you imagine 200 people crowded in here? The floor you are standing on is brick that is covered in cement made from the saliva, urine and excrement of the slaves who were kept here – they were not given any toilets. In the female dungeons, menstrual blood was also in the mix. You can see that there is no light in here, or even much air. The smell must have been unbearable. And can you guess what is on the floor above? A church. The slaves had to listen to their captors singing hymns while they suffered down here in the dark, terrified of what would become of them.'

The guide led us to a small section of the dungeon where a shrine of several ribbon-bedecked wreaths and a sheet splattered with chicken blood had been set up.

'Descendants of slaves often visit us to see for themselves what their ancestors endured,' he said. 'They pour gin over the shrine as libation. Michelle and Barack Obama came here in 2009. She is the descendant of slaves. The President said this place reminded him of a concentration camp.'

He led us back out into the sunlit courtyard before ushering us into a small room and shutting the door.

'This is the condemned cell,' he said, turning out the light.

A child on the tour let out a shrill scream. 'If any of the slaves rebelled, they were put in here without food and water and dragged out once they were dead. The slavers wanted to send a clear message to the other slaves that rebellion meant certain death.'

We were led down a steep cobbled path to a door that, when thrown open, revealed a picturesque harbour sheltering colourful fishing boats from the crashing Atlantic. 'The door you have just stepped through is called the Door of No Return. This harbour was where boats waited to take slaves to the ships anchored offshore. For every 100 slaves who survived the journey across the Atlantic, as many as 150 died on the way. Some of the slaves had never seen the sea before and were so terrified they committed suicide by throwing themselves overboard.'

'When I was a child, my mother showed me an engraving of the interior of a slave ship,' said Lisa. 'I remember being horrified that to carry as many slaves as possible, slaves were chained together and crammed below deck on a series of shelves like sardines in a tin. It gave me nightmares.'

'We need to remember,' said our guide, 'that Europeans avoided going into the interior to capture slaves as that would expose them to deadly tropical diseases. Bands of African slavers were the ones who actually caught the slaves and then sold them to the Europeans in exchange for weapons and goods. Male slaves could be bought for 40 guns and some cloth; female slaves cost a fraction of that.'

As we left, our guide pointed out a small plaque set into the castle wall bearing the words: 'In everlasting memory of the anguish of our ancestors. May those who died rest in peace. May those who return find their roots. May humanity never again perpetrate such injustice against humanity. We, the living, vow to uphold this.'

Although our guide said it had been placed there by Ghana's chiefs to acknowledge their forefathers' role in the slave trade, by not including this detail the plaque avoided acknowledging the role played by Africans in facilitating such unimaginable atrocities.

That night, we met up with our Lupine West Africa tour group at a smart, modern resort hotel complete with horizon pool on a hill overlooking Elmina, another slaving post about 14km west of Cape Coast. The sound of Highlife pop music drifted up from the town. Sarnor, from Liberia, was our tour leader, and had with him two travellers, Ernestine, a day trader from Vancouver who spent half of every year travelling the world and had so far visited 143 countries, and Luisa, a tiny but redoubtable Filipino from Miami, who'd once been taught by none other than Imelda Marcos and who'd been to 167 countries, including Iraq when it was a war zone.

The next day after breakfast we met our local drivers, Kojo and Elolo, and Kaatachi who was to be our 'guide'. I say 'guide' advisedly because Kaatachi was a local Elmina boy and seemed not to have left its city limits before landing himself this gig. He knew very little about not very much.

'Hello, my name is Kaatachi, but you can call me Kaa or Chief,' he said smiling, shaking my hand Ghanaian-style, which involved three different hand clasps and a click of the fingers as a finale. I, of course, shook his hand English-style, so between us we made a complete hash of our greeting.

'I'm Graham, and you can call me Graham,' I told him, 'as that's my name.'

Unperturbed, Kaa continued: 'During this trip I will be your local knowledge and fixer man. You are not in England, Canada or America, you are in Africa, so you have to be careful. There are bad people about. Every day we will have a briefing. We will always drive in convoy and be in phone contact between the two vehicles. Tell me if you want the car to stop and I will decide if it is safe to do so. Your safety is my priority. Does anyone have any questions?'

I had one, but for Sarnor, not Kaa, and it was, 'Where did you get this prize chump from?' We were in Elmina, a sleepy fishing port, next stop Kumasi, the cultural capital of the Ashanti tribe, not the strife-ravaged Mogadishu of *Black Hawk Down.*

Lisa and I took the back seat of one car while Kaa sat up front with Kojo in what we always call the 'suicide seat'. Sarnor, Luisa and Ernestine travelled with Elolo in the second vehicle. It seemed a shame that we weren't all in one larger car, but Sarnor said it was far cheaper to have two smaller vehicles.

We headed out to Elmina Castle, a fortification built by the Portuguese in 1482 that was wrested from them by the Dutch, who later lost it to the British. Elmina Castle is the oldest European structure in sub-Saharan Africa and, like Cape Coast Castle, a place of great sadness. While the governor enjoyed spacious quarters with fabulous views of the ocean, the shackled slaves, who were kept for up to three months in the dungeons below, had no space to lie down.

'Governors often didn't bring their wives to West Africa because of the malaria risk,' our guide Robert informed us, 'so whenever they wanted a woman to sleep with they would choose one who would be brought up through this trapdoor into his bedroom. The slaves were kept in filthy conditions so the chosen woman would first be given a bath before being led up here to be raped.'

'This story,' whispered Lisa, 'is making me feel ill.'

The nightclub breakfast

After an uneventful four-and-a-half-hour drive north from Elmina, we pulled into the carpark of our Kumasi hotel.

'Mmm, it looks a bit like a bordello, or a love hotel,' said Lisa under her breath.

'I know what you mean,' I agreed, surveying the giant billboards advertising hot stone massages and the virtues of the attached casino. The room we'd been assigned had a peculiar smell, there were cigarette burns on the desk and the sheets, and the ceiling smoke alarm let out an ear-splitting and headache-inducing squawk every 20 seconds, so Lisa insisted on being given another. The receptionist's pained response made me think that our request was unreasonable, as if Lisa had asked her for one of her kidneys.

Breakfast was something of an experience. Walking from our room to the end of a long, marble-floored corridor, we pushed open the door at the end of it and found ourselves in a gloomy room with purple-and-silver décor.

'This looks like a nightclub,' said Lisa, before spotting the bottles of alcohol behind the bar. 'Oh, I see that it is.'

We settled into a booth that smelled of stale beer and stale bodies. Through the low glass table a discarded pink stiletto, a casualty from the night before, lay forlornly waiting for its owner to reclaim it. Lisa kicked it to one side. A few minutes later, a surly waitress shuffled over to take our order.

'I'll have an omelette, toast and coffee, please,' said Lisa.

'And I'll have fried eggs, toast and tea,' I said.

'That will be extra.'

'What do you mean by extra?'

'It is one breakfast per room,' said the waitress, 'so if you order a second breakfast, you will have to pay for it.'

I looked over at the mashed-up scrambled eggs Sarnor was quietly choking down and thought better of it.

'Just bring us the omelette breakfast, please, but with two sets of cutlery. We'll share it.'

Half an hour later a plate containing two fried eggs was dropped on our table, along with a side plate of toast. The toast slid onto the finger-smudged table. The waitress reached over, picked it up and plonked it back on the plate. I was going to remind her I'd ordered an omelette, but as we wanted to see at least something of Kumasi, zipped my lip.

Ghana Armed Forces Museum, located in a colonial-era fort, was our first stop of the day. A motley collection of armoured cars and artillery pieces were set out on the pavement outside. Inside, there was an exhibition room of militaria depicting the proud history of Ghanaians' armed service to the British, plus lots of hideous-looking 'genocide weapons' captured by Ghanaian UN peacekeepers in Rwanda. Most were machetes that the Hutu used to amputate the hands or arms of Tutsis. Our knowledgeable guide informed us that victims were asked one chilling question before their amputation: 'Do you want long or short sleeves?'

In 1900, during an Ashanti rebellion against the British, the Ashanti laid siege to the fort for over 12 weeks. 'The rebellion was led by the Queen Mother, Yaa Asantewaa, who had taken offence when the British Governor demanded that the Ashanti hand over their Golden Stool, the symbol of Ashanti kingship, so that he could sit on it,' our engaging guide informed us. 'The sacred stool, covered in pure gold, floated down from the sky into the lap of the first Ashanti king. According to the king's head priest, Okomfo Anokye, the stool possessed the soul of the Ashanti people – he prophesied that if it was ever destroyed or captured, the kingdom would fall.' Eventually the siege was relieved, the Queen Mother was imprisoned in a tiny cell in the fort before being exiled to the Seychelles and – so our guide said – the British got their hands on the sacred stool. Except they didn't. The wily Ashanti, knowing the Brits had no idea what the stool looked like, allegedly handed over a replica instead.

'What a cheek! I can't believe that the British would demand that the Ashanti give them something so sacred. It's an act of cultural genocide,' frowned Lisa.

'The Golden Stool is displayed to the public once every five years,' continued our guide. The next scheduled outing was 2019, so we were a year early. Or four years late.

Luisa, of course, immediately wanted to set off in search of it, and knowing her, would probably have managed to wangle access to it. She'd already demonstrated her persuasive charms when it came to taking photographs. As a white-haired elderly woman she was accorded great respect wherever she went, to the extent that she could take photographs in places where photography was prohibited, which was nearly every museum across West Africa.

'Would it be all right for me to take one or two pictures, please?' she'd sweetly ask the male curators and guides, often while gently pressing their arm. 'Okay, Mama, but just one or two, and only you.' Whereupon Luisa would photograph and film *everything*. If she was ever challenged for exceeding her remit – frankly, she was always tearing the arse out of it: 'Mama, you should not take so many pictures, it is not allowed and I will get into trouble' – her invariable response was to widen her eyes in innocent surprise and double-down on flattery and charm: 'Oh, but this is *so* beautiful and interesting and you are *such* a wonderful guide. Just *one* more picture?' Each evening Luisa would share with us via WhatsApp the many dozens of fantastic pictures she'd taken. We loved her for it.

From the fort we drove to the Okomfo Anokye Sword Site, Kumasi's own slice of Arthurian legend: Okomfo Anokye summoned the sword – as he did the Golden Stool – from heaven, planting it at this exact spot over 300 years ago. Only the hilt of the Ashanti Excalibur is visible above ground in a gravel-filled pit, surrounded by empty bottles of liquor used for libation. According to legend, if the sword is removed then the Ashanti nation will be destroyed. Muhammad Ali reportedly tried to remove it. What could he have had against the Ashanti such that he was prepared to risk bringing about their downfall? I wondered.

'Sarnor, I need the loo,' said Lisa. Sarnor found her a toilet, and when she emerged, Lisa commented that it was, as usual in Ghana, pristine.

'What is it with you guys, haven't you seen a clean toilet before?' he asked, amused.

We had, but generally not while travelling. Sarnor had obviously never been to India. Perhaps the numerous signs we spotted in Ghana's public toilets exhorting patrons to keep them clean had something to do with it. In one, Lisa told me the public advisory read: 'Ladies, our aim is to keep this bathroom clean. Please remain seated throughout the entire performance!' Staying with the comedy theme, the sign in the gents was: 'Gentlemen, your aim is to stand closer. Life is shorter than you think!'

The afternoon's planned activity was a foray into Kumasi's vast, sprawling Kejetia Market, which vied with Cotonou's Dantokpa Market for the title of biggest in West Africa.

'It also has a shot at being Africa's most daunting,' I said apprehensively as we contemplated plunging into the maze of 11,000 rusting tin-roofed shacks interspersed with a rainbow of beach umbrellas. Jogging hawkers crossed our paths from every direction – they were portering tall stacks of cardboard, foam blocks into which were inserted rows of cheap Chinese sunglasses, steel bowls of cooked food and massive bundles of clothing. Had we bumped into one I feared it would have had a domino effect on at least a dozen close-set stalls where goods had been piled so high they threatened to topple over at the slightest waft of a breeze.

To Ghanaians Kejetia Market is probably just a very big market providing life's staples – plastic utensils, groceries, woven *kente* cloth, underwear and second-hand shoes – but to tourists Kejetia is a challenge and an adventure and not for the faint of heart or those of a claustrophobic disposition. A thunderstorm was brewing so we briskly scuttled through it, with Luisa tightly clutching Kaa's hand for fear of becoming separated and spending the rest of her days wandering the market as The Lost Lady of Kejetia. For braving the melee, Kaa named her 'man of the match'.

Back at our hotel, Luisa and Ernestine retired to their rooms for the evening, leaving Lisa and me free to walk to the corner shebeen where we each had a cold beer, drinking it down quickly to escape the ear-bleeding thumping music. Ghana is a noisy place. The people are loud, they play their music loud and their televisions broadcast at full volume.

There is no escaping loudness.

'Today's breakfast is an improvement on yesterday's – at least we got the eggs we ordered,' I said to Lisa over our one-for-two breakfast in the nightclub. Fortified, we set off for Accra, arriving at our hotel six hours later. In reception, Lisa struck up a conversation with the receptionist Doris, whose magnificent braids she'd admired.

'How are you liking Ghana?' asked Doris.

'Oh, we love it,' said Lisa. 'Everyone's so friendly and welcoming. This is my husband Graham. He was born here.'

'You are Ghanaian?'

'I'm British,' I said, 'but I was born in the Military Hospital as my parents were diplomats.'

'You are Ghanaian if you were born here,' said Doris smiling. 'Great to have you back. Welcome.'

The conversation turned to names.

'On what day of the week were you born?'

'Sunday, I think,' I replied.

'Then your Ghanaian name is Kwesi. In Ghana we often name people after the day on which they were born, so Kwame Nkrumah was born on a Saturday and Kofi Annan was born on a Friday. What day were you born, Lisa?'

'Thursday,' Lisa replied.

'Ah, that makes your name Yaa.'

'Like the courageous Queen Mother Yaa Asantewaa who led the rebellion when the menfolk were too cowardly to do so?' Lisa asked.

'One and the same.'

Feminist that she is, Lisa was dead chuffed by this.

'But we also name children after the circumstances of their birth,' Doris continued. 'So, for example, Obímpɛ̀ means "Nobody wants", and it means your father refused to acknowledge you as his child. My own Ghanaian name is Nyamékye, which means "God's gift" as my parents had trouble conceiving me. But do not worry about them. They had five more children after me!'

Doris said it was really hard for her to be the eldest child. She was 32 and juggling studying tourism with holding down the reception job which involved working from 7pm till 7am.

'That is one of the reasons I am still not married. I am always working. You are nothing in Ghana if you are a woman and you are not married. People laugh if a woman is not married by 30, but I do not have time to go on dates. I have to earn enough money to ensure that all my siblings are educated as otherwise I will have to support them later on.'

We expressed sympathy for her predicament, agreeing that it must be very hard to have to 'parent' your siblings.

'Oh yes, it is indeed a hard job, a very hard job,' Doris sighed. 'There is no child as stubborn as a black child. You have to beat them. In fact, I beat my 20-year-old sister before I came to work today because she refused to visit our sick father in hospital.'

Before we could learn more about Doris's disciplinary tactics, a businessman arrived.

'You will have to excuse me. I have to check this gentleman in. Have a lovely time in Ghana.'

That evening we were given the choice of eating at a Chinese or an Italian restaurant.

'I vote for Chinese,' said Ernestine. 'I can help you order.'

At Noble House restaurant, a dancing nightwatchman opened the door for us.

'I've never eaten Chinese food before, but this is truly delicious,' said Sarnor, when our food arrived.

Ernestine beamed. 'It helps if you have a Chinese person to order for you, but I have to say this is really good.'

'Sarnor,' said Lisa, tucking into her fish in black bean sauce, 'I was speaking to the receptionist, Doris, and she told me you're nothing in Ghana if you're an unmarried woman. I've been a feminist since I was about five and I really struggle with that. What's it like for women in Liberia?'

'Pretty much the same. A woman like you would have a

very hard time in Liberia.'

'That's really sad. But you treat me as an equal. And the way you talk about your wife, it sounds as if you treat her like an equal, too.'

'Yes, Lisa,' he said smiling broadly, 'my wife is a feminist, too. But the difference between her and you is that you have taken your rights, whereas it is I who have granted my wife her rights.'

The conversation moved on to Sarnor's childhood.

'I was four when the Liberian civil war broke out, so I had to flee to Guinea. I grew up in a United Nations refugee camp. That's where I learned to speak English. I once met a man who called me a coward for leaving Liberia during the war and I told him I'd rather be a coward than be dead. It's the same with the 2015 Ebola crisis. My family and I live on an island and we didn't leave it for a year. A whole year. Can you imagine that? My wife begged me to let her go to visit her sister because she missed seeing her so much, but I wouldn't agree. It was the right decision as her brother-in-law died of Ebola and I was the one who had to arrange for an ambulance to take him to an Ebola treatment centre where he was pronounced dead. If I'd let my wife go, my entire family could all have died. Entire homes were emptied by the virus.'

The Kwame Nkrumah Memorial Park and Mausoleum looked a little worse for wear. Dedicated to the man who led Ghana to independence in 1957, and who famously danced the foxtrot with Queen Elizabeth II when she came to Ghana in 1961, Nkrumah arguably rose to a position beyond his competence and his star quickly waned. He was overthrown by the army in 1966 while in China on a peace mission aimed at ending the Vietnam War. Ironically, Nkrumah had welcomed Nigeria's military coup a few weeks before.

Back home, statues of him were torn down and smashed, and the head of one in the museum grounds was only returned by a loyal supporter 40 years later. Time heals all wounds, however, and the true indication of Nkrumah's lasting impact is how much better he has done in retrospect. He has statues and a museum and a mausoleum; not so the generals who overthrew and succeeded him.

'I always thought of Ghana as one of the most stable countries in Africa,' said Lisa. 'I had no idea they've had three coups since independence.'

Nkrumah spent five years in Guinea writing and cultivating roses, waiting for the people of Ghana to call him back. They never did. When he died in 1972 he was buried three times: in Guinea, in Nkroful, the village of his birth, and finally under a monument of upside-down swords in the park next to the museum.

The park was studded with trees planted by visiting dignitaries and we took quiet satisfaction from noting that the tree Mugabe had planted was wilting, whereas the one planted by Mandela was thriving.

At nearby Black Star Square, a soaring triumphal arch like one half of the famed McDonald's golden arches, commemorated independence. The eternal flame of African liberation, on the opposite side of the square, lit by Nkrumah, had long been extinguished, I suspect because the municipality of Accra had failed to pay the gas bill. We dodged the traffic to get to the Arc de Triomphe-like Black Star Gate, engraved with the words 'Freedom and Justice' and topped by a large black star.

'Please only cross the road when I tell you to, Graham,' admonished Kaa when he caught up with us. 'The traffic is very dangerous. Watch out for the cars, they are driving very fast. Wait until I tell you it is safe to cross.'

'I'm 55 years old and I've been crossing roads without someone holding my hand since I was six,' I muttered to Lisa.

'He's just trying to make himself useful,' she said. 'Why don't you just humour him?'

'He'd be more useful if he actually knew something about Ghana that our guidebook hasn't already told us,' I sniffed.

Coffin up

We'd been looking forward to visiting a 'fantasy' coffin maker's workshop in Teshie, some way out from the centre of town, as some coffins were such works of art that they'd been exhibited in museums in Paris, Milan and Hamburg. Instead of a shop sign, the workshop announced its presence with two coffins, which were visible from the street on the building's open-sided first floor. One was shaped like a haughty-looking yellow-beaked eagle, and the other was a sweetly smiling goldfish. After a few words with the owner, Sarnor urged us to look around. There wasn't much to see: perhaps most of that week's production was already six feet under, or in a museum.

'I'd expected these coffins to be coffin-shaped,' I said to Lisa as we inspected a Coke vending machine coffin painted with Japanese signage. 'I thought they'd just paint things onto them, not shape them to resemble things such as an eagle or fish.'

'Yes, they're incredibly detailed,' said Lisa. 'I can see why they're considered artworks. It must take ages to carve them.'

'These coffins are popular with Ghana's Ga tribe,' said our genial guide, the workshop's owner. 'People who can afford to do so take great pride in being buried in coffins that reflect what they have achieved in life, their character or what they did for a living. Some of these coffins can cost as much as 6,000 *cedis*. For a Ghanaian earning the minimum wage that is more than two years' pay.'

I could see the logic of an eagle coffin; it could represent majesty, pride and soaring success. A cannon might represent power and strength, and a fish quiet dignity and depth of character. But, I wondered, what positive attributes could I associate with the coffin in the form of a soft drink vending machine? Was the deceased cool, sweet and popular, or did they just like Coca-Cola very much? The coffins were impressive, and it seemed a waste to bury such craftsmanship.

'Do you suppose that grave robbing is common?' I asked Lisa.

'Why, do you think people might see one of these at a funeral and think, "Man, that would look good in my lounge next to the television"?'

'More like "I'll have that for my own send-off. I'll come back tomorrow night with a van and dig it up. Uncle so-and-so can keep it in his garage until I pop my clogs."'

'On our way back, can we go past the Military Hospital?' I asked Kaa once we were back in our vehicle.

'Why, are you feeling ill?' he asked, turning around in the front seat with a look of concern.

'No, I'm fine. It's just it's the place where I was born.'

'You were born in Ghana?' said Kaa, his eyes widening with surprise. 'Is that for real?'

'Yes, my father was a British diplomat and he was posted here in 1963 for three years.'

'Man, that is so cool,' purred Kaa.

A short while later we drove by the hospital, with Kojo slowing the car so I could take pictures for Ma back home. The hospital was unremarkable, just a cluster of low-rise buildings behind railings.

'How does it feel to come back to the place where you were born?' asked Kaa.

'I can't say it feels like anything. I left before I turned three and I haven't any memories of Accra. All I know is what my mother has told me. Her friends back home were amazed that she didn't stay in London to have me, but she didn't want to be away from my father so she came out here. She said the hospital was quite good when I was born but two years later, when she gave birth to my brother Rod, it wasn't, and patients had to bring their own sheets and pillowcases. But I suppose it's nice to think of my young mum and dad starting their family and creating so many happy memories here.'

Lisa told Kaa that we'd like to be dropped off at a supermarket and that we'd walk from there back to our hotel.

Kaa, with thoughts only for our health and safety, did not think this was a good idea.

'It is too late. It may be closed. You do not know the way back. If you insist then I will accompany you.'

'Actually, Kaa,' I retorted, 'the supermarket is on the same road as our hotel. And if the supermarket is closed well, then, it's closed. But we are getting out. Kojo, when I tell you to, please stop the car.'

Kojo nodded his assent. Kaa turned away, his lips pursed in frustration that we weren't taking his paternalistic advice, more like strictures, seriously. One can usually intuitively feel if a place is sketchy, and neither Lisa nor I was picking up that vibe from central Accra.

Kojo put us down where I asked him to. It was good to be on our own, just the two of us. We took a table outside a pavement bar and ordered a couple of beers.

A young man selling bolts of wax-print cloth approached, smiling. I asked him to show us what he had. Putting the pile on the chair next to Lisa, he held up in turn something like 15 different fabrics. An attractive aquamarine cloth patterned with yellow mussel shells caught Lisa's eye and, to give us an idea of just how generously large it was, he gave me one end to hold and walked away from the table, unfolding the bolt as he went. He came to a stop six metres from us. Holding the fabric just under his chin, it reached almost all the way to the pavement.

'A lot of the wax print in West Africa comes from Holland,' the salesman informed us, pointing to the word 'Vlisco' printed on the edge of the unrolled cloth.

'It's much bigger than I thought it would be,' remarked Lisa. 'Let's get it for Loren. We can keep looking for a nice piece for ourselves.'

We paid the salesman his asking price, plus a little extra for his trouble, and ordered two more beers.

As the cold lager revived and refreshed us, we happily watched the passing show of homeward-bound commuters, shoppers, traffic and hawkers. Threading its way along the broken paving stones, a lone goat sniffed at and ate a piece of discarded newspaper before moving on to snack on some fruit peelings.

'I'm so glad you were born in Ghana, Graham,' said Lisa. 'If you hadn't been, we wouldn't be sharing this very special moment together.'

Togo à gogo
Togo

The two-hour drive north from Accra to Akosombo to see the dam that had created Lake Volta, the largest man-made lake in the world by surface area, and which covers a third of Ghana's land area, was interrupted by a series of bizarre questions from Kaa.

'Tell me, what's your biggest fear?' he asked.

I politely resisted expressing my initial response, which was 'Dying on a Ghanaian road'.

'Heights,' said Graham. 'I really don't like heights. And I don't like flying much either.'

'What did you want to be when you grew up?'

I gamely answered that question, leaving Graham to stare out of the window.

'A doctor.'

'I always wanted to be a tour guide,' continued Kaa. 'The reason I am not married is because I am focussing on my career.'

'That's good,' I said grimly, wondering how narrow Kaa's focus was if he knew almost nothing about his own country.

The dam was indeed an impressive sight, but it was hard to believe that the six small hydroelectric turbines were capable of generating 85 per cent of Ghana's electricity needs, and some for export to Togo and Benin.

The following morning, Sarnor informed us that we'd have

to drive all the way back down to the coast, cross the border into neighbouring Togo, and then motor back north up to Kpalimé in the Togo interior.

'That doesn't make sense to me,' said Ernestine. 'Why can't we just cross the border opposite Kpalimé? It's a lot closer.'

'The drivers say that if we take that road we'll have to sleep in the mud if we get stuck as it's in a very bad state of repair,' Sarnor said. 'I agreed we should go the long way round.'

'Oh yes,' I concurred, 'we must always travel the safest way. I definitely don't want our cars to break down.'

'If the drivers say it's a bad road, then I suppose we'd better listen to them,' said Graham.

For lunch we told Sarnor we wanted to eat at a local restaurant and not, as was his preference, in a hotel. Ernestine ordered chicken and *fufu* – a starchy, stiff porridge made from pounded cassava and green plantain – but, when it arrived, pushed the food away.

'I'm not eating *that*,' she vowed. 'Is this what I ordered? I don't think so.'

Granted, *fufu* is pretty tasteless and the chickens in West Africa, though undoubtedly free range if not organic, were scrawny runts compared with the plump birds that grace our dinner tables at home. From her handbag Ernestine whipped out a tin of tuna she'd bought in Accra, devoured it with a teaspoon and rose from the table to pace in circles around the restaurant to get in her daily 10,000 Fitbit steps. You've got to admire her dedication. Graham and I chewed our way through our meal as scrawny chickens who'd avoided the pot ran about between our feet.

At the Ghana-Togo border we were hassled by moneychangers, pestered by taxi drivers and frustrated by the lethargic African bureaucracy of exiting one country and entering another. A notice reminded staff to desist from extorting money from travellers in exchange for emergency visas. No one put their hand out for 'dash', as bribes are called in Ghana.

'Please, Luisa, don't take any photos here,' pleaded Sarnor. 'They are very sensitive about photos at borders in African countries. You may have a government that will rescue you if you get arrested, but I don't.'

The mischievous twinkle in Luisa's eye betrayed that she hadn't taken his advice seriously.

'Luisa, I'm serious. I was once guiding a German tourist in Guinea-Bissau and he took a photo of a hut full of soldiers. They came out and confiscated his camera. I had to spend half an hour on my knees begging to get it back. This is Africa, not America, and it's how things are done here.'

Luisa got the memo. Her iPhone remained in her pocket.

At Ghana emigration we caused a little merriment when honestly listing our address in Accra as Somewhere Nice.

'I believe you when you say that it was nice,' observed the mirthful official, holding out our emigration form so that his colleague could share the joke. 'But we need to know the name of the place you stayed, not whether you liked it.'

'The place was Somewhere Nice. And it was somewhere nice,' I told him.

Kaa, Kojo and Elolo had to remain on the Ghanaian side, so I organised a whip-round and we said our goodbyes. Kaa and Graham shook hands, he Ghanaian-style and Graham English-style. They botched it when they first met, and they botched it when they parted, laughing.

We walked across the border into Togo and sat in the shade people watching while Sarnor went off to organise onward transport. All signs were now in French and baguettes replaced the fluffy white loaves on sale in Ghana. And whereas in Ghana men tended to wear jeans and T-shirts or football-team tops, in Togo many men had adopted a fashion of trouser suits cut from the most hallucinogenic and Esher-like wax print. They weren't loud, they were screaming.

'Lisa, you should sit in the front passenger seat,' suggested Sarnor when he returned accompanied by a single station wagon and its driver. 'Graham, Luisa and Ernestine can share the back seat and I'll ride in the trunk. It's just a short distance to the place where I've arranged to collect a second car.'

I hate sitting up front so demurred, offering the seat to Graham on the grounds that he has longer legs.

'No, I really think it's best if you sit with the driver,' Graham said, reasoning that my child-bearing hips would need more room than Luisa's and Ernestine's.

'Yeah,' agreed Ernestine, 'you should have the front seat as you have the biggest butt!'

'Be very careful,' I said laughing, 'in this part of the world a bottom like mine is widely admired.'

The local men gathered about us broke into confirmatory laughter.

'Blimey, I didn't realise everyone was listening to what we were saying,' I said, blushing as I went to take my seat.

Having rendezvoused with a second driver and car, we again split into two parties and set off for Kpalimé, 120km to the north, arriving there nine hours after we'd set out that morning. The entire journey had been on hair-raising single-lane roads where we faced the possibility of a head-on collision every five minutes as oncoming overtaking vehicles hogged our lane and only pulled back in at the last moment.

'Emmanuel, please stop doing that,' I said to our driver as he once again attempted to overtake in the face of oncoming traffic. 'I don't want to die today. We're not in a flaming hurry to get to Kpalimé, and I want to arrive there alive.'

To his credit, Emmanuel listened.

'I've just found out that we could have used the border crossing in the north,' Sarnor said apologetically later that night at our hotel. 'I've been chatting to two truck drivers and they said the Ghana drivers lied to me. I think they wanted to earn another day's pay.'

After seeing what little there was to see in and around picturesque Kpalimé the next day – a German-built cathedral, a forest, a ruined château erected by a French-German lawyer, and a few waterfalls – we made the 120km trip back south to Lomé, Togo's capital.

'I can't believe we risked our lives to see that stuff,' I harrumphed. 'I could murder those bloody drivers. And I now really regret tipping them so well. I hate spending time in cars at the best of times but spending nine hours in one when we could've done the trip in two is utterly galling.'

The fetish pharmacy

In Lomé, we stayed at the Hotel Magnificat. Our simple room was windowless, but the narrow balcony off the breakfast room looked over to the city's cathedral and down on the two-storey Art Deco Grande Marché famed for its Mama Benz – sharp businesswomen who rule the market. The 'Benz' in 'Mama Benz' is a respectful acknowledgement of the fact that they'd made enough cash to be chauffeured around in their own Mercedes Benzes. The palm-fringed coast was a short walk from the hotel, so we headed there while it was still light. It was rubbish-strewn and felt a bit unsafe, and so we didn't venture too far.

There wasn't much to keep visitors in Lomé. Naturally, it had an overlarge monument to the country's independence which, in Togo's case, was at the same time a monument to the start of dynastic rule by two father-and-son dictators: Étienne Gnassingbé Eyadéma, who ruled for 38 years, and his son Faure Gnassingbé, who's been president since 2005. The expansive traffic circle enfolding the monument was almost deserted save for the occasional scooter puttering round or a car entering or exiting one of its access streets. We'd walked there from the Magnificat to visit the Musée National, which shares space with the Palais de Congrés where the month before, 22-year-old Ichabatou Gnongbo Tchoro had been crowned Miss Togo 2018. Like the election of a new Pope at St Peter's, her victory had been signalled to those outside the Palais by a plume of white smoke. Eager to make a sale, two young men pushing a steel-and-wood handcart loaded with bags of dried dates approached us. Sarnor introduced us to them not by name but by our countries of origin, and the men shook our hands. Did we want to buy some dates? We replied that we did. Luisa, though, was more interested in the half-dozen plastic drinks pouches on top of the dates. On the reverse of each pouch were four pictures: one of an elderly man nursing an aching back; one depicting a cut-away male genitalia, the kind of picture found in a school biology book; the third of a couple having sex on a brass bed; and the last an engorged penis of quite prodigious proportions. It was this image that demanded Luisa's – well, *all* of our attention – to the great merriment of the two vendors who happily posed for photos holding up the drinks.

'What's the drink they're selling, Sarnor?' asked Ernestine.

Sarnor inspected one of the bags.

'It says that it cures backache and haemorrhoids. And "*erection molle*" I would translate as something like "curing a soft penis".'

'It's a miracle remedy for all midriff ailments then,' I remarked. 'How much is it? I want to get one for Graham.'

'Very funny, Lisa,' Graham said. 'You and I both know that I don't need help in the downstairs department.'

'Oh, I'm not buying it for *that* reason – I'm buying it for your piles!'

'I'm getting museum sickness,' Graham complained to me as we toured the impressive National Museum. 'I'm going to suggest to Sarnor that we pop by the fetish market.'

When making this proposal Graham wasn't suggesting we take in an 'adult' latex-and-leather shop flogging rubber gimp suits, nipple clamps and harnesses for dressage-play, but the Marché des Féticheurs, the world's largest voodoo market. Over a quarter of Togolese are adherents of the voodoo religion – or Vodun as it's known locally – and the Marché is *the* place for them to consult traditional healers and buy fetish prescriptions: objects invested with 'magical' properties such as statues inhabited by spirits and dried animal parts that are able to help and heal.

'I can't be sure I'm in a fetish market and not a Chinese grocery,' Graham remarked as he surveyed the rows of tables sagging under heaps of desiccated pangolins and porcupines and the weight of baskets of dead grey parrots. There were *lots* of severed heads: tables were piled high with blackened serpent, antelope, baboon, crocodile and cat heads with eyeless dark sockets and lips drawn back from their jawbones to reveal vicious fangs and teeth.

In one corner of the earth-floored compound stood a circular concrete altar, its centre studded with metal tridents covered in the ash of sacrifices burnt there. Next to it, a row of dried whole goats, seated on their hindquarters, stretched their scraggy necks skywards as if they were Satanic priests performing a dark ritual.

Picking up two bound twigs, the mandatory guide explained that they were a fetish for love meant to be thrown into the sea; for safe travel a small bottle with a thorn stopper to be plugged in before leaving and unplugged on arrival was the must-have voodoo talisman. I tried to imagine what prescriptions the traditional healers doled out. Suffer from migraines? Try ground cat skull. Afflicted with psoriasis? A bat-skin poultice, applied twice daily. You want the girl next door to fall in love with you? Then prepare her a tasty tortoise-shell broth.

'I don't think I'll be doing too much voodoo in Miami,' said Luisa, politely declining to buy a travel talisman.

'I can imagine the witches in Macbeth shopping here,' I said. '"Eye of newt and toe of frog," and all that. It's a grisly voodoo pharmacy with not an aspirin in sight.'

Surprisingly, there were no zombies either, as they are a myth originating in Haiti in the 17th century, when African slaves were worked to death on brutal French-run sugar plantations. Those who committed suicide, it's said, wouldn't find freedom in the afterlife but would instead be condemned to linger in the plantations as soulless zombies for eternity.

'Zombies do exist, Lisa. You know as well as I do that London's pavements are clogged with "phone zombies",' Graham teased.

At the tamer, less taxidermic end of the market were simple wooden fertility statuettes and voodoo dolls studded with cowries and iron nails. Knowing that a dried baboon head wouldn't go down too well with British Customs, but wanting a Vodun souvenir nonetheless, we bought male and female fertility fetishes for ourselves and a voodoo doll for each of Graham's nieces. Emily and Grace have seven children between them, so we figured they hardly needed help in the fertility department.

How do you voodoo?
Benin

'Oh my God! Is that a penis?' asked Luisa, pointing to a mound of baked mud, jutting out from which was a vaguely phallic shape, as we approached a voodoo temple on the outskirts of Abomey. 'I have a friend who *loves* penises and photographs them *all* the time. I have to take a photo of this penis.'

'Jesus, Luisa. The Elephant Man's old man may have been as misshapen as that,' I conceded, 'but I spent seven years at boarding school and saw many penises. It's true, they do come in all shapes and sizes, but not one todger I've seen looked like that.'

The voodoo priest standing on the threshold of the walled compound was expecting us. He was an elderly wizened man dressed in a white knee-length shirt and a woollen beanie that pressed the tops of his ears down and forwards like small horns. The whites of his eyes were English-mustard yellow and his smile showed that he needed to see a dentist. He motioned us to remove our footwear, and having done so we followed him into his hut-like temple where four voodoo figurines and a mess of pots and bowls had been collected into a floor-level shrine set in front of a dirty length of cloth. In the dark left corner, behind a stout figurine, a hen and four chicks nested, intermittently clucking and chirping. In time they would no doubt be sacrificed in the name of voodoo, and afterwards fried in the name of supper.

We took seats on low stools as the priest went about his incomprehensible-to-us rituals of singing an incantation, stroke-touching the avatars and dripping water on others before taking a swig and blowing water noisily onto the shrine. Ernestine let out an involuntary squeal. Whatever he'd done, whether it was pray for rain or wealth or wish a scrotal hernia on his neighbour, the priest was finished and it was time now for him to sell a fetish to the tourists: CFA12,000 (£17) for a protective ring. I wasn't sure if it was a ring for a fat finger or for a slim cock.

'Sarnor, please use your French and ask him if we can take a photo with him,' said Luisa. The priest nodded his assent and stood alongside Luisa as Ernestine used her mobile phone to take a picture. Ernestine was next, bringing into the picture Barry, the miniature stuffed toy bear from Bolivia she travelled with and that appeared in all her selfies.

'Eek!' said Ernestine, stiffening. As Lisa stepped forward to have her picture taken, Ernestine whispered as she passed, 'The priest grabbed my butt!'

Surely not. The priest closed the narrow gap between himself and Lisa and placed his hand on her shoulder. As Lisa smiled for posterity he casually slid his hand down her back and onto her bottom. Lisa's smile vanished.

'Ernestine was right. He fondled my bum. He's a priest and he fondled my bum!'

I put my arm around Lisa's shoulder and gave her a squeeze. 'It isn't the first time that a man of the cloth has taken advantage of his position, Leecy,' I said. 'And sadly I don't think it will be the last.'

Abomey, formerly the capital of the pre-colonial Kingdom of Dahomey, is home to the Royal Palaces of Abomey, a UNESCO World Heritage site. There were 12 kings between 1600 and 1900 and, when one died, his palace became his burial place and shrine and a new palace for his successor was constructed next door. Only two of the 12 palaces remain, those of kings Ghézo and Glélé, and they housed a sprawling museum exhibiting, among other things, Ghézo's throne mounted on four skulls of his defeated enemies.

'It gave the king great joy to sit on his enemies' heads like that,' said our guide. 'The Dahomey were fearsome warriors and were big on human sacrifice.'

Bas-reliefs on the external walls recorded the kings' strengths, war victories and achievements. To Ghézo's everlasting glory, one depicted a Dahomey about to insert a large ball of clay into the anus of an enemy. 'It gave the king great joy to watch his enemies receive a lethal anal insertion,' our guide didn't say.

Like many indigenous West African powers, the Dahomey sold many of their enemies into slavery and continued trading slaves long after it had been abolished. The last known slave ship to land in the US, in 1860, brought slaves from the Dahomey Kingdom. Dahomey kings weren't much kinder to their own: when, in 1858, Ghézo died, 41 of his wives were drugged and buried alive, and when his son Glélé died in 1889, his funeral included 41 male and 41 female human sacrifices, 41 being a sacred number in Dahomey society (and a *very* unlucky number for some). Monarchy in England wasn't always any kinder and gentler – you only need think of Henry VIII and his fondness for beheading his wives – but when the Queen dies the days of her funeral and Charles' coronation will be national holidays.

The feminist in Lisa at first delighted in the descriptions of Dahomey's Amazons, formidable female soldiers who inoculated themselves against the trials of war by scaling thorn hedges and spending up to nine days in the forest with only subsistence rations. In the 1840s, King Ghézo swelled their number to 6,000 after a surprise raid by a neighbouring tribe succeeded in capturing his sacred stool. Nawi, the last Amazon, died at the age of well over 100 in 1979. However, when Lisa learned that Amazonian 'insensitivity training' included chucking bound and gagged prisoners off a 16ft-high platform, she was less sure of Amazons' suitability as role models for modern women.

Our next stop was the python temple in Ouidah, the voodoo capital of Benin. The temple houses as many as 100 pythons, though never at one time as they are released once a month to slither into town to catch rats.

'The guardian says that, to accidentally kill a python – if it is driven over, for example – brings very bad luck,' Sarnor told us. 'The person must perform libation.'

'That's a novel way to control traffic,' I thought. 'Drive carefully or sacrifice good liquor rather than drink it.'

'He says the snakes return here when they feel like it. Or if someone finds one in their house, they bring it here.'

After politely knocking on the wooden door to the python sanctuary, the guardian unlocked the door and beckoned us inside. There were tangled knots of pythons at ground level, in a circular recess in the centre of the floor and on a head-height ledge around the inside wall. Most were perfectly still, but one or two showed an interest in their visitors by raising their heads and sniffing us with their flickering tongues.

'I've never been so close to a snake,' said Lisa, 'and certainly not so close to so many.' She stepped away as an inquisitive python silently closed in on her from behind, thereby positioning herself closer to one of the inert knots. 'I'm not sure how happy I am being in here. I'm leaving.'

'The guardian says these snakes are harmless to humans,' reassured Sarnor as Lisa stepped outside.

'I don't care. There are too many.'

First in and last out, the guardian emerged with a glossy

black-and-bronze mottled snake in his hands. He held it out for Ernestine to take. She poked it with an index finger, much as one would summon a lift.

'Ugh!' she shivered.

Translating from French, Sarnor explained that we should each take turns to 'wear' a snake as doing so would confer good luck on us. Luisa didn't hesitate – no one doubted that the 'power pensioner' would – and Sarnor looked as though he'd been wearing pythons as neckties his whole life. Not everyone was as keen to have a cold-blooded silky-skinned serpent draped around their neck, though, even if it would confer 'showers of blessings'. When her turn came, Lisa forced a very fake smile for the camera, which was more than a wincing Ernestine could manage.

'I was literally crying and peeing my pants at the same time!' she said afterwards.

Known as the 'Venice of West Africa', Ganvié village on Lake Nokoué was accessible only by boat. Built in the 17th century by the Tofinu to escape Dahomey slave hunters whose religious beliefs prevented them from fighting on the sacred lake, its 30,000 residents lived in huts on tree-trunk stilts driven deep into the lakebed, and farmed fish in enclosures made from reeds staked out in the shallows. The departure jetty thronged with traders, and it took a while for our hired boatman to fetch his launch. On the water, sailboats – canoes given wind power by the simple expedient of a few sticks and a patchwork quilt of rice sacks – bobbed among women deftly manoeuvring their dugout canoes laden with baskets of dried fish. The inhabitants of Ganvié don't appreciate being photographed, apparently because they don't tend to benefit financially from day visitors, so the crews of the boats we passed all turned their backs on us.

On reaching Ganvié we stepped off at Chez Raphael bar-restaurant-hotel-souvenir shop, like most structures built from crooked wood and sheets of gaily painted corrugated iron. From a bedroom window we could see women in wide-brimmed straw hats paddling slimline dugouts piled high with baskets of yams, plantains and cooked food. The moment they caught sight of our camera, they hid their faces. As most toilets in Ganvié do, those in Chez Raphael emptied straight into the lake, no doubt providing food for the fish but also creating a health hazard for its citizens.

'I've never been to a region that's more photogenic and camera-unfriendly,' said Lisa as our boatman took us back to the jetty, passing the turquoise village church with a white cross nailed to its façade. 'Here I can understand the locals not wanting to be photographed, but in the museums the prohibition is a mystery. You'd think they'd want tourists to take photos to show their friends back home. It's the equivalent of banning free advertising.'

Selling fuel out of school

It was only two hours on to Porto-Novo, Benin's capital. Our accommodation was fabulous: separate rondavels overlooking a lagoon in which clumps of water hyacinth drifted slowly past, and next to a short jetty from where joyous adult baptisms took place in the still, warm water. For supper that evening we had biblical bread and wine in the lagoon-side restaurant. It was heavenly.

Porto-Novo was quiet, relaxing and friendly. Not quite so friendly was the sign at the Musée da Silva prohibiting, surprise, surprise, photography.

'It is rigorously forbidden to snap picture inside the museum,' it read – 'Of course it bloody is!' groaned Lisa – 'Any visitors surprised in taking picture will be amended at the price of CFA20,000 [£28] and his camera will be sized [*sic*]! Thank you!' This didn't deter Luisa, who, as always, surreptitiously took photos left, right and centre.

Our tour ended that day. Luisa and Ernestine took a taxi to Cotonou to fly home and Sarnor moved on to Nigeria to fly home to his family in Liberia.

Our flight didn't depart for another 30 hours, so Lisa and I were on our own. We made the most of it, and of Porto-Novo, a sleepy, leafy city that reminded Lisa of Pretoria when she was growing up. We wandered the market and bought a length of green cloth with a repeat design of a pink sun rising over a white sea. Perfect for a tablecloth for home. In the late afternoon we spent a couple of hours in Rina's Restaurant Bar, drinking ice-cold beers pulled out of an ancient chest freezer as Rina diligently swept the front yard with a broom made of bundled twigs. Rina broke off from her sweeping duties to pluck two more beers from the freezer before disappearing into the room behind the bar. Half an hour later a man on a moped pulled up and called to Rina to come outside. A few words were exchanged in French and Rina scooped up her toddler, who'd fallen asleep on the pavement, and brought her inside.

It was a lovely reminder of the African saying that it takes a village to raise a child.

On the last day Rina's was closed so we drank our final beers just across the road from our hotel. As we arrived the owner was opening up, sweeping away fallen leaves and wind-blown sand and setting out plastic furniture under a towering tree. He pointed to the best table outside and went to fetch two beers. I moved the table into the sunshine.

As Lisa and I recounted what West Africa had shown and taught us, and how it had been the people who had made our trip – as they usually do – informal petrol sellers plied their trade on the road 50 yards either side of us. Since crossing the Ghanaian border we'd seen tens of hundreds of these roadside petrol sellers – many of them young children unsupervised by adults – competing for the passing trade. Though illegal, they made no effort to disguise what they were about: receptacles ranging from one-litre alcohol bottles to enormous fluorescent green bulbous glass jars were set atop makeshift wooden tables, with larger plastic containers stacked in the dust underneath.

We were seeing only the last step in an extensive distribution network. Lubricated by dash, contraband petrol is smuggled out of Nigeria, where it's cheaper as it's heavily subsidised, into Benin, with fuel for the Togo market forwarded on from there, often by sea. Barrels of petrol are thrown overboard from boats offshore, towed by swimmers to the beach and then distributed to the sellers in smaller containers by scooter drivers, popularly known as 'human bombs' or 'kamikazes' because transporting highly flammable fuel in this way is so dangerous.

'I'm worried about those kids inhaling petrol fumes,' said Lisa as children no older than eight rushed to fill the tank of a truck. 'If the police took this seriously, they could fill an entire jail in 15 minutes.'

'Yes, but judging by how many petrol sellers we've seen in Togo and Benin, selling illegal fuel is probably a huge source of informal employment. It must suit the governments to let the trade continue.'

Midway through our second beer, uniformed children coming home from school passed us. Most playfully pointed and screamed '*Yovo! Yovo!*' ('White man! White man!'). To their delight I stood up, tapped my bare forearm and, dancing from foot to foot, hollered back '*Yovo! Yovo!*'

Two expensive cars pulled up and a quartet of Beninese dressed in their wax-print finest nodded and smiled greetings to us as they sat and ordered beers at a table in the shade.

'I'm guessing that the two women are Mama Benz,' observed Lisa, admiring the women's regal turbans.

'Could well be. My French isn't good enough to ask. And, despite your protestations to the contrary, your French is worse than mine.'

The two hours we stayed at the bar were the perfect sign-off to Benin and our trip, and after waving goodbye to the '*Yovo!*' kids and the manager, we strolled back across the road to pick up our luggage and make our way to the airport. But

West Africa wasn't done with us quite yet.

The previous afternoon we'd arranged for one of our drivers to come back and take us to the airport.

'We need you to be here at two o'clock,' I said. 'That's two o'clock on the clock, not Africa Time two o'clock.'

The driver smiled and assured us he'd be there at two o'clock on the dot. We'd already dashed him handsomely, so we were confident he'd return to get another tip. Our flight was at 11pm and we wanted to be 100 per cent certain we'd catch it.

Two o'clock came and went. So did three, and four o'clock.

'Just as well we factored in so much extra time to get us there,' I said to Lisa, growing concerned.

When our contracted driver hadn't arrived by 5pm we picked up our rucksacks and went to stand on the road adjoining our hotel, hoping to flag down a taxi. The Sunday traffic was light – it wasn't the best day to be selling petrol from glass bottles – and the few taxis there were already had fares. I pulled from my wallet the last of our West African CFA francs.

'Let's see if we can thumb a ride. If a car or truck stops, I'll tell them we want to go to the airport and show them the cash. Hopefully we'll get a ride that way.'

After an hour we gave up.

'We'll miss our flight if we don't get a lift soon,' said Lisa. 'Let's go to reception and see if they can help.'

The hotel owner listened sympathetically to our plight and agreed that, as long as we covered the cost of his petrol, he'd drive us the 40km to Cotonou. He was going there anyway to check on one of his restaurants, he told us.

Despite the extended delay, we made the airport in time. In time to queue for two hours outside the small terminal as the security guards adamantly refused to let anyone inside until two hours before their flight departed.

Once inside, we sat in the cramped departures lounge on hard plastic seats for another two hours. We'd hoped to have a farewell beer inside the airport but we couldn't even buy water, so I dropped our remaining francs into a charity box.

'This trip started off on the wrong foot with that Ghanaian visa malarkey. It's ended a little off-key with our taxi driver not showing up. It had a wobble in the middle with that unnecessary and terrifying nine-hour road journey, but Sarnor was an amazing guide and we had such fun being "photo spies" with Luisa and Ernestine that I'm really glad we came,' said Lisa as our plane took off.

I agreed. 'There are a lot worse things to be than being born Ghanaian. From now on I might start telling people that my real name is Kwesi.'

'If you do that,' said Lisa, 'I'm going to tell them that it's really Obímpɛ̀, unwanted child. Only no one will get the joke.'

CHAPTER SIX

2019: The Axis of Evil Year
Iran & North Korea

When you're plunged into the crazy world of cancer, you never know what's coming. One of the first things our former oncology nurse friend Sue said to us on hearing of Graham's diagnosis was 'Expect the unexpected.' So at least we were forewarned before we attended our first appointment.

'We wouldn't ordinarily operate on someone like you,' said the young oncologist in the claustrophobic windowless consulting room where we'd been summoned so the doctors could discuss Graham's illness and spell out our options.

My heart hit the floor. Was Graham really so ill that he was beyond saving? I'd read countless research papers and knew that a multi-disciplinary approach of surgery, chemotherapy and radiotherapy gave the longest survival outcomes.

'Really?' I said, shocked. 'What's my husband's staging?'

I asked because I knew that staging mattered. Doctors use a staging system called TNM to categorise cancer, where the T stands for Tumour, the N for Nodes and the M for Metastasis. Being a suitable candidate for surgery depended whether your TNM was 'good' – the tumour was small and hadn't spread to your lymph nodes or other organs – or 'bad' – the tumour was large and cancer cells had metastasised. A 'bad' TNM meant there was no point in operating as the surgery wouldn't do much good and might even prove lethal.

'I don't know,' admitted the doctor.

'You don't know?' I asked incredulously.

'I thought *you* knew,' he said defensively.

'No, we've come here today hoping you'd tell us that,' I replied.

And in that way the scariest hospital appointment of our lives was turned into a farce, with no one in the room knowing what was going on. Like the proverbial kid whose dog had eaten his homework, the oncologist hadn't bothered to read Graham's file before our meeting.

Concerning though that meeting was, it was a huge red warning sign from the universe that if Graham was going to get the best treatment, we couldn't leave it solely up to individual medical professionals, we'd have to become super-informed so that we could speak to medical staff as equals not ignoramuses.

Extensive research finally got Graham the treatment he needed – at a different hospital as we felt the first one had broken our trust. Surgery by one of the world's foremost thoracic surgeons was followed by six rounds of chemo which Graham tolerated quite well, and which gave us the chance to travel and to work on this book, and its predecessor *Travel Seekness*.

For several check-up appointments Graham remained in remission and we'd take a long deep gulp of gratitude every time his doctors said, 'I'm going to get this out of the way really quickly as there's no point in keeping you in suspense. There's no sign of any cancer in your body. You're in remission.' Every time we heard that news it was like being given a three-month extension to life, and then the tension would build up again in anticipation of what the next scan might reveal. There's a portmanteau name for it – 'scanxiety' – putting it in the league of words such as 'cockapoo', 'bromance' and 'banoffee', though it's far from funny.

Then one meeting there was nothing to get out of the way, and a lot to discuss. The cancer was back: one grape-sized tumour in the centre of Graham's chest. The radiologist opined that a course of stereotactic radiotherapy was the best course of action, but there was a 'but'.

'But I'll have to check that the hospital trust will fund it,' she cautioned. 'I should be able to give you an answer in a week or so.'

We waited on tenterhooks for a week before the call came. The trust had found the money, and after eight sessions of radiotherapy and a follow-up CT scan Graham was given the all-clear again.

We knew there was no time to waste. While researching surgery in 2017 I'd also researched travel insurance and had been horrified to discover that few insurers would cover Graham, and those that would said they wanted an eye-watering £1,200 for a two-week trip to South America. With Graham now well, we needed to strike while the iron was hot. I'd longed to visit Iran ever since reading, as a 16-year-old schoolgirl, the Afrikaans novel *As 'n Pou Kon Vlieg* (*If a Peacock Could Fly*), the story of a South African diplomat's wife forced to flee Tehran during the 1979 Islamic Revolution. I'd initially planned a visit to mark our 20th wedding anniversary in 2011 but ditched the idea when Israel began making noises about attacking Iran to prevent it from developing nuclear weapons.

'Being vaporised by an Israeli rocket is not the way I want to celebrate our anniversary,' I'd told Graham.

2019 seemed the perfect time to go as Tehran had recently reopened its London embassy after an eight-year closure so we wouldn't have to fly to Dublin to get visas. And as long as Iran didn't find out we'd visited Israel, all would be well.

At the same time I explored booking a trip to North Korea with Lupine Travel, the same company that had taken me to Georgia, Abkhazia, Armenia and Azerbaijan.

'I can't say I'm not jealous, Leecy,' admitted Graham when he heard my plans. 'But there's no way I can go to North Korea as long as the Foreign Office advises against it. After all we've been through you deserve a break. And besides, I'm thinking that we should meet up in South Korea afterwards.

I can take a week's leave. You do realise that this means you'll have visited two of the three "Axis of Evil" countries in one year. You only need Iraq to complete the hat trick, but I really don't want you going there. I know Luisa visited, but it's far too hairy.'

'Now that you mention it, Lupine does do a trip to Iraq,' I said, half-seriously, half-teasingly. 'But it's to Kurdistan, the safe bit in the north, apparently.'

'I don't care how safe it is in the north, I don't want to go there – and I don't want you going there either.'

'Oh, Graham, you're such a stick in the mud.'

Touchdown in Tehran
Iran

'You'll probably get one, but when they know where you work they'll think you're a spy,' said a colleague when Graham enquired about his chances of getting an Iranian visa. Encouraged, we duly put in our applications and our passports with visas were returned to us within a week. It seemed that the Iranians positively wanted us to visit.

At Imam Khomeini International Airport our guide, a diminutive, stocky man just shy of 30 with stubbled, chubby cheeks, a cheeky smile and a thatch of dark, wavy hair, introduced himself.

'Hello, I'm Milad. Your tour company has appointed me as your guide. Welcome to Iran.'

'This is my wife Lisa. I'm Graham,' said Graham, shaking his hand.

'Graham,' said Milad slowly, as if he'd never heard the name before. 'Can I call you Gary?'

'No,' said Graham, 'my name's Graham.'

'Oh, I thought Gary was short for Graham.'

Milad ushered us to the taxi and, as we sped northwards along the highway to central Tehran, reminded me that I had to wear a headscarf at all times.

'That's the tomb of Ayatollah Khomeini,' he said pointing to a monumental floodlit dome with four missile-like minarets to our right. 'Should we go and see it now?'

'I don't think so,' said Graham, 'it's three in the morning.'

Milad shrugged, obviously not impressed by our lack of sightseeing stamina.

The first inkling we had that Milad may not have been all that he seemed came the next day when he took us to the Treasury of National Jewels.

'You see, I brought you here first thing so that you wouldn't have to queue,' said Milad, pointing to a nondescript building. 'I'm a guide who always does his best for my tourists.'

He exchanged a few words with the guard.

'Mmm,' he said, perplexed, 'it seems that this isn't the right building.'

Graham and I looked at each other. That would explain the absence of a queue.

Within a few minutes Milad located the correct building, the only one on the street with a queue outside.

Thankfully, the wait was worth it. Twinkling away in the dimly lit, heavily guarded vault were so many exquisitely crafted crowns, tiaras and necklaces that they made the Tower of London's crown jewels look as if they'd been purchased from the Argos catalogue. The standout pieces were a beach-ball-sized globe with the oceans fashioned from shimmering emeralds and the continents from glittering rubies, and the famous Peacock Throne, a gilded platform studded with priceless jewels. The throne was a copy of the one commissioned by Shah 'Taj Mahal' Jahan that was looted in 1739 by the Persians, and which had once been adorned with the 186-carat Koh-i-Noor diamond, now part of the British crown jewels. The museum's ostensible purpose was to show Iranians how degenerate and profligate the Pahlavi dynasty had been, but it seemed to have the opposite effect: like us, they were entranced rather than disapproving.

After a day of sightseeing under the benign gaze of Ali Khamenei, the white-bearded Supreme Leader who'd succeeded Khomeini as the country's head of state, gigantic posters of whom were everywhere, we boarded the Metro for the railway station to pick up our train to Shiraz.

'Shiraz is my hometown and it's super-nice,' Milad promised us as we settled into our four-berth sleeper cabin. 'I can get you wine in Shiraz, if you like.'

'Yes, and you can get us arrested there, too,' said Graham warily. 'We're not doing anything that could land us in jail.'

Milad told us there was a thriving black market in wine sales in Shiraz and, although the wineries had been shut after the Islamic Revolution, grapes continued to be grown there.

'Officially, the grapes are used for vinegar,' he said, grinning.

I retired to the upper bunk while Milad chatted to Graham about his heroic humanitarian efforts during the recent floods. When night fell, it was time for Milad to turn in.

'Excuse me while I get undressed. I'm so hairy,' he chuckled as he removed his shirt to reveal a white vest bordered by voluptuous crops of dark hair.

I pretended I hadn't looked but silently wondered why the authorities insisted on laying on women-only Metro carriages but were quite happy for a female tourist to share a train compartment with a shirtless hirsute man who wasn't her husband.

In Shiraz we picked up Milad's uncle's car, a small dove-grey Renault Tondar, which he'd borrowed for our two-week trip. I was appalled at Milad's driving: lane discipline had obviously not been drummed into him as it had been into me when Graham taught me to drive. I clutched my seatbelt with both hands as he navigated the honking chaos of the city's traffic, seemingly aiming to position the lane markings directly under the centre of the Renault. After five minutes it came to me that his driving style made perfect sense: simply everyone drove like him so if he'd driven between the white lines, as I was tempted to instruct him to do, he would most certainly have crashed.

Shiraz's most famous attraction is the Pink Mosque, whose stained-glass windows cast – to stunning effect – psychedelic, kaleidoscopic patterns into the interior and onto the faces and bodies of visitors who crowd its Persian carpets to pose and pout for carefully staged photos.

Two hours' drive from Shiraz stands the tomb of Cyrus the Great, celebrated as the founder of the Persian Empire, which covered much of the then-known Ancient world. Despite his greatness, Cyrus was apparently a modest man, choosing to spend eternity inside a man cave: an unimposing shed-like stone structure set atop six stepped platforms.

All the time we were at the tomb Milad was glued to his phone, animatedly chatting in Farsi.

'I've just arranged for us to have lunch with a farmer,' he said, obviously chuffed with his organisational skills. 'And after that we will visit a jungle. You'll like it. It's super-nice. There are bears.'

'How far is the farm?' I asked, worried that it was already past midday and that we wouldn't have enough time in Persepolis, where we'd planned to spend the afternoon.

Milad replied that the farm was an hour away and the jungle 30 minutes on from there.

'Unfortunately, I don't think we have time,' I said. 'We want to see the tombs cut into the rocks near Persepolis, too.'

'The ones at Naqsh-e Rostam? They're almost identical to the ones in Persepolis, so most tourists give them a miss.'

I thumbed through our guidebook until I found photos of four monumental cross-shaped tombs cut high into the cliff face, showed them to Graham – who nodded his agreement – and persisted.

'Milad, we really do want to see those tombs. It says here that one of them is the tomb of Darius the Great, so they must be really important. Wasn't he the guy who founded Persepolis?'

Milad remained stubbornly silent, like a sulky, bored teenager at an adult party where the discussion is all about home renovations and medical ailments.

'We also want to have enough time to do Persepolis properly, so please cancel lunch and the bear jungle. And please, from now on, you need to ask us what we want to do rather than make decisions on our behalf.'

Obviously keener on a languid lunch than he was trudging round the dusty ruins of the ceremonial capital of the Achaemenid Empire yet again, Milad looked disgruntled.

'Trust me, I know what I'm doing. Persepolis only needs one or one-and-a-half hours.'

'I haven't been there before so I can't comment,' I replied, hoping for a bit more support from Graham, 'but I am 100, no 200 per cent sure that I want to see the cliff tombs, so let's get going.'

As we returned to the car after viewing the tombs and the incredibly detailed bas-reliefs below them, one depicting the vanquished Roman Emperor Valerian bending the knee to the Persian King Shapur I – who later used the humiliated man as a footstool when mounting his horse – I hissed at Graham: 'You could have backed me up back there. If we're not careful this whole trip is going to turn into a series of "super-nice", "super-long" lunches, and we're not going to see half of what's on my to-see list.'

'Why are you having a go at *me*? I didn't know about those tombs and I don't know how long we need at Persepolis. Stop being so mean to me.'

Not wanting to let Milad know that he'd divided and conquered, I seethed in silence as we climbed back into the stifling-hot car for the 15-minute journey to Persepolis, which turned into a 30-minute one as Milad stopped several times to ask for directions to the car park.

'He's a tour guide, he lives near here and this is Iran's most famous tourist site, and he doesn't know how to get to the parking lot?' I mouthed to Graham as the lights dimmed in the visitor centre auditorium for the start of a 45-minute movie introducing the ruins.

The film gave us a great introduction to what we could expect to see, which was just as well as Milad seemed to have forgotten most of what he'd been taught at tourism school.

'I studied a long time ago and there's a lot to remember,' he shrugged at the stunningly beautiful Apadana Staircase, decorated with a frieze depicting 23 delegations bearing gifts for King Darius. Milad pointed out what we were quite capable of identifying for ourselves – camels, sheep, lions, bulls, horses – without being able to properly remember whether the gift-givers were Ethiopians, Libyans, Parthians, Syrians or from elsewhere in Darius' extensive empire, something all the other guides seemed to do effortlessly.

Instead of listening to Milad's kindergarten commentary I'd have preferred to read the informative English signs, but whenever I tried to he'd leap in front of the sign and give me an indignant look as if to say, 'There's nothing on there I haven't told you already.' Judging by the two or three I did manage to read by craning past his wavy-haired head it was clear there most certainly was.

Persepolis is hard to describe. It's huge, grand and, as Milad told us several times, 'super-impressive'. Painted in garish colours as it would have been 2,500 years ago, it must have been the Las Vegas of its day. At the entrance – the Gate of All Nations, flanked on either side by two colossal, bearded bulls with outstretched wings – numerous vandals had been at work. One was none other than journalist Henry Morton 'Dr Livingstone I presume' Stanley, who in 1870 had seen fit to carve his surname, and that of the *New York Herald*, his employer, into the soft stone.

After 90 minutes of ruin-rambling we climbed a low hill to get a better view of the complex. Standing so close to me that his head almost rested against my shoulder, Milad related how in 1971 a vast tent city had been erected to celebrate the 2,500th anniversary of the Persian Empire. The steel frames of the million-dollar campsite could still be seen, standing skeletally among the grove of trees specially planted for the three-day, £165 million event. To bring the new forest to life, 50,000 European songbirds had been imported; within three days, the searing desert heat had killed every last one of them. The Shah's hurrah was a celebration so inappropriately extravagant that it helped fuel the Iranian Revolution seven years later.

'Your Queen was one of the guests,' said Milad.

Our guidebook begged to differ. Perhaps reluctant to be seen kowtowing to the autocratic Shah, who called himself the 'king of kings', Her Majesty had sent her husband Phil the Greek and daughter Anne to help consume the sumptuous banquet laid on by Maxim's of Paris. 'I'll never eat another peacock!' Princess Anne is reputed to have said afterwards. Well, she shouldn't have been so greedy as to eat a whole one.

Gazing across Persepolis I tried to fix it in my mind. Even though the grand ceremonial capital was now reduced to a field of columns and crumbled colonnades it was still a very special place.

'I know, you can't tear yourself away,' said Milad as the guards started herding visitors to the exit and closing the entrance gates. 'You see, I *told* you you'd see everything.'

'Yes, only because we skipped the lunch you'd organised with the farmer and the visit to the jungle full of bears,' I thought, biting my tongue.

Melon balls with the secret police

Back at our guesthouse in Shiraz, we had surprise guests.

'I've just been told the "diplomatic" police are here and want to talk to me,' said Graham when I brought him a mug of green tea in the covered central courtyard.

'You're joking!'

'I'm not. They want me to join them in the room across the passage from ours.'

Milad seemed thrilled, like a puppy thrown a chew, and bounded up the stairs behind Graham to the room where the police were waiting in order to volunteer his services as an interpreter. The police had brought their own. Crestfallen, Milad shook my hand and said dejectedly that he was going home to his family.

Watching him go I finally twigged that the many phone calls he'd pulled over to take on the road from Persepolis back to Shiraz hadn't been from his Mum, as he'd claimed, but from the police enquiring when we'd return.

My heart pounding, I retired to our room and to distract myself answered work emails on my iPhone. 'I can't hear any sounds of torture,' I thought, 'only occasional laughter, so Graham must be okay.' An hour later I finished emailing and had started to worry. 'If we're going to be detained, I'd better let someone know where we are,' I thought, sending a message to the friend least likely to panic.

Relief flooded over me when Sarah replied that if she didn't hear that we were safe, she'd alert the British Embassy. 'Anthony and I are here for you,' she texted. 'And sending lots of reiki. You'll be absolutely fine I'm sure, but it's as well that you let me know.'

It was gone 11 when Graham slipped into our room. He'd been 'detained' for two hours.

'Nice melon,' he said.

Convinced they'd bugged our room, I understood his cryptic comment to mean 'I don't want us to discuss what just transpired across the corridor' so we both pretended nothing unusual had happened as we brushed our teeth and readied ourselves for bed.

The next morning, as we breakfasted on freshly baked flatbread, sheep's cheese and honey, and waited for Milad to pick us up, Graham filled me in on the evening's events.

'It was all very civilised. Mr Mahdavi was very polite and

broke a smile now and then. I was served melon balls and tea, asked what I thought about Jeremy Corbyn and Brexit and then, more pointedly, about Britain's relationship with Saudi Arabia and why the UK didn't stop the war in Yemen. They questioned me about my family, and yours, too. I told them that your dad had worked in engineering but had retired many years ago.'

My dad had spent his entire career working for South Africa's nuclear enrichment programme, so I could see the wisdom of being economical with the truth.

'I'm pleased you did that. Anything "nuclear" would, I'm sure, have piqued their interest.'

'Mr Mahdavi said he would like to see me again. I tried to put him off by reminding him that we were on holiday. Oh, and they asked me if I'd grown my beard specially for my trip to Iran.'

We fell about laughing. Graham loves any excuse not to shave and I'd given him permission not to, provided he lost the fuzz when we returned to London.

Farhad, our guesthouse owner – who'd also arranged our tour – walked over to offer us more hot bread and I took the opportunity to complain about Milad's overzealous minding of us.

'We know it's the law for British and American tourists to be on a guided tour, but does Milad *have* to spend every waking minute with us, Farhad? We both work long hours and don't get to see a lot of each other back home, so we were hoping that we could at least eat some of our lunches and dinners alone.'

So far Graham and I hadn't exchanged more than two words in private, except at breakfast and when we were in bed, and even then I couldn't help but wonder if Milad's curly mop would pop up from under the covers.

'Of course, you can have meals on your own,' said Farhad soothingly. 'I'll have words with the boy and tell him you two honeymooners need your space.'

Guided by a gig-aloo

'I'm super-tired,' yawned Milad as we piled into his car after breakfast, 'because last night I had to drive all the way from here to my house on the other side of town, and then come back again today.'

'Are you sure it wasn't because you were playing computer games till 2am this morning?' I teased him, knowing he was an avid gamer.

Abashed, Milad confessed that he had gamed for several hours before turning in.

'Anyway, we have a 600km journey today and so my mother is very worried. She's given me a duvet and pillows so that if I get sleepy I can take a rest at the side of the road. Is that okay by you guys?'

We nodded, sympathetic to the fact that it would be tiring for Milad to make the seven-hour trip non-stop. We made good progress, stopping only once at a roadside stall so we could buy a large bottle of fresh, lightly bubbling *doogh*, a fermented yogurt drink somewhat like *lassi*, that I'd grown fond of and that had taken the place of alcohol at all our Iranian meals.

Two hours after leaving Shiraz we drew into Estahban. Its streetlamps, as in towns and cities throughout Iran, were adorned with poignant portraits of the hundreds of thousands of fresh-faced local boys and stoic-looking men who'd met their death during the 1980s Iran-Iraq war. The Iranians had been militarily ill-equipped, and their most formidable 'weapon' had been the leagues of young volunteers who answered Ayatollah Khomeini's call to defend their country and marched straight into hails of Iraqi machine-gun fire. Now, 30 to 40 years on, family members can't go anywhere in town, not even to the shops, without being reminded of the ghastly, needless slaughter.

Milad mentioned that his uncle lived in Estahban and asked if we could stop for tea. We assented, provided it was a quick visit, reminding him that we still had a long drive ahead.

'Just for tea,' he confirmed. 'Thirty minutes. No longer.'

At his uncle's house we were warmly greeted by Milad's uncle and aunt and his female cousin Minoo, who placed a doormat-sized tray of biscuits on the coffee table and invited us to help ourselves. Only Minoo spoke any English, so our conversation was rather awkward.

'Graham, would you like some pyjamas?' Milad, chomping on his third biscuit, asked me.

'Pyjamas?'

'You know, pyjamas. They're much more comfortable than sitting around in normal clothes.'

'I'm good, thanks,' I said as Milad's uncle brought out several pairs for him to choose from. Milad disappeared into an adjacent room, re-appearing a few minutes later attired in a pair of blue-and-yellow gingham baggy drawstring trousers and his white vest.

'Lisa, it's fine to take off your headscarf, you're with family here,' said Milad. Lisa reluctantly removed her headscarf. 'And my family say they want us to stay for lunch. Iranians are very hospitable, and it would be rude to refuse.'

Thinking of the long road ahead I looked pleadingly at Lisa but she didn't offer a way out.

'All right, but it really does have to be a quick lunch as we don't want to travel in the dark.'

'Sure,' muttered Milad unconvincingly, now engrossed by the football on TV.

Minoo laid a disposable plastic tablecloth in the centre of the living room floor and, once plates of kebabs, vegetables and locally grown truffles had been placed on it, invited us to tuck in. The food was excellent.

Lunch over, I was eager to leave, but Minoo was equally eager to show off her musical talent by playing us her *santur*, a stringed, xylophone-like instrument. Encouraged by our enthusiastic response to her daughter's performance, Milad's aunt dashed off to fetch her *daf*, a tambourine-cum-drum with small metal rings set into the frame. She was also an accomplished musician, and after her set was over, she passed it to me and Lisa to have a go. To the amusement of the family, we were irredeemably useless.

'I need a nap,' announced Milad suddenly, getting to his feet and stretching exaggeratedly. Before we could object, he disappeared into a bedroom and shut the door. Silence.

'Would *you* like a nap?' Minoo asked Lisa who, after weighing up the awkwardness of going to sleep in a stranger's bedroom against the awkwardness of making small talk, demurred.

'Would you like to see our fig factory?' suggested Minoo as an alternative. 'It's just down the road.'

This was an improved offer on stilted small talk, so we agreed. Minoo and her mother went to fetch their *chadors* while Milad's uncle brought the family Peugeot round to the front gate.

It wasn't fig season so when we got there, the cold, silent factory didn't offer much of a diversion.

'Would you like to see our fig farm?' asked Minoo, handing us the bulging gift packs of dried figs and fig syrup her parents had assembled for us.

'We *really* need to get going,' I said. 'Kerman is a very long way from here.'

'Oh no, it's fine. My father called Milad and he says he wants to go on sleeping.'

'I bet he does,' I said under my breath.

Resignedly, we got back in the Peugeot and half an hour later pulled off the main road and drove up a rutted track. As far as the eye could see stretched acre upon regimented acre of fig trees. By now the sun was dipping behind the mountains. I knew that Iran had one of the world's worst road safety records and that it was very dangerous to travel after nightfall.

'We need to go, please,' Lisa insisted.

'No, we can stay, Milad is still feeling tired.'

'No, we still have at least five hours to drive.'

We duly returned to the family's house to rouse Milad from his slumbers.

'Did you like the fig factory?' he enquired as we drove out of Estahban.

'Yes,' said Lisa through gritted teeth.

'And the fig farm?'

'Yes.'

Nodding towards a stepped fountain down which water was cascading, Milad offered to stop so that we could photograph the town's waterfall.

'No!' Lisa erupted. 'No more quick stops for *anything*! You said we were only stopping for tea, and that was at *noon*. It's now *five hours* later and we've still got *five hours* to drive. Graham told you it's unsafe to drive in the dark!'

'It's not late,' mumbled Milad, clearly taken aback at being scolded by a woman. 'We'll get there before dark.'

'It's almost dark *now*!' raged Lisa.

'We'll be in Kerman at eight, maybe nine.'

'No, we won't! You said it was a seven-hour trip so we're going to get there at 10 at the earliest.'

All her frustrations – Milad spying on us 24-7 on behalf of the police, his unwillingness to consult on our itinerary, his thick-skinned refusal to respect her personal space – boiled over. She was letting rip. I'd been on the receiving end of similar tongue-lashings a few times and knew only too well how uncomfortable it felt. Embarrassed, I sat in silence, trying not to catch Milad's eye in the rear-view mirror.

Just as Lisa was getting into her indignant stride, something happened that enraged her even more: she was blinded by something cold, wet and white. Startled and momentarily silenced, Lisa wiped her eyes and face, looked at her hands and, now comprehending what had happened, turned to me in red-faced fury. I was looking down in horror at the bottle wedged between my thighs, from which *doogh* was erupting like lava. It was everywhere – saturating us, dripping off the rear of both front seats, collecting in the footwell and spattering the back of Milad's carefully coiffed hair.

'We need to stop *right now*!' Lisa barked. 'If we don't clean this mess up we're going to spend the rest of our trip in a car that smells like vomit and I, for one, am not going to do that.'

Milad pulled over onto the hard shoulder.

'How *dare* you interrupt me when I was reading Milad the riot act!'

'Lisa, it was an accident. Calm down. We can clean this up.'

Fifteen minutes later – 15 minutes during which Lisa vented her spleen at me and forgot about Milad – the car interior was as clean as we could get it and Milad pulled back onto the road. Lisa's wrath hadn't abated but, finished with me, she resumed tearing the hapless chap a new one.

'We are *not* going as far as Kerman tonight. Sirjan is much closer and we are *not* driving in the dark. You *will* phone Farhad and tell him that you slept and that he needs to cancel our room in Kerman and book us a new one in Sirjan.'

'All right, all right,' Milad murmured, continuing to drive eastwards.

Several miles further on, miles Lisa spent noting with increasing anxiety how reluctant Iranian drivers were to turn on their headlights, she returned to the fray.

'Are you going to make that call or not?' she snapped. 'I can assure you that under no circumstances are we staying on this road now that it's dark.'

'Okay, okay, I was just looking for a good place to pull in,' said Milad sulkily.

We did find room at the inn in Sirjan, and for the first time in a week we ate dinner alone. At a KFC. Making his excuses Milad, as tired of being harangued by Lisa as we were of being shadowed by him, said that he wasn't hungry.

Waking refreshed the next day we joined Milad in the car, which smelled only vaguely of stale *doogh*. He was still smarting, and to show his pique turned up the stereo full blast. 'Alejandro, Alejandro, Ale-ale-jandro, Ale-ale-jandro,' blared Lady Gaga from the loudspeakers behind our heads. He did that whenever he wanted to show he was unhappy. But the irrepressibly gregarious Milad was only kicking himself in his balls: his puerile attempts at 'torture by tune' gave Lisa and me time to talk without him listening in, which we knew he hated. Milad couldn't abide his own company. And besides, what would he report to the secret police? 'I slept and the wife shouted at me and the husband spilled *doogh* so she shouted at him and then she shouted at me again and they went to Kentucky Fried without me and I cried alone in my room and I played music loudly in the car and I couldn't hear them while they spoke about secret things?'

Milad turned off the music. 'I'm sorry about yesterday. I was a bad guide, and I shouldn't have slept for quite that long,' he said.

'Apology accepted,' I said graciously, 'and we shouldn't have been quite so cross with you. I'm sure that from now on we can get along.'

Much as Lisa's outburst had been justified, she felt a little shamefaced about it and was happy to let me do the talking.

Amicable relations restored, Milad regaled us with stories of his romantic entanglements.

'I'm such a gig-aloo,' he said, running a hand through his pomaded hair and casting admiring glances at his reflection in the rear-view mirror. 'I used to have a girlfriend who was a model. I took up smoking when we broke up.'

'Why did you break up?' Lisa asked.

'Because she smoked weed and drank far too much,' he said sorrowfully. 'And because she left me for a bodybuilder.'

'That's too bad,' Lisa sympathised.

'Oh, it's fine. I've got another girlfriend now. But she lives in Jakarta in Indonesia.'

'That's really far away. How often do you see her?'

'It's super-far. I haven't seen her for over a year. And she never calls me. Why doesn't my girlfriend ever call me?'

'You could try calling her,' Lisa suggested.

'Oh, I guess I could,' he said, sounding unconvinced.

After a brief visit to Kerman we motored on to Yazd, a city renowned for its Zoroastrian 'towers of silence' where vultures – not flames or worms – disposed of the dead. We had a tense hour on the outskirts of town when we were stopped at a military checkpoint.

'They need to see your passports,' said Milad.

We handed them over and waited.

'I need the toilet. What's taking them so long?' Lisa asked.

'I'll go and check,' he said. Returning to the car, Milad leaned in through the open window.

'They apologise for taking so long. They just need to make a few more phone calls and then we'll be on our way. It's all going to be okay; this is just routine. As long as you haven't visited Israel.'

'No, we haven't,' I lied, trying to sound convincing. There was nothing in our passports to show otherwise.

Farhad had arranged accommodation for us at a farm, in an atmospheric stone tower that had been turned into a guesthouse. After a tour of the expansive property and every single crop grown thereon – 'Carrots,' intoned our eager-to-please hostess, pointing to a row of feathery green leaves. 'You know carrots? Thyme. You know thyme? Potatoes. Here onions. And here figs. And apricots. Let me take you up the hill to show you the dam' – a tour so long it had to be concluded by the light of our mobile phones, supper was ready. Given the choice of eating communally or in our room, we asked that our meal of chicken smoked in a clay oven be brought to us so that we could dine *a deux*.

'Quick, they've brought three sets of cutlery. Portion out the food and leave Milad's outside his room,' I whispered to Lisa when the food was brought in and placed on the floor. Lisa hastily began heaping jewelled rice decorated with crimson barberries, yellow saffron threads and orange carrot strips onto a plate. Milad entered without knocking.

'Is it okay if I join you guys?' he said, rubbing his pot belly hungrily and sidestepping Lisa's rucksack, from which some of her underwear was overflowing.

I looked up, startled, and weighed up how bad I'd feel if I said 'No' compared with how annoyed I'd feel with myself and with him, and how bloody pissed off Lisa would be with me if I said 'Yes'.

'No, I'm afraid it isn't okay Milad. We want to eat on our own tonight. I'm sure that you understand.'

Milad looked crestfallen, and grumpily accepted the plate of food Lisa held out to him.

'I hope you enjoy your meal,' he said a tad sarcastically on the way out. 'See you tomorrow.'

'Sleep well,' I replied.

The next morning Milad tried to exact his revenge.

'Do you mind if I give this old lady a lift?' he said as we passed an old woman dressed top-to-toe in black carrying a large bundle.

'Of course not,' said Lisa. 'We give rides to hitchhikers all the time when we're travelling.'

'You are good people,' flattered Milad. 'In our culture we respect the elderly.'

The woman got into the front seat and we sped off. Forty-five minutes later she got out. Barely a minute afterwards Milad again asked if we could give someone a lift, this time an elderly gentleman.

A few kilometres down the road the old man got out, bidding us farewell in Farsi.

'Hang on a minute,' I said suddenly. 'Doesn't that road sign say that we're leaving Yazd?'

'Yes, it does,' replied Milad innocently.

'But we told you yesterday that we wanted to see the towers of silence. They're the most important tourist sight in Yazd. It was too late to see them yesterday, but you said we could come back in the morning.'

'The towers of silence,' repeated Milad slowly, as if this was the first he'd heard of them and that he hadn't been present yesterday. 'You want to see the towers of silence?'

'Absolutely!' said Lisa brusquely. 'You know very well we do. We told you that yesterday. Twice. And you agreed it would be the first thing we would do today.'

'But I'll need to turn around and go back to Yazd.'

'Best you do then, Milad,' I said, amazed at his brazen deceitfulness.

'Well, when we get there, you can only have 20 minutes as we have a long way to drive. You can only go up the one that's easy to climb.'

'Milad, we will certainly need longer than 20 minutes. If we hadn't spent all morning giving lifts to strangers, we'd have plenty of time. And I don't care if you've got uncles every 30 miles between Yazd and Isfahan, there'll be no pyjamas and sleeping on the way.'

Yazd had two circular towers of silence built, apparently in the 19th century to an Indian design, by Iran's Zoroastrian community. The tower with steps built into the hill leading up to it was the most impressive, and the one most visitors chose to climb as it didn't involve scrabbling up a stony, unpaved path. Conscious that Milad's taxi antics had cut into our time, we followed the string of visitors up to the summit. Inside, a stone floor sloped down to a well in the centre of a walled courtyard. There was no roof, and there never had been: towers of silence are open to the sky so that vultures can feast on the dead. Zoroastrians believe that dead bodies are impure and so must be kept well away from the four 'sacred' elements of earth, air, fire and water, ruling out burial and cremation.

We spent quite a bit longer than the 20 minutes Milad had allotted to us.

'I'm glad we insisted Milad turn back,' said Lisa. 'Driving all the way to Yazd and not coming here would have been utterly pointless.'

'Should we climb the other one?' I asked, looking at my

watch and then over to the tower on the adjacent hill.

'Isfahan is four hours from here so let's not repeat Kerman-gate and find ourselves driving in the dark again. It's great to have come here and seen inside one tower. The other is probably identical, so I think we can skip it.'

Milad met us at the entrance gate.

'What did you think of the towers? They're super-cool, aren't they?' he said enthusiastically, as if it had been his idea all along to visit. 'Now we must hurry to get to Isfahan.'

'They are,' replied Lisa. 'We tried to see the towers of silence in Mumbai when we were travelling in India many years ago, but we couldn't even get close. They were still being used at the time.'

'These days Zoroastrians bury their dead in cement-lined coffins because our government banned this custom back in the 1970s,' said Milad.

'Why's that?' asked Lisa.

'Because so many people complained that hands and feet were falling from the sky when vultures decided they'd prefer take-aways to eating in,' chuckled Milad.

'Really?' asked Lisa, sounding a little unconvinced.

'It's true. You don't believe me, but I always tell the truth.'

The mantis & the lily

On the first morning in Isfahan, over coffee in a café, Milad began scrolling through his phone looking for a clip from *Game of Thrones* he wanted to show us.

'You have *Game of Thrones* in Iran?' I said, mildly surprised, remembering how HBO's 'the more nudity the better' policy had caused a stir in the UK.

'Sure. We know how to stream all those series for free. America thinks they're so smart putting sanctions on us but they're losing out on big bucks by not allowing us to legally watch shows like that.'

A few minutes later Milad started giggling like a schoolboy and passed his phone to Graham, who drew back in surprise, frowning disapproval. Milad turned the screen to show me a short clip of a couple having alfresco sex, the man's 'moving bits' obscured by a cartoon caterpillar with a cheesy grin.

'Milad!' I chastised him. 'Put that away!' I looked around to see if anyone had seen me looking, but the café was almost empty. Unabashed, he continued scrolling through his phone as if nothing had happened.

He turned to Graham.

'Do you know what a MILF is?'

Late that afternoon, after exploring the bazaar and the Aali Qapu Palace overlooking the huge fountain-filled Naqsh-e Jahan Square, where black-clad veiled women picnicked with their families in the spring sunshine, we returned to our caravanserai lodgings. I'd been cold the previous night so I asked at reception if someone could fix the heater in our room. The caretaker was summoned and five minutes later was on his hands and knees with a spanner in hand tinkering with the ancient contraption. Belatedly realising that if he ever got it working – which seemed unlikely – we risked carbon monoxide poisoning, I told Milad to tell him that I'd rather have some extra blankets.

'Never mind extra blankets. You are like a relative, like an aunt to me, so you can share my room.'

I half-swallowed a guffaw. 'Blankets will do just fine.'

That evening we met up with a young couple travelling independently whom we'd first chatted to at breakfast. Felix was a German journalist and Anna, a Hungarian, worked for the Erasmus scholarship programme. As they were the only English-speaking travellers we'd encountered since arriving in Iran, we were keen to have new company and to compare notes with them.

'Where do you want to go for dinner?' I asked Felix.

'I know a good place,' interjected the ever-present Milad.

'I wasn't asking you, Milad, I was asking Felix.'

'I don't know, maybe we can walk into town and find somewhere?'

'I can take you to a great place,' persisted Milad.

I felt my blood starting to boil.

'Milad, if we need a recommendation from you, we'll ask you. Graham and I just want an evening on our own with our new friends. Can't you just leave us alone for a single night?'

'You are so *rude*!' blurted out Milad.

Embarrassed by Anna and Felix seeing me argue with Milad without knowing the back story, I kept my cool.

'Milad, you don't have to come with us tonight. Farhad said it's fine for us to eat on our own.'

'Well it's not,' said a peeved Milad. 'I have to accompany you, even when *I* don't want to.'

'If you insist on coming then you can sit at a different table. We just need some space.'

'I don't want to sit at your table anyway. I've got a sore stomach.'

'I'll tell you all about it at the restaurant,' I whispered to Anna and Felix as we walked back to the narrow alleyways of the bazaar. 'Milad hasn't let us out of his sight for five seconds and it's starting to bug the hell out of me. Consider yourselves lucky that the Iranians don't insist that Hungarian and German tourists are accompanied by a guide. Graham and I really envy you travelling independently.'

We emerged from the bazaar onto the pavement outside the many tourist shops on Naqsh-e Jahan Square.

'Where are you from?' asked a man casually dressed in a T-shirt and jeans.

'England,' said Graham.

'Germany,' said Felix.

'Ah, Manchester United, Bayern Munich,' said the man.

'Yes, that's right,' said Graham good humouredly.

The man's tone changed. 'Where's your guide?' he asked sternly. 'From England you must have a guide.'

My heart lurched into my throat. I'd been ignoring Milad who'd been sulkily keeping his distance behind us, and now I hoped he was still with us.

'Over there,' said Graham, turning to point to Milad.

Without a word, the man disappeared back into the bazaar.

'Blimey,' I said, 'so Milad really does have to stick with us all the time. I wonder why Farhad said it was okay for us to go out on our own.' I started to feel sorry for my outburst at Milad, but not so sorry that I would relent and eat yet another meal with him.

In the brightly lit restaurant I made sure that I seated myself with my back to Milad, alone at a nearby table. We knew he'd try to overhear every word of our conversation so we kept the volume low as we filled Anna and Felix in on our many run-ins with him, Graham's meeting with the secret police and what we'd seen and done in Iran.

'I can see why your guide is getting on your nerves,' said Felix. 'It would drive me nuts if we had to have someone shadowing us all the time. I can't believe you've had so much hassle in Iran. We've had no trouble at all. We've used public transport and Snapp, the Iranian equivalent of Uber, and everyone's been so helpful and friendly.'

'Even though we had our visas refused twice,' said Anna, 'I'm really glad we persevered.'

'What's been your favourite sight so far?' I asked them.

'I loved Kashan, where we not only had the kindest Couchsurfing host but also went on an amazing trip into the desert to see the sunrise,' said Felix.

'Yes, Kashan was incredible,' agreed Anna. 'The strangest moment I had was during our tour of the giant mosque in Qom, one of the holiest cities in Iran. The male guide only addressed Felix and completely ignored all of my questions, most probably because I'm a woman. That was when we experienced the other side of Iran.'

Back at the caravanserai, as we drank green tea from the communal samovar, we enrolled Felix and Anna into our one subversive act: getting rid of the bottles of fig syrup and packets of dried figs we knew we couldn't take in our hand luggage or consume before we left Iran.

'Milad mustn't see us doing this,' I said to Anna quietly, 'as the figs were a gift from his family, who were truly lovely and very generous to us, and I don't want to hurt his feelings. We tried "accidentally" leaving them in our room in Kerman, but he searched it straight after we left to check out and brought them back to us.'

In our room I hid the figs and two bottles of syrup in a shawl and then, back outside, slipped them into Anna's daypack as guiltily as if I'd been smuggling Semtex.

'I can't believe we're doing this – I feel so guilty and there's nothing to be guilty about,' said Anna.

'That was a really great evening, thank you,' said Felix. 'See you at breakfast tomorrow.'

'Yes, we'll be there at about nine.'

'I want to leave at nine, so you need to have breakfast at 8.30am,' said Milad from the shadows where he'd been lurking, smoking a cigarette.

'Alright, 8.30am,' I said to Felix, rolling my eyes.

It was 20 past midnight by the time I'd brushed my teeth, taken off my trousers and slipped into bed. We'd come to Iran with only hand luggage and I hadn't had room for pyjamas, so I kept my shirt on to ward off the chill. As Graham sat on the bed to take off his socks there was a soft knock on our door. Thinking it was Milad wanting to change our plans for the next day, Graham opened the door four inches. A pungent fragrance barged into the room.

'Hello again,' said a male voice that wasn't Milad's. 'Would you mind if I came in?'

'Er… Really? Sure. If you have to,' answered Graham, opening the door fully.

Struggling to manoeuvre a huge floral arrangement with a nauseatingly smelly lily at its centre through the doorway, the stranger entered. He was six foot five, rake-thin and dressed in a pink shirt and baby-blue suit. His dark-rimmed, oversized Austin Powers spectacles, and the way he tilted his head, made me think of a praying mantis. I had no idea who he was or why Graham had let him in.

'Good evening, good mother,' he said, putting the flowers down on a side table. 'This is for you.'

'Thank you, that's… very kind,' I said, drawing the bedsheets up to my chin while looking searchingly at Graham for an explanation. I was conscious that I was half naked and bare headed.

'It is my pleasure, good mother. Mr Mahdavi wanted to thank you for allowing him to talk to your husband in Shiraz.'

I clocked who he was: the interpreter for the secret police.

'How have you found your time in Iran, good mother?' he asked, getting out a pen and small notebook. I wasn't sure if this was the start of my own interrogation, so I thought carefully about what I was about to say.

'It's been absolutely fantastic,' I said truthfully. 'We have been charmed by your beautiful country but especially by its friendly people. Absolutely everyone has been amazingly kind to us, and we were blown away by Persepolis. And of course, the Pink Mosque and the magnificent Peacock Throne.'

The interpreter smiled and wrote down what I'd said. I hoped he wasn't going to ask me who we'd been in contact with as I was fearful of getting anyone into trouble, though we'd been so closely minded by Milad – as well the interpreter knew – that we hadn't exchanged more than the most basic of pleasantries with any Iranians we'd met.

Turning to Graham, he invited us to join Mr Mahdavi, the man for whom he'd translated Graham's answers in Shiraz, for dinner the following evening.

'It'll be a very nice dinner, at a nice restaurant, and your wife can come, too,' he smiled.

'We're here on holiday so we'd rather just have dinner on our own,' replied Graham.

'Ah yes, but it is Mr Mahdavi's way of thanking you for your time. You have a highly scientific mind and Mr Mahdavi was very grateful.'

'It's quite all right. The beautiful flowers you've given my wife are all the thanks we need.'

'Can I sit down?' asked the interpreter, yawning. 'It's so late and I'm really tired.'

'Of course,' said Graham, gesturing towards our double bed, the only place the man could sit. He sighed heavily, sat on the edge of the bed and resumed his pleading.

'It'll only be a short dinner.'

'I can't accept official invitations from your government when I'm not here on official business.'

'It's not an official invitation, it's a way of saying thank you.'

'I cannot accept. Please thank Mr Mahdavi and explain to him why I cannot, we cannot, accept his generous invitation.'

'The thing is, when you get to the airport you may be asked a lot of tedious questions. I'm not saying you definitely will be, but you could be. But if you come to dinner tomorrow there definitely won't be any tiresome questions.'

'That sounds like a threat to me,' said Graham.

'No, no. I'm not threatening you. I am your friend.'

'Please, you must understand, I can't accept an invitation to dinner,' repeated Graham.

'So, the answer is yes?' said the interpreter hopefully.

'No, it's no.'

On and on it went, with Graham politely declining and the interpreter equally politely insisting.

Addressing me, the interpreter desperately implored: 'What do you think, good mother? Would *you* like to go to dinner with Mr Mahdavi? I promise it'll be at a very nice place.'

By now I was shivering, as much from fear as from the cold. It was 1am and I was feeling ground down by the wrangling. I was about to accept his offer when I glanced over at Graham who frowned a very stern 'No'.

'I'd have loved to,' I said, before uttering words I never thought I'd hear myself say, 'but I'm an obedient wife and I can't go against what my husband says. If he says no, then it has to be no.'

'I can't leave here without you saying yes,' the interpreter pleaded. 'Please, I am just trying to make things easier for you. How about breakfast? Will you have breakfast with Mr Mahdavi tomorrow?'

'Okay,' said Graham wearily, 'but it has to be a short breakfast as we're leaving for Kashan tomorrow.'

'I know,' said the man, rising to his feet, reminding us that the secret police were aware of our every move even before we'd made them. 'Good night, good mother. Good night, Dr Williams. Mr Mahdavi will see you in the morning at 9am.'

'Bloody hell, they are nothing if not dogged,' said Graham as he shut the door behind the praying mantis. 'I need a beer. Oh, I forgot, we're in the Islamic Republic of Iran and there is no beer.'

Sure enough, at the appointed hour the interpreter, still in his pink shirt and blue suit, returned to the caravanserai with Mr Mahdavi. Hastily wiping the lipstick off her lips and adjusting her headscarf so that it covered more of her hair, the caravanserai manager led the duo from the courtyard to one of the upstairs bedrooms and returned to fetch Graham. An hour later he was back. Helping himself to tea from the samovar, Graham reported to Felix, Anna and myself that he'd been invited to return in September for an all-expenses-paid conference, but had told Mr Mahdavi that as a civil servant he could only do so if the invitation was passed to him through the British Embassy in Tehran.

'The interpreter – who I must say looked worn out – said they didn't want to do that because that would make it "political". I insisted that there was no other way.'

The conversation had then turned to gifts.

'I said they'd already given us some beautiful flowers but the interpreter said that Mr Mahdavi said they were not enough,' said Graham. 'After some toing and froing we agreed that they could buy us one of those copper-and-turquoise vases we'd seen in the bazaar. The large, Holy Grail-type chalice would be nice, but I don't think it would fit in our hand luggage and I told Mr Mahdavi that and said that a small one would suffice. Mr Mahdavi is going to drop it off personally at the airport.'

'Really, hasn't he got anything better to do?'

'It seems not. I genuinely think that Mr Mahdavi likes me.'

Ayatollah Khomeini & 'Lady Gaga'

For the remainder of our trip we had no more contact with the secret police. Lisa even used them as leverage when Milad expressed reluctance to take us into Tehran to see the former US Embassy, now rebranded the US Den of Espionage Museum, where in 1979 52 Americans had been held hostage for 444 days by Iranian college students.

'I'll think about it,' he said when she made the request. Man, but Milad was a slow learner.

'Mr Mahdavi told Graham that he wanted us to have the best possible holiday in Iran and we really want to see the US Embassy, so if you can't make it happen we'll give him a call and see what he has to say,' she said. 'I'm sure the secret police wouldn't want to hear that you won't take us where we want to go.'

The threat had the desired effect. Complaining that the traffic would be 'super-hellish', Milad refused to drive into the centre of Tehran, but instead agreed to park at Ayatollah Khomeini's mausoleum where there were no fewer than 20,000 parking spaces. We'd pay a quick visit to the tomb and take the Metro from there.

We had to split from Lisa so that she could use the separate ladies' entrance, and when she rejoined us inside, draped in a bedsheet-like modesty cloak, she told us that she'd been challenged by an overzealous guard for not having a guide.

'I'm just so sick of the petty enforcement of all the tourist rules and regulations that I didn't even look at him and just said "He's a man! And he's with my husband!"' she related. 'He immediately let it drop.'

Ironically, the vast carpeted building with its lofty glittering ceiling, uplit columns and vaulted arches had more than a touch of Liberace – or Pahlavi – excess about it. For all its reported US$2 billion-worth of grandeur, the mausoleum was like an Amazon parcel: an overlarge box, professionally wrapped, full of packaging, but with not much inside. A handful of elderly women cloaked in black ankle-length *chadors* brandishing polyester flick dusters alternated between 'cleaning' the spotless green-and-gold tomb and instructing everyone to 'Shh'.

A few snaps later, we walked to the nearby Metro. It was crowded, and salesmen pushed through the length of the carriages selling tissues, combs, inner soles and lipsticks. Mindful of her dad's upcoming 80th birthday, Lisa bought three deflated green balloons the size of Swiss balls from a man whom I thought deserved to be rewarded for his skill in squeezing past everyone with inflated examples of his unwieldy wares.

'Did you notice he spoke English?' asked Milad. 'He's probably got a university degree, but it's so hard to get a good job in Iran that selling balloons is probably the only one he can find. When Trump abandoned the nuclear deal, the value of our currency halved – can you even imagine? – and unemployment shot up to 35 per cent. It's very hard in Iran.'

Milad continued his running commentary. 'See those two women over there, the ones with bandages on their noses? They've had them straightened. Iran is the nose-job capital of the world.'

Iranian women with their aquiline noses, and dark eyes accentuated by winged eyeliner, were stunning, so to learn that they thought they needed to be surgically enhanced was disheartening. As elsewhere in the world, the 'beauty' industry was succeeding in making beautiful women feel ugly.

A young woman got on at the next stop, one unlike any we'd seen all trip. She was wearing the compulsory headscarf, only hers was tipped far back on her head, exposing a long fringe and waist-length dyed platinum blonde hair. With enormous fake white eyelashes, brothel-red lipstick and gold glitter eyeshadow she was a dead-ringer for Lady Gaga.

'Hi there,' she smiled. 'How do you like Iran?'

'It's been amazing,' Lisa replied.

'Where are you going?'

'To see the former US Embassy.'

'When you get there, you'll see posters with "Death to America" and stuff like that written on them. I hope you know that most of us don't think that way.'

I turned to see if Milad was eavesdropping. True to form, he was ardently sticky-beaking. I didn't know how to warn Lady Gaga that she shouldn't speak too freely in case he reported her. He had Mr Mahdavi on speed-dial.

'Where do you come from?'

'London.'

'I would love to go to London,' she said wistfully. 'You have freedom in London. There's no freedom here.'

Lady Gaga got off at the next stop, leaving me time to reflect on the contradictory 'and yet' nature of Iran: women could work and drive – and yet couldn't leave home without a headscarf and were prohibited from attending football matches, forcing some die-hard fans to don fake-beard disguises in order to sneak in; *Game of Thrones* was an underground hit and Michelle Obama's best-selling book *Becoming* was openly on sale in many roadside kiosks – and yet satellite dishes were banned and literature was censored. The country's young people wanted to travel and dress as they pleased – and yet its theocratic rulers sanctioned lashings for dancing. Iranians were some of the most friendly people we'd met – and yet Iran's government seemed determined to live up to its 'axis of evil' status by hating America and funding armed groups such as Hamas and Hezbollah.

The *haram* hug

The lanky interpreter, still attired in his blue suit, was already at the airport when Milad dropped us off the next day. He shook Graham's hand and greeted me as 'good mother' before saying that Mr Mahdavi wished to meet Graham alone.

'That's fine by me,' I said, thankful that I would be spared an encounter with Graham's interrogator. 'In fact,' I blurted out, 'I really don't want to meet him because all of this is really starting to... *freak me out!*'

Taken aback, the interpreter led Graham downstairs to a coffee shop and a short while later he and Graham returned, with Graham clutching a presentation box with a vase inside, and another smaller box with a beautiful silver-and-turquoise necklace – a gift for me from Mr Mahdavi.

After bending over to hug Graham farewell, the interpreter turned to me.

'I'd hug you too, good mother,' he said, smiling awkwardly, 'but it is *haram*. Forbidden.'

As we settled into our plane seats and I removed my headscarf I felt an enormous sense of liberation, and relief that we'd survived our trip to Iran unscathed.

Our families and friends, too, were hugely relieved that we'd made it home in one piece and that they hadn't had to get out the poster paint. 'Iran is such a safe country,' I said at a family get-together. 'There are loads and loads of foreign tourists. It's no big deal.' Talk about famous last words. Within 10 weeks of our departure from Iran the UK was embroiled in a stand-off with Iran: Royal Marines had boarded an Iranian-owned oil tanker off Gibraltar and Iran had retaliated by attempting to seize a UK-registered tanker in the Strait of Hormuz. Fifteen days later, Iran captured the British-flagged tanker *Stena Impero*, holding it hostage for 10 weeks. And on 3 January 2020, America goaded Iran by assassinating Qasem Soleimani, the most senior military commander of the Islamic Revolutionary Guard Corps, in an air strike at Baghdad Airport. Five days later, a jittery Islamic Revolutionary Guard shot down Ukraine Airlines Flight 752 shortly after it took off from Imam Khomeini International Airport. All 176 passengers and crew died. We'd been on Flight 752 from Tehran to Kiev only eight months before.

Keeping up with the Kims
North Korea

'I'm so paranoid my guidebook will be confiscated that I've torn it into sections and I'm going to stuff the pages down my trousers the moment we get to Pyongyang,' confessed Amelie, a flame-haired tax accountant from Paris as our train crossed the border from Dandong in eastern China and trundled towards North Korea's capital.

'The tour organiser's instructions didn't say guidebooks were illegal, only that we shouldn't bring any Bibles, pornography or political satire films such as *The Interview* with us, so I'm going to take my chances,' said a relaxed Bruce, a builder from Melbourne, as he took a swig from a bottle of beer he'd purchased from the smartly attired train attendants. They'd done a roaring trade selling drinks and snacks from their trolleys. 'They can't possibly search every single one of us on this train before letting us in.'

Now that he mentioned it, most of the passengers on the train were Chinese so the authorities would only need to search the tour groups. That wouldn't take long. Perhaps I should follow Amelie's example?

Our group of 17 were mostly seasoned travellers who'd on average each visited almost 100 countries, but all the same, the excitement was palpable as we stood in the carriage passage taking snaps of the yellow fields edged with fluttering crimson flags as if none of us had ever seen a farm before. Long rows of red metal propaganda boards ending with exclamation marks had been erected to encourage an ardent work ethic: 'Let us praise the sacrifices of the farmers and labourers who have worked tirelessly to realise the vision of Marshal Kim Jong-un!' I imagined them proclaiming. Among the haystacks of harvested rice stalks, toiling agricultural workers cut rice by hand. It was Monet's 19th century *Haystacks* paintings brought to life in the 21st century.

'I've read that about 16 per cent of the rice harvest is lost each year because the North Koreans don't have enough trucks and tractors to get it to the threshing centres before it goes mouldy in the fields,' said Amelie. 'Can you imagine so much of your backbreaking work going to waste like that?'

Waiting on the platform were our state-appointed guides, Joo and Sonu. One of the first things Joo told us was that it wasn't just farmers who laboured in the fields. Townsfolk did their bit by volunteering to bring in the harvest.

'In the Democratic People's Republic of Korea we work six days a week,' she informed us in perfect English, only her accent giving away that she wasn't a native speaker, 'but one of those days is a study day where we can study history or the writings of our Great Leaders. I was on the farm this weekend helping to harvest rice on my day off.'

'*Can* study history, or *must* study history?' I wondered. North Korea has a reputation for being a country where a lot of activities are compulsory.

'You mean you worked a seven-day week last week?' I asked incredulously.

'Sure, I enjoyed it. It was great to get out in the fresh air. It's important that us city folk learn where our food comes from – and also lend a hand to our farmers to make sure it gets harvested in time.'

I wondered how this form of education would go down in the UK where we relied on petting zoos and city farms to do that job, not people getting their hands dirty by reaping their own food.

'Let me tell you a little more about life here,' continued Joo.

'The state takes very good care of us. It gives us all homes to live in, healthcare is free, there's 100 per cent literacy and we get vouchers for free rice, meat, soap and toothpaste. Until I asked my mother, I had no idea how many of our groceries were given to us by our government. There's also a voucher for beer. Koreans love drinking.'

We'd been warned to ask only innocuous questions of our guides: any about Kim Jong-un's personal life, where he lived or how many children he had, were strictly off limits. That left us the choice of asking about a handful of things such as local customs, wedding traditions – and the personal lives of our guides.

'Can you choose what jobs you want to do?' Amelie asked.

'After university we submit a list of our three favourite jobs and the government decides for us,' said Sonu, the quieter, and sterner of our guides who later told me her first choice had been to become a teacher.

'Do you get paid a salary?' I asked.

'Of course. But I live at home with my parents, so I generally tend to spend it on snacks. I love snacks. And handbags. This is one I bought only yesterday.' Joo held up a smart polyester satchel, no doubt made in China.

On arrival at the Yanggakdo International Hotel there was no check-in – probably to prevent us from having contact with anyone other than our guides: Joo and Sonu simply distributed our room keys in the gleaming marble lobby.

'Welcome to Pyongyang,' said Joo. 'Tomorrow we visit the International Friendship Exhibition. It's two hours away by bus so we need to get an early start.'

'That's not what our itinerary says,' complained Maria, an interior designer from Argentina. 'It says here that we're going to the Demilitarised Zone.'

Joo didn't dignify Maria's act of defiance with an answer.

'You must wake up tomorrow at 6am – we'll give you a wake-up call every morning – and breakfast is at 6.30am. The bus leaves at 7am. Don't make us late.'

She didn't need to add 'or else'.

Our guides had obviously never met my nieces-in-law who, in their youth, needed at least two hours to make themselves presentable for public consumption, so didn't factor in that some people might need more than an hour to 'scrub up and grub up'.

'Then we're going to Kaesong, the Victorious Fatherland Liberation War Museum and the supermarket or fun fair – it's a great place to go if you want to hear North Koreans scream!'

'The HQ of the secret police is the best place,' whispered Bruce.

'The next day we'll visit the Mansudae Grand Monument and the Kumsusan Palace of the Sun, attend a Mass Dance and then go for a ride on the Metro. We will also visit the circus and perhaps go to the Mass Games, but these two are not compulsory.'

'Blimey,' I thought, 'that's a jam-packed itinerary, with no room for hesitation, deviation or repetition. It seems they've deliberately designed a programme that will exhaust us so we'll have no energy for rebellion.'

Already there were mutters of disquiet among our group.

'I thought this was supposed to be a holiday,' grumbled Maria. 'I don't even get up at 6am when I'm working.'

'And finally, when you use the lifts, *do not* get off on any floor other than your own,' warned Joo. 'The ones marked "staff only" are strictly for staff.'

I knew that Otto Warmbier, the American student who'd returned to Cincinnati from North Korea in a vegetative state, and who died six days later, had been imprisoned for 17 months as punishment for stealing a propaganda poster while staying at the Yanggakdo. Otto had allegedly wandered into off-limits areas of the hotel used either as staff lodgings or guest-surveillance suites. There was no way I was going even vaguely off-piste in the lifts.

Secrets & lies

I found it curious that, whenever I told anyone I was going to North Korea, their response wasn't 'How?' but 'Why?'. I was surprised to find that few people were as inquisitive as I was about 'the world's most secretive state'. For me, if you stick the word 'secret' in front of anything, you've got me. Secret Santa? Love it. *The Secret*? Bought the book *and* watched the movie. Secret Service? Leaves me both shaken *and* stirred.

But when I investigated if it was difficult for tourists to get in I found any number of tour companies would escort you there, and that getting a visa wouldn't be a problem unless you were a journalist or a human-rights activist. That didn't stop me feeling anxious, however, as I packed my bags for Pyongyang. As they'd done when we'd visited Iran, several friends joked that they'd already bought the paint to make campaign posters for my release.

It turns out I wasn't the only one on the tour who was nervous.

'Just before we got on the train in Dandong, my legs were shaking and I did wonder what on earth I was doing,' admitted Louise, a 40-something PR from London who'd joined the trip with her husband Felipe, an events manager. 'All my friends and colleagues think we're nuts for coming – and Felipe and I aren't going to tell our parents we've come here until we're safely back home!'

Day one, though it did include a lengthy visit to the International Friendship Exhibition where over a quarter of a million gifts from 178 countries given to members of the Kim dynasty are on display, thankfully broke us in gently. After depositing our watches and phones at reception we were led to two rooms where we were asked to bow to waxwork models of North Korea's founder, Kim Il-sung, his first wife Kim Jong Suk and their son Kim Jong-il.

I couldn't imagine Madame Tussauds asking visitors to

bow to their dummies but I could imagine the chaos that would ensue if this were required.

'I won't bow to Boris,' I could envisage someone saying, 'but if there's a waxwork of Beyoncé, I'll happily bow to that.'

'It would take you several months to see all the presents that world leaders have given our Great Leaders over the years,' said the exhibition guide, a woman wearing pastel-coloured traditional dress comprised of a wrapover top and a delicately embroidered, high-waisted, floor-length balloon skirt that made her look like a fairy-tale princess, 'so if you tell me which countries you're from, I'll take you to see only those exhibits.'

After a quick tour of the Oceania room in Bruce's honour, where I spotted a gift of a gardening book inscribed with the message 'To Kim Il-sung, with grateful thanks from an Australian citizen', and of the South America room, so that Maria could feast her eyes on a grinning Nicaraguan caiman crocodile rearing up on its hind legs and holding a tray of wooden cups, we were shepherded to the Africa room. I was dismayed to see that the only gift from South Africa was a bedraggled African National Congress flag.

'South Africa isn't exactly generous in the gift-giving department,' I thought as the far more exotic gifts from other African nations caught my eye. Robert Mugabe had gifted a rhino horn, as one does, and Muammar Gaddafi a less endangered ornate chess set. As no one in our group had any connection to Cambodia, Russia, Cuba or Palestine, we were denied the privilege of seeing Pol Pot's gift of a cutlery set, Putin's Siberian bear rug, a crocodile-skin suitcase from Castro and Yasser Arafat's gem-encrusted sword.

After an afternoon exploring Kaesong, where we were treated to a royal banquet served in a dozen golden cups, and a trip to the Victorious Fatherland Liberation War Museum to see the bullet-riddled spy ship the *USS Pueblo* seized by North Korea in 1968, we stopped off at a supermarket.

'This is the only place where you're allowed to convert

foreign currency into *won*,' said Sonu. 'There's a lady over there who will change your money. You then have 20 minutes to do your shopping – and then you must change any *won* you haven't spent back into *yuan*, dollars or euros. Remember, it's a criminal offence to take *won* outside our country.'

Eager to purchase souvenirs, we stampeded as one into the supermarket, changed money as quickly as we possibly could, and then roamed the aisles. My mental arithmetic is worse than my ability to juggle chainsaws, and I usually leave the money side of things to Graham, so I struggled to convert *won* into euros and euros into pounds, while deciphering products whose labels were mostly in Korean. I failed to figure out a single price. Painfully aware that I was running out of time, I jogged to the checkout queue, my arms laden with several bottles of *soju* (Korean rice or grain wine), a bottle of red wine, an expensive-looking box of chocolates and some dried squid snacks of the type I'd grown fond of in Taipei. I dutifully converted what was left of my *won* back into euros and clambered onto the bus.

'Did you spot the Nutella and the Nescafé?' asked Louise. I nodded. 'You do realise this is all put on for show. Apparently, all the people in there are actors and no ordinary people from Pyongyang are allowed to shop there.'

I had my doubts that the state would go to so much trouble to put on a display requiring not only the requisitioning of Western groceries but an enormous array of fresh fruit and vegetables, too, but later in the tour, when Bastien, a Swiss schoolteacher, who'd hung on to some *won*, tried to use it to buy a bottle of water, he was told it wasn't valid currency.

'They gave us Monopoly money in that supermarket!' exclaimed Bastien laughing.

When I got my purchases back to the UK, I found that the squid and the *soju* were the real deal. The wine, however, was good only for clearing drains and the fancy chocolates weren't chocolate at all but a box of plasticky, shiny-white, sickly sweet pineapple-flavoured confectionary.

A mausoleum & a messed-up Mass Dance

Day two of bootcamp started with a uniform inspection in our hotel lobby. Joo had swapped the previous day's casual outfit of trousers and trainers for a skirt suit and pumps.

'No, Lisa, I'm afraid that's not smart enough,' said Joo, who'd been doubtfully eyeing my ensemble of black trousers, a long-sleeved navy blouse and court shoes. Our tour briefing email had advised us that in order to be allowed to visit some of the sights, we'd need to bring along sombre, smart clothes without any cheerful designs such as floral prints. 'If in any doubt, bring clothes suitable for a funeral.'

'But I actually wore this exact outfit to my friend Pat's funeral,' I replied.

'It's not the clothes, it's the jacket and hoody you're wearing. The hoody's considered sportswear, not formal clothing, and that padded jacket isn't very smart.'

'It isn't a hoody, Joo – it hasn't got a hood – but I don't have anything smarter. Can I just please wear them on the bus as it's really cold outside and then take them off when we get there?'

'Sure,' said Joo. 'You need to understand that you're going to visit the bodies of our leaders today, so you must show them respect.' She turned to inspect the next member of our group who playfully gave her a twirl in her 'funeral' outfit.

A short bus ride transported us to the Mansudae Grand Monument, comprising two giant statues of Kim and his son Kim against a mosaic background of Mount Paektu.

'Does anyone want to guess why we all wear a badge with Presidents Kim Il-sung and Kim Jong-il on the left side of our jackets?' said Sonu as our bus chugged up Mansu Hill.

'So they don't get shot?' answered Bruce under his breath.

'No guesses? It's meant to show that no matter where we go, our Great Leaders are always close to our hearts.'

It was a sign of how thoroughly indoctrinated North

Koreans are. Sure, some Americans wear 'I love Trump' badges, but in North Korea you'd never see the equivalent of a bumper sticker reading 'Elect a clown, expect a circus'. Actually, that's probably because there are no private cars in North Korea to stick bumper stickers on, as much as it's down to unquestioning loyalty to the Kims.

'It's traditional for visitors to lay flowers here,' Joo informed us. 'It's not compulsory to buy flowers but we have some in the bus that you can buy. Who wants flowers?'

Most of the bus put up their hands and within minutes Joo and Sonu had distributed an armload of blooms. The posy I bought – a triangular sleeve of polythene containing three or four twigs of what looked like chrysanthemums – was decidedly past its 'best by' date as several of the flowers had petals tinged brown with age. I wondered whether they'd been recycled.

'There are quite a few rules you need to be aware of when visiting this monument,' said Joo over the bus loudspeaker. 'Firstly, you need to bow to the statues. I will tell you when it is time to bow. If you don't want to do that, that's fine; we don't force people to do things in our country.'

'Why would you *not* want to do that?' whispered Louise to me. 'In my view, if you don't want to do that you should stay on the bus.'

'In my view, you should stay at *home*!' said Bruce.

'Anyone who doesn't want to bow must stay on the bus,' said Joo, echoing Louise. I later learned that two members of our group did indeed choose the bus option as they didn't want to show obeisance to the dictator duo.

'The second rule is that when you photograph the statues you need to include the whole statue – you are not allowed to chop off the feet, for example, or the heads. Thirdly, please don't kid around or laugh while you're here. And please don't do silly things in your photos like imitate the way our Eternal President is pointing – that's disrespectful.'

I thought of all the times I'd imitated statues around the

world – the Statue of Liberty in New York, the kung-fu pose of Bruce Lee in Hong Kong and the arms-aloft Rocky in Philadelphia – and was glad I'd been warned off.

We strode purposefully up a tree-lined road and were greeted by two 20-metre tall statues of Kim Il-sung and Kim Jong-il, which looked as if they'd been crafted from melted-down penny pieces. There are 35,000 Kim Il-sung statues in North Korea – one for every 750 people – but this one was by far the largest. Kim Il-sung was depicted in a suit and coat and Kim Jong-il, who'd initially been cast wearing a long coat like his dad's, was decked out in a parka to make him look more like a man of the people.

'Kim Jong-il always wore that jacket,' Sonu informed us. 'When someone asked him why he didn't get a new one he said that until everyone in our country could afford a new one he would keep wearing the one he'd had for years. That was the kind of man our Dear Leader was, and why all Korean people love him so much.'

Pre-trip reading had taught me that it wasn't just Kim Jong-il who'd had a costume change. His father had originally been depicted in a Mao suit, but when the statue of his son was added to the monument after his death in 2011, the builders took the opportunity to update his statue by giving it a more benign expression and a Western-style suit and tie. The monument makeover didn't come cheap: some estimate the extra statue cost US$10 million, and apparently North Koreans working abroad were ordered to cough up US$150 each to fund the alterations.

'I'd like you all to stand in a row now, please,' instructed Joo, 'and when I tell you to, once that group of soldiers has laid their flowers, we'll all walk up slowly together, lay our flowers at the base of the statues and bow.'

Our group, though full of jokers, did Joo proud, and our synchronised bow was judged a success.

'Thank you everyone for showing your respect for our leaders,' she said.

Just as we were congratulating ourselves on mastering North Korean Leader Etiquette, both guides rushed up the aisle of the bus to pick up one of the newspapers they'd distributed to us that morning, which had fallen on the floor.

'The Supreme Leader!' Sonu called out crossly. 'We told you that you need to show him respect at all times. It's not respectful to let Kim Jong-un's face touch the ground like that. We told you that you should never wrap anything with newspaper showing his face. You really must be careful.'

'Just as well fish and chips isn't a staple in North Korea, like it is in the UK,' I whispered to Bruce, who grinned.

Our next stop was the Kumsusan Palace of the Sun, the mausoleum where the bodies of Kim Il-sung and Kim Jong-il were on display. An enormously lengthy airport-style travellator carried us to the rooms where the embalmed leaders lay.

'This is another place where we need to bow,' said Joo. 'We're going to line up in rows of four, and then bow three times: once to the feet, once to the left, and once to the right. There's no need to bow to the head.'

I paired up with Joo, Andrew and Kieran, two brothers from The Wirral near Liverpool, who'd taken the 'clothes for a funeral' diktat one step further by dressing like undertakers.

Soft music played in the dimly lit halls where the bodies lay in state in their climate-controlled glass sarcophagi, separated from us by rope barriers. Soldiers stood ramrod stiff to attention at the sides of the cavernous rooms. I'd seen the bodies of Ho Chi Minh, Lenin and Mao, allegedly pickled by the same team of Russian embalmers, but these two – if they were the real thing and not waxworks – were undoubtedly their finest work, and looked as if at any moment they would get up and join us for a stroll outside. But I suppose at an alleged annual cost of £320,000 to keep them preserved, you'd expect the bodies to look pretty darn good.

After a tour of the rest of the palace we emerged into the large square outside for a group photo.

'Please don't do any silly poses here,' instructed Sonu. 'A foreign student once did a handstand in front of this building. We Koreans find that very insulting.' As well they should.

'Hurry up, we can't miss the Mass Dance,' said Joo, ushering us back to the bus. 'Today is Party Foundation Day and so it's traditional to hold Mass Dances in all the squares around the country.' They're also held when the North Koreans have successfully launched a missile, tested a nuclear bomb or completed a major construction project, so they're the human equivalent of celebratory fireworks. Featuring thousands of women dressed in gossamer-like traditional kimono-style robes paired with men dressed identically in black trousers, white shirts and red ties, it truly was one of the most thrilling spectacles I'd ever seen. I hate taking photos but within minutes, standing on the steps overlooking the square, I'd shot off 300.

'That's my favourite dress, no that one, or maybe that one, or that one, in fact they're all just unbelievably gorgeous,' I thought as the couples swirled past, making circular patterns that expanded and contracted as they pranced towards the centre and back out again. The music, blaring from huge loudspeakers, was incredibly catchy, and soon I was clapping along delightedly.

'Who wants to join in?' asked Joo, smiling encouragingly. I noticed a few tourists had already taken up the offer and were having a whale of a time, but thought my lamentable 'gross motor co-ordination' score from primary school precluded me from having a go. After another minute or two, though, I knew I'd regret not participating.

'Will you take some photos of me please?' I asked Joo.

'Of course. Good for you. Let me go and find you a young man to dance with.'

Joo raced to the edge of one of the circles, tapped a stunning young woman on the shoulder and explained that a tourist wanted to borrow her beau. Unsmiling, the woman stepped out of the circle and I took her place. My male partner remained impassive as I stumbled and staggered through the moves, clapped out of time, and headed for the centre of the circle at the moment everyone decided to skip the other way. I wondered what my partner thought about having to hold hands with a clumsy Westerner dressed in a bullfrog-green puffer jacket, black elasticated-waist trousers and a bulky bum bag, rather than with his vastly more accomplished, orchid-pretty former companion. A galloping galumpher rather than a light-on-her-feet fairy.

Breathless, I returned to the steps and was truly sorry when the display ended.

'You liked that?' asked Joo as we left.

'I loved it! If I were Korean, I'd wear one of those dresses every day – they're the loveliest outfits I think I've ever seen. Do you have one, Joo?'

'Of course. I have several. Come on everyone, back on the bus. Hurry up, we have a lot to see today.'

In the centre of town, as devoid of people and litter as it was of traffic, we disembarked outside Puhŭng Metro station.

'We don't need private cars in Pyongyang as our Metro is so cheap it's almost free,' said Joo when we reached the bottom of the incredibly long escalator. 'Our Metro is one of the deepest in the world, so if we need to we can use it as a bomb shelter. Its heavy blast doors will protect us against a nuclear attack. Before he would let his people use the Metro, our Eternal President Kim Il-sung rode the entire network to assure himself that it was safe.'

Considering there were only two lines and just 16 stations, that would thankfully not have chewed up too much of the Eternal President's time that could otherwise have been better spent supervising missiles tests.

Like Moscow's world-famous Metro, Pyongyang's doubled up as a cathedral to transportation, complete with flower chandeliers and exquisite murals. It was the complete opposite of the grim, pigeon-dropping-spattered arches of London's Victoria Station and its grubby Tube platforms infested with mice that I'm more familiar with. The mural I found particularly striking depicted a bespectacled Kim Il-sung in a trench coat and blue Mao suit and cap: he was striding beside heroic officials and housewives – all smiling blindingly white Hollywood-dentist smiles – below some powerlines and smokestack factories outlined against a sunflower-yellow sky. Powerlines? Factories? I hadn't seen even a single tractor out in the fields, let alone any signs of industry. Perhaps the mural depicted Kim on a visit to China.

After spending a few minutes perusing the free newspapers posted up in glass cabinets for the edification and instruction of commuters, it was time to hop aboard the red and peppermint-green Metro train. The wood-panelled interior was spartan because, like on the escalators, there was no advertising, though above the door linking the two carriages the now familiar portraits of the two deceased but beloved leaders beamed down benevolently.

'We can only go one stop because the rest of the Metro doesn't exist,' whispered Bruce to me. 'It's rumoured that all the locals on this train are actors.'

Again I found it a bit far-fetched that the North Korean government would go to so much trouble to fool us – I mean, considering our itinerary was as strictly controlled as a muffin top in a pair of Spanx, wouldn't it just be simpler to omit a Metro visit rather than stage a *Truman Show* experience just for us? Metro visits are hardly top of tourists' must-see lists.

'Apparently, the trains are second-hand from Berlin's U-bahn,' said Dieter, a gruff German mechanic, pointing out a manufacturer's logo worded in German, 'but the North Koreans bought twice as many as they needed so there may be secret Metro lines and stations no one knows about.'

'Quick,' said Sonu, 'we must hurry now as we need to get to the circus. We love the circus and our performers have won many awards in international competitions.'

I had a culture-rich childhood sprinkled with visits to art galleries, museums, the ballet and opera – for goodness' sake, my mother took us to a lunchtime symphony concert almost every week – but even I was starting to marvel at the cultural riches our guides were laying on for us. It reminded me of children in London whose helicopter parents, frantic to keep their little darlings entertained, organise mud play, water play, sandpit play, bubble blowing, macaroni-necklace making and cookie baking all in one day.

The circus, though indeed a spectacle, was nothing compared to the grand finale to the most action-packed day of my life: the 2019 Arirang Mass Games. Our tour operator had said we might be lucky enough to attend, but it was possible that Kim Jong-un had cancelled them. The previous year's Games had been the first in five years and North Korean state media had reported that Kim Jong-un had 'seriously criticised' the current Games for 'their wrong spirit of creation and irresponsible work attitude', whatever that meant.

'Do you know whether the Mass Games are going ahead or not?' I'd asked Sonu on our first day.

'I don't know,' she'd replied evasively.

'But I thought you said they go on every night for a month?'

'They do.'

'So how come you don't know?'

Sonu wandered off. She was very adept at avoiding questions she'd rather not answer.

I'd marvelled at how a spectacle involving over 100,000 participants could work on a 'shall we, shan't we?' basis. Surely all the performers needed to know whether they should keep their evening free?

Joo took a seat beside me in the cavernous 150,000-seat Rungrado May Day Stadium, the largest in the world by seating capacity.

'Remember everyone,' she said addressing our group and pointing to the bank of seats directly opposite, 'when you see the images of our leaders over there, we all need to stand.'

I looked where she'd pointed and saw the stands were filled with 17,000 children, each holding a small placard to create gigantic images. Every now and again a small, dark inquisitive head could be seen popping above the top of a placard, but the timing of the scene changes was so precise that there was no other indication that we were watching a living screen rather than a digital one.

Intended as a propaganda tool, the Games managed to outdo the best bits of every Olympics and World Cup Opening Ceremony I'd seen. In the stands opposite us the human pixels continued to create scenes of incredible beauty and imagination. An image of an old bearded man holding up a plump child waving a North Korean flag appeared as if by magic, to be almost instantaneously replaced by one showing a group of children running through a flower-strewn field with a pair of white doves. An image of two red-eyed adult rabbits coyly nibbling on a lush lawn clacked to one of four, then eight, then 16, then 32 baby rabbits hopping about happily, as an example of either exponential growth in farming output, how the country intended to feed its often malnourished populace or a Korean telling of the traditional story of the birds and the bees.

It was impossible to take everything in: cheerleader-style pyramids; kung-fu brick breaking; uniformed marching bands. Anything that could be waved – fans, flags, capes, outsize foldout paper pom-poms, garlands of flowers – was waved with immense enthusiasm. Mixed in was almost every type of dance imaginable, including one where men wearing skullcaps with ribbons attached rotated their heads to make them swish in rapid circles, much like burlesque dancers twirl nipple tassels.

True to her snack-loving persona, Joo proceeded to munch on a gigantic bag of popcorn. 'Take some photos,' she said, nudging me.

'This is just too special to miss. I'd rather see it with my own eyes,' I said, humouring her by taking a few snaps before sitting back and trying to comprehend what I was witnessing.

The pixel scene changed to depict a portrait of Kim Jong-un surrounded by fireworks, the music changed and the audience, as if programmed, rose as one and gave his image a standing ovation. Kim Jong-un's image disappeared. As one, everyone sat down. The stadium filled with hundreds of dancing gymnasts: while the boys, dressed in the red, white and blue colours of the national flag, performed synchronised headstands and flick-flacks, the ranks of little girls, wearing pink-and-white tutus, suddenly bent over backwards into a bridge with as much ease as if they were touching their toes. Cartwheels and tumbling followed.

Walking back to the bus I quizzed Joo on how the human-pixel effect had been achieved. I'd seen footage of people at mass events being issued with placards that had to be held up at specific times, but just couldn't imagine 17,000 children with laps full of cardboard sheets managing to choose and hold up the correct ones with such precise timing.

'Oh, they simply have flipbooks in their laps,' she said.

'Flipbooks?'

'Yes, give me your travel journal. If I hold it like this,' she said, opening the notebook, 'you can see how easy it is to turn one page at a time to create a new image.'

Easy perhaps for North Koreans, but I couldn't imagine myself tasked with dropping down pages on cue every 10 seconds for 90 minutes. I'm sure that if I'd been involved there would have been a piece of bunny tail visible long after the scene had changed to the picture of the North Korean flag, and that Kim Jong-un would most definitely have frowned upon my 'irresponsible work attitude'.

'Some people where I come from say the Mass Games are actually very cruel as the adults, and especially the children, have to practise for hundreds of hours to get it all perfect. Do you think it's cruel?' I asked Joo, my heart still pounding from the excitement.

'Not at all. I participated in the Games when I was young and I loved it,' she replied.

I marvelled at how North Korea's PR machine had worked its magic on me. No matter how much I reminded myself that it was ruled by a truly brutal regime that thought nothing of executing 'traitors' in public by shooting them to pieces with anti-aircraft guns – none other than Kim Jong-un's uncle had met this fate – I couldn't help but feel deliriously happy. I wasn't alone.

'God, that was absolutely amazing. Did you see the ice skaters doing pirouettes on the mini ice rinks? And the Taekwondo fighters?' gasped Felipe.

'Ice skaters? You're kidding me! No, but did you see the human cannonballs?' I replied.

'I missed that. There was so much going on I didn't know where to look.'

'For me, one of the best bits was how they made giant clouds roll across the stadium floor just by having runners hold up a gigantic white sheet,' said Louise. 'I imagine there were quite a few bloody noses and bruised shins when they practised that part of the show as it must be hard to see where you're going under there.'

'I guess you all enjoyed that?' asked Joo, beaming from ear to ear.

'No, Joo,' I joked. 'Back in London we watch something like that every Tuesday. It's no big deal.'

As our bus passed the floodlit North Korean Workers' Party Monument – a stone hammer, sickle and calligraphy brush – the group begged to be let off to take photos. I hate the faff of taking photos and usually leave this to Graham, so wasn't too bothered.

'It's not on the itinerary but we are going to allow a very quick stop,' conceded Joo. 'It's a present from us guides to Kieran as it's his birthday today.'

The group let out a cheer and hastily spilled out of the bus like happy puppies.

'I'd already taken a "drive-by shooting" photo of the monument earlier today,' said Louise when she returned to the bus, 'but it was great to get a close-up one.'

The minute we got back to our hotel I rushed off to make a hugely expensive phone call to a rather bemused Graham, who had just had lunch. Unable to join me on the trip because the UK Foreign Office had advised against all but essential travel to North Korea, he'd agreed to join me in South Korea after my trip ended.

'Graham, can't talk long or I'll bankrupt us, but I've just had one of the most interesting and exciting days of my life.' Conscious that the phone, like my room, was most likely bugged, I told him in one stream-of-consciousness sentence about all the amazing things we'd crammed into one day. I kept my misgivings about seeing workers toil in the fields picking rice by hand to myself, along with the fact that besides our guides we'd not been allowed to interact with a single North Korean.

'I wish I were there with you, sweetie, but I'm just so pleased you're having a fabulous time. See you in Seoul on Wednesday.'

Still buzzing with adrenaline and almost giddy with over-stimulation from the day's events, I hung up and retired to our hotel's top-floor revolving restaurant where the rest of our group was already tucking into Taedonggang beers in celebration of Kieran's 24th birthday.

'I hate to break it to you, Kieran,' I said as we clinked bottles, 'you're only 24 but I don't think that, as long as you live, you'll ever have a birthday party quite as spectacular as the one you've had today. Every single one of them is going to be a massive anti-climax.'

'I think I have to agree with you,' he said, laughing.

Bastien and his Hungarian friend Csaba arrived.

'Sorry we're late folks. We've just been to the casino in the basement because we wanted to see if we could get Wi-Fi. It's so weird being cut off from the world without email access.'

'Did you manage to get Wi-Fi?' asked Kieran.

'Yes, but the way we got it was quite funny actually,' said Bastien. 'Despite gambling being illegal for the locals we had to buy 10 dollars of gambling chips before the staff would give us the Wi-Fi code.'

'Yes,' added Csaba, 'we didn't want to waste our precious internet-access time gambling so we told the staff to gamble on our behalf. Only problem was, they kept winning, and wanted to know what they should do with the chips. We kept telling them to keep on gambling. I think we must have made about 30 dollars from our little Wi-Fi adventure.'

'Just to let you know, in case you were wondering, there's no Tinder in North Korea,' said Bastien.

'Tinder?' the group asked in unison.

'Yes, we always go on Tinder wherever we are in the world – we've met some great women that way – but it's obviously not reached North Korea yet.'

Propaganda posters & axe murderers

'Come along, come along, has everyone got their cosy clothes?' asked Joo as she ushered us into the bus at 6.59am. 'We need to get to the DMZ as soon as we can. If we're not first in the queue we'll be behind dozens of other tour buses and we'll have to wait a long time to get in.'

The road down to the Demilitarised Zone was smooth and, like all the roads, eerily empty.

'That monument is the Arch of Reunification,' said Joo over the loudspeaker as we made a half-moon detour around a stunning giant stone statue of two elegant women in traditional dress jointly holding up a ball with a map of a reunified Korea on it. 'The North longs to be reunified with the South.'

I'd previously thought the two countries were sworn enemies, judging by the military build-up on both sides, and had never considered that North Korea wanted reunification with the South.

Our bus continued southwards and Joo continued chatting over the loudspeaker.

'I'm 32 and nearing the end of the marriage season. Most women in our country marry before the age of 30, so I'm in danger of becoming a spinster.'

'Do your parents choose whom you should marry?' asked Louise.

'No, I have wonderful parents and they've said I can marry the man I choose. I'm going on a lot of dates but I haven't met anyone I like yet.'

'Why don't you like them?' Felipe asked.

'I don't know. It may be because I have a wonderful father and no one I've met so far is as good as him. I test all the men I date by turning up late. If they are annoyed I tell them immediately "I'm sorry, but this is not going to work," and go home. I just can't be bothered to waste my time taking it any further.'

'That's a bit harsh,' I said. 'My husband Graham really hates lateness and has always told me that if I turn up more than 15 minutes late I can't expect him to still be waiting where we arranged to meet.'

'No, it's a good test. I mean this is someone I have to spend the rest of my life with, and I can't imagine doing that with anyone who's unkind or impatient.'

Joo proceeded to tell us that in North Korea female beauty was based on the law of threes: three whites (skin, eyes, teeth), three blacks (hair, eyebrows, eyes), three bigs (eyes, breasts, bottom) and three smalls (mouth, hands, feet). Unlike in the West, where small 'heroin chic' bottoms were fashionable one minute, and voluptuous Kardashian rears were in vogue the next, North Koreans obviously liked to keep things simple and standardised.

I loved Joo's spirit. Her love of snacks meant she didn't conform to the North Korean petite and highly feminine ideal of beauty, and having a wife who was as intelligent, funny and headstrong as she was probably wasn't on every North Korean man's wishlist. But the man who managed to overcome a distaste for a lack of punctuality would be a very lucky man indeed.

'I hope to be married by the time you come back to our country,' she said grinning. I told her that I hoped so, too.

In 1993, President Bill Clinton called the Demilitarised Zone (DMZ) the 'scariest place on Earth,' but it certainly didn't feel like it. A strip just 2.5 miles wide and 160 miles long, it was peppered with the same workers bent double in the fields that we'd seen from the train on our way to Pyongyang. Our guidebook, however, assured us that these were special farmers who were paid a premium to live and farm there – farmers who could be trusted not to try to defect.

The first sign that we were in a military zone came when the road narrowed. On either side, huge square concrete anti-tank blocks had been erected at regular intervals: if ever an invasion came from the south their foundations would be blown up and they'd topple into the road like dominoes.

'Quick, get off the bus! You can buy propaganda posters and paintings here,' said Joo. I loved the matter-of-fact way she said 'propaganda posters' – I'd expected them to be called 'revolutionary zeal posters' or 'productivity encouragement posters' in an attempt to disguise their true nature, but at least in this instance there were no smoke and mirrors. You got what it said on the tin. There was a flurry of excitement as everyone rushed to the gift shop and began speed-shopping.

'Quick, you need to get back on the bus,' Sonu called out after 20 minutes.

Worried about my brim-full bladder, I asked whether there was time to go to 'uncle's house' first, using the euphemism for visiting the toilet our guides had taught us.

'No, we have to go right now or we'll miss our slot in the armistice huts.'

Minutes later the bus dropped us off outside a single storey building with a corrugated tin roof. I raced to the loo and was just in time to enter the huts with our group.

'This is the North Korea Peace Museum,' said the guide. 'And this table is where the armistice was signed that ended the Korean War. However, North and South Korea are technically still at war.'

Our group jostled to be photographed at the historic table so I left to explore the museum, stumbling across the one exhibit I'd dearly wanted to see. The relics from the 'tree-trimming incident' didn't look very impressive: just a single axe and an axe handle missing its blade in two separate clear plastic bags inside a nondescript glass case. None of the other tourists seemed remotely interested in them. But I'd read my guidebook on the train from China and knew that these axes were murder weapons, and that the murderers who'd used them had seized them from US Army officers who were trying to prune a 30m-high poplar tree in the DMZ that was obstructing the view of a United Nations command post. When they defied North Korean instructions to desist, the 19-strong team was attacked and two officers were subsequently bludgeoned to death with their own axes. Three days after the incident, American and South Korean forces launched Operation Paul Bunyan – named after the legendary giant American lumberjack – to cut down the tree and show North Korea who was boss. While nuclear-capable strategic bombers, attack helicopters and fighter jets circled overhead, the tree was cut down using chainsaws in what's been called 'the most expensive tree-felling operation in history'.

Ten minutes later we were ushered outside to visit the world-famous lookout where tourists on the North Korea side could stare across the border at South Korea, and curious South Koreans and tourists could stare back. Peering from the balcony, I saw the light-blue huts straddling the border. Once again, a bunfight ensued as everyone strove to get a photo of themselves against the iconic backdrop without being photobombed by a fellow tourist.

'Quick, give me your camera,' hissed Joo. Her command startled and unnerved me: I wasn't sure if she wanted to inspect my camera and mentally raced through the images I'd taken that day in case I'd 'chopped off' any part of the two leaders in some of them. Apprehensively, I handed it over.

'The minute that group moves on, go and stand next to that soldier and I'll take your photo. Don't be polite, and don't wait for anyone else to join you, just rush in and stand next to him. It's the only place in the country where it's okay to have a photo with a soldier.'

The Wonsan 'torture massage'

Most of our group headed home after day three, but I and four others elected to add a further three days to my North Korea trip. Although this part of the trip wasn't nearly as full-on as the first three days, I'm pleased I did it for it gave me an insight into life outside Pyongyang, where only the elite were allowed to live.

The ill-maintained road eastwards was incredibly rough and our luggage on the back seat of the minivan levitated with every bump. It was lovely having a chance to chat with the guides and, after I'd shared my Bolivian barricades story, Joo shared one of her own: the time she'd almost been kidnapped by Boko Haram in Nigeria, where she'd worked at the North Korean Embassy.

'A colleague and I had to catch an overnight bus to Abuja,' she told us while shelling sunflower seeds. 'People told us to be very careful, and that if the bus was held up we should not let the hijackers know that there were yellow people inside. Halfway to Abuja our bus suddenly stopped. When I peeped out of the window I could see figures outside with guns, so I told my colleague to sink down into her seat hoping they wouldn't find us. We were right at the back of the bus, and thankfully they never came that far back. In Abuja I met another North Korean who'd also nearly been kidnapped. "You and I are either the luckiest, or the unluckiest, North Koreans alive, depending on how you look at it," I told him.'

Just then our minibus hit a huge pothole and Joo's sunflower seeds, and the hulls she'd so carefully placed in a makeshift packet constructed from a folded piece of newspaper – not a piece with a photo of Kim Jong-un – shot into the air.

'Oh no!' she shrieked with laughter, rubbing her head where it had hit the minivan's roof. 'Now I'll have to spend the rest of the journey picking up sunflower seeds from the floor. It's not good to litter and I'm a good citizen.'

At a rest stop along the way I thought I'd like to find some of the seed bars I'd bought at Heathrow, intending to share them with Joo, so I asked our driver, a slim, grey-uniformed man in his 50s, to help me extricate my backpack from the pile of luggage on the back seat. A few minutes' rummaging produced a fistful of snacks and I offered one to him as thanks for his help. He didn't say a word, but he didn't need to. Looking visibly shocked, he recoiled, waved away my hand and retreated to the front of the minibus as quickly as his legs could carry him.

'What was that all about?' I wondered. 'Was he scared to be seen fraternising with a foreigner? And if so, who would report him?' The reality of life for ordinary North Koreans was becoming clearer.

When we finally reached it, Wonsan was a total anti-climax. Yes, there was a passable beach – though it was too chilly to swim – but all we got to see of the acclaimed Wonsan Special Tourist Zone, supposedly boasting 680 tourist attractions, 140 historical relics, 10 sand beaches, four mineral springs and several bathing resorts was a distant skyline.

The state doesn't like to show outsiders unfinished sites, so we were kept at arm's length from the resort, being built at vast expense to rival Las Vegas. Even small-scale building work was not deemed fit for tourist consumption.

'Please don't take their picture,' said Sonu quietly but firmly when Bastien paused to take a photo of two women laying paving stones.

Why that was an issue was anyone's guess. Was it because the pavers were women? Or because they were using their bare hands to do construction work? Or because, simply, the need to lay paving stones was an indication that Wonsan wasn't perfect?

Anti-climax notwithstanding, whether I want to or not, I will forever remember Wonsan because it was the town where I paid good money to be tortured.

'Kim Jong-un is magnificent and amazing. He builds bridges, he opens dams and factories, he sends great rockets into the sky,' sounded the sing-song narrator of a propaganda film playing on a small portable television in one corner of the massage room. 'Kim Jong-un could fire a gun when he was just three and hit a lightbulb 100m away. He is so great he doesn't defecate. He drove a truck at 80 miles an hour when he was eight. He is incredible, unbelievable and totally, undeniably awesome.' The sole word of Korean I could speak was to say 'thank you', pronounced 'go-map-seup-ni-da', which poor Joo had encouraged us to memorise but which few of us managed, so I can't vouch for what the semi-hysterical narrator was really saying, but the hummingbird-wing fast synchronised clapping of Kim's audiences and blissed-out bowing, smiling and furious note-taking of those he walked among when doling out 'on the spot guidance' certainly gave the impression that this was the gist of her autocue script. To promote the idea of his omniscience, Kim Jong-un surrounded himself with soldiers, apparatchiks and officials who wrote down his sage advice about everything from the best way to launch a missile (upwards before downwards was probably a good start) to how to steer a battleship (presumably away from rocks) to how to run a maternity hospital (fill it with doctors and midwives, then invite heavily pregnant women).

I'd decided to have the €20 massage because the months of stress over Graham's health had taken their toll. As had happened after my mother died, my shoulders were so tense they were sore to the touch and I knew a good massage would help to put things right. The room was small and furnished with just the TV, a small towelling-covered massage bed and a table laden with lotions and potions. The masseuse, a diminutive but sturdy woman, gestured for me to strip to my underwear and then pointed to some ceramic cups lying on the table. I'd heard about Chinese cupping, so was eager to try it. I nodded, and lay face down on the bed.

The massage started gently enough, with the masseuse working to untie the macramé-like knots in my shoulders.

'That feels really good,' I thought, now beginning even to enjoy the incomprehensible propaganda soundtrack, which was a far cry from the usual whale song and windchimes played during previous massages I'd had back home. But gradually the woman started to ramp up the intensity of her kneading, pressing and rubbing.

'Er, I actually have an incredibly low pain threshold,' I thought. 'Perhaps I should have mentioned that? But how, if I didn't speak Korean?'

The pummelling became more intense and I felt an elbow dig so deeply into my hamstrings that I almost let out a yelp. Then it was the turn of my triceps. Whatever the woman used on them – her knees, knuckles or chin – almost caused them to go their three separate ways. I next felt something weighty on my bottom.

'Tell me she's not actually walking on me,' I speculated as the pain moved from my glutes all the way down to my calves and ankles. Oh, good grief, she was. I didn't think it possible for the pain to get any worse, but somehow the masseuse homed in on every tiny pressure point with the aim of causing maximum agony.

'What's she doing now?' I thought fearfully as she lifted first one and then the other of my legs so high that I thought they would snap like breadsticks. She nimbly hopped off the bed and stood next to me, her cotton smock brushing against the tops of my thighs, and proceeded to give me 10 Chinese burns on each arm, twisting the flesh so hard that my eyes watered. I've had a few agonising sports massages in my time, ones that brought me out in a sweat and had me biting my lip – in fact, during one of them my massage therapist said he suspected only someone who was tough-as-nails as Paula Radcliffe could cope with the kind of unbearable pain he was going to inflict – but this was by far the most intense. I chewed on the towelling bed cover, trying not to scream. And then, as abruptly as it had started, the pain ended. I recalled the marathon saying that running is like hitting your head against a brick wall; it feels good only when it stops. With the pain turned off, my whole body was a zinging cocktail of endorphins and adrenaline. I felt invincible, like I could personally launch a rocket if Kim would let me.

Then the *real* torture started. The masseuse dropped a heated cup on my back: it felt as though I'd been scorched with a branding iron and my body shook with shock. When the second hot circle was imprinted on my back I nearly levitated off the bed. The third, which felt larger than the others, was pressed between my shoulder blades. No matter how much I reflexively jerked in agony, the masseuse seemed not to notice or to care and methodically stuck more cups on my naked skin. Guilty or not, at that point I would've readily confessed to anything.

'You've just *got* to say something,' my brain screamed. 'Who cares if you upset her by telling her you're hating what she's doing, just say it. Surely she understands the English word "No"?' I regretted not paying more attention when Joo had tried to broaden our Korean vocabulary.

'Nooo!' I screamed as the ninth red-hot circle created a vacuum that sucked on my skin, simultaneously arching my back like a flailing trout that's just been landed by a fisherman. No more cups were added. Either my torturer realised I couldn't take any more punishment, or else there simply was no more space on my back to plonk more cups. A few minutes later the cups were deftly plucked off. Bowing, the masseuse gestured that I was free to go. Wiping a tear from my eye, I saw two circular smears on the bed where I'd cried off my mascara.

On the way to my room I stopped to chat to Bastien, and then dropped by the hotel gift shop. While I was browsing through the uninspiring piles of propaganda pamphlets and some of the 890 works 'written' by Kim Jong-il – one dating from when he was just 11 – Dieter strolled in. He'd had a massage right after mine.

'How was your massage? Good, *ja*?'

'I wouldn't exactly describe it as good,' I laughed nervously. 'More like the worst pain I've ever experienced.'

'Come on,' said Dieter, 'she was really good. And she was certainly determined to give us good value for money. She left no muscle untouched.'

'True, she certainly wanted to show she knew what she was doing, but I can promise you I've never been in more pain, and that includes how I felt after running all 56 miles of my first ultramarathon in three pairs of socks that gave me excruciating blisters from mile one. It was utterly brutal.'

'Did she also use the cups?'

'Yes, that was even worse. I felt like my whole back was on fire and that all the blood in my body was going to be sucked out by those cups.'

'I know what you mean, it was pretty intense. Have you had a chance to look at your back yet?'

'No, have you?'

'No, but I spotted a mirror in the corridor outside this shop. Let's go and take a look.'

Dieter and I stepped out into the hall and stood before the long gilt-framed mirror that stretched away down the corridor. I lifted up my top, looked over my shoulder and was horrified to see nine large, angry-looking circular welts on my skin. It looked as if the masseuse had turned my back into an outsized domino. I turned to Dieter, who was inspecting his own damage, and we burst out laughing.

'My back looks like a pepperoni pizza!' gasped Dieter. 'And yours looks like you've got salami slices all over it! Oh my God, I wonder how long these are going to last? What am I going to tell my wife when I get back home to Duisburg?'

'You could tell her that you were tortured in North Korea. Actually, that's not funny.'

Just then we caught sight of the gift shop sales assistant through the glass wall of her store. The whole time I'd been browsing she'd stood in impassive silence, eyeing me warily. 'I'm hardly going to shoplift a book of propaganda speeches and go to prison for life,' I'd thought, feeling uncomfortable under her scrutiny.

The assistant was doubled over with laughter, her eyes twinkling. In an instant she'd been transformed from stern shoplifting deterrent into a giggling schoolgirl. Dieter caught her eye, too, and all three of us convulsed with laughter as I pointed to Dieter's injuries and he to mine. On our entire trip we hadn't once had any meaningful interaction with any North Koreans besides Joo and Sonu, and now all three of us were communicating effortlessly through the international language of laughter.

'North Koreans are actually just like us,' I thought. 'They're definitely not the unsmiling automatons the media would have us believe.'

After an uneventful trip to Mount Kumgang, the second highest mountain in North Korea famed for its forest scenery and spectacular waterfalls, it was time to head back to Pyongyang along the same bumpy, broken road that had taken us eastwards.

Saying our goodbyes on the station platform the next day, I was overcome with emotion. I'd grown fond of feisty Joo and it seemed such a shame that I would never see her again or even be able to stay in touch. I'd loved the almost motherly way she'd always asked if we had our 'cosy clothes' and how she'd managed to make the fact that she or Sonu had to accompany us wherever we went – even to the loo – feel less oppressive by referring to it as 'visiting uncle's house'.

'This has been an amazing group,' said Joo. 'You probably think I say this to all my groups, but this Extended Tour Group really is one I loved taking around.'

We posed for photos outside the train carriage and then got on board.

Joo and Sonu waited to wave us off. Tears welled up in my eyes and soon I was sobbing.

'You must be the only person who's cried when *leaving* North Korea,' said Dieter.

'I probably am,' I said, blowing my nose.

POSTSCRIPT

Travel has changed our lives for ever. The life we'd once mapped out for ourselves – marriage then mortgage then munchkins – became secondary to cramming in as many adventures as possible. We've joined the dots between distant destinations and packed in as much as we could, experiencing more in some years than we envisaged we would in a lifetime.

Travel changed another life, too. The way we spoke of our affection for Taiwan's friendly and enterprising people and fascinating culture inspired my much younger brother Mark to visit in 2003. He fell in love with Taiwan's wild east coast and made his home there. Teaching English. Much as we had done. Today Mark, together with his girlfriend Yong Yi, runs WaGaLiGong, a thriving hostel and surf school in Dulan, cultivates a plot of land with sweeping views of the ocean and has a half-Taiwanese daughter, Leoné, named after my dearly beloved Mum, who loves drumming, drawing, swimming, singing, dancing, windsurfing, sailing, skateboarding and stand-up paddle boarding. We hope that one day, when she's grown up, she'll add travelling to that long list.

We thought that *Travel Seekness* and *Travel Agents* would be completed six months after we started writing them but, like some of our Indian train journeys, it took much longer than that. And had the Covid-19 lockdown not wrested away our ability to travel, it would have probably taken six times longer than that! The pandemic forced us to dig even deeper into our stockpile of memories, now more precious even than loo roll, and spend our empty weekends and stay-indoors holidays completing our two books. And, like some of those journeys, the process was hold-onto-your-hat exhilarating but also incredibly exhausting and frustrating. When our rows got too heated, we took to poking each other in the ribs and shouting 'Pologise! Pologise!' to induce fits of laughter to defuse the tension.

Writing our books was a welcome distraction from illness and death, this time not just what Graham and I were going through, but the whole world. Reflecting on our travels became a way of re-connecting with the life we've shared together and the adventures we fervently hope still lie ahead.

It's a cliché, but life is a terminal illness – let's face it, none of us is getting out of here alive – so we aren't feeling sorry for ourselves, asking 'why us?' or giving in to despair. Instead, we're determined to make the most of what the Pulitzer Prize-winning poet Mary Oliver called our 'one wild and precious life' by continuing to travel. That's why, after Graham's diagnosis, pre-Covid-19, we went backpacking whenever he was well enough, glorying in the joy of travel by visiting his birthplace in Ghana, spending three weeks touring the Adriatic coast and returning to South America for a four-country holiday that was a lot less nerve-jangling than our 2003 Bolivia trip.

In January 2020 we finally saw the Northern Lights when we flew to Tromsø to celebrate our 29th wedding anniversary and run our first on-ice race, a 10K. After a six-hour drive to chase them down the lights graced us with an appearance: we lay on our backs in the snow gazing up at them, our faces glowing with delight and biting cold, as they played out a spine-tingling display, dancing and swirling in psychedelic swathes of splendid greens. Like the travel journalist I'd seen on TV who cried when he saw the lights for the first time, I shed a tear, too – not only in response to their other-worldly beauty but because, in a reprise of our near-death minus-nine experience at the Grand Canyon, I was so cold that my extremities felt as though they were on fire.

We returned from Tromsø to the good news that Graham

would be enrolled in a clinical trial where he had a 66 per cent chance of getting a fearsomely expensive immunotherapy drug not normally available on the NHS. Fortunately he was assigned to the group who got the drug. Unfortunately, the side-effects, including nausea, crippling arthritis and severe swelling of his legs and feet, were intolerable and, sadly, the drug didn't work. So Graham had to battle through a second cycle of chemotherapy, which thankfully did.

The American journalist and author Hunter S Thompson once wrote: 'Life should not be a journey to the grave with the intention of arriving safely in a pretty and well-preserved body, but rather to skid in broadside in a cloud of smoke, thoroughly used up, totally worn out, and loudly proclaiming "Wow! What a ride!"

Graham and I don't know how much of life's journey there is yet to come, but what we can unreservedly say is 'Wow! It's been one hell of a ride!'

EPILOGUE

Thank you for reading to the end of *Travel Agents*. We hope you've enjoyed the time you spent with us as much as we've loved sharing our experiences with you.

Whether you loved or loathed *Travel Agents* we'd be chuffed to bits if you'd write us a short review on Amazon and Goodreads. We promise to read every single one. Reviews can be as short as 'Hilarious' or 'Tedious in the extreme' and you don't have to have finished our book to leave one. We don't have an advertising budget, but your reviews will ensure that Amazon does most of our marketing for us, which means we'll be able to raise more money for lung cancer research.

If you want to meet us in virtual 'real life', see photographs from the travels featured in *Travel Seekness* and *Travel Agents*, or get an update on how much money this book has raised for mesothelioma research, you'll find us at Little Bandit Books on Facebook and @lisajackson43 on Twitter.

And please, don't be a stranger: you're more than welcome to drop us a line at LisaAMJackson@gmail.com. We love getting emails from fellow travellers rather than from scammers or the bank, so we will always write back.

Happy travels!

Graham & Lisa

ABOUT THE AUTHORS

Graham Williams is a research analyst for the British government. Terrified of turbulence, he nonetheless braves the scary skies in devoted service to Her Majesty. Graham's job has taken him to one or two hairy places such as Afghanistan and Pakistan's Khyber Pass, but as a long-time resident of Croydon he reckons he's acquired the street smarts to get out of any trouble. Despite bouts of diarrhoea so bad he's needed penicillin to cure them, Graham still maintains that if you can't peel it or boil it or wash it, you should eat it anyway, for it may well be very tasty.

Lisa Jackson is a latecomer to almost everything: sushi, mobile phones, social media. She only started travelling at 24, previously having set foot outside her native South Africa just once, as a surly, sulky teenager. Aged 31 she discovered marathon running and, never one to do things by halves, combined this new interest with her post-pubescent passion for travel, going on to run over 100 marathons and ultras, almost half of them abroad.

A hypnotherapist, health writer and 2020 Women of the Year nominee, Lisa is also a *Runner's World* columnist and the author of the best-sellers *Your Pace or Mine?* and *Running Made Easy*. On the road Lisa will always favour a hostel over a swanky hotel because, she reasons, if you're going to spend money it's always better to do so with your eyes open.

Married for three decades, Lisa and Graham live in Croydon, south London, with a tame squirrel called Pecan, two overfed wood pigeons called Fletcher and Sedaris and four very noisy foxes who visit from next door.

Travel Agents is the sequel to their travelogue *Travel Seekness*.

ACKNOWLEDGEMENTS

A huge round of applause to…

■ You, our readers, for buying this book. Not only have you made us happy but you've also contributed to the National Centre for Mesothelioma Research. That's two good things you've done, so please give yourselves a congratulatory pat on the back.

■ Sarah Owen, our 'book doula' and sharp-eyed editor, who cared about our two books as if they were her own 'babies'.

■ Rita Brass, dear friend and proofreader, whose idea it was to write our books on a chemo ward, who has always wanted only the best for us and the best for this book.

■ Teresa Schenk aka CM, for neverending stellar support and secret-squirrel snacks. And lovely Louise Wilkie!

■ Dragana, John and Thomas 'Slipperfetcher' O'Dowd, for sustenance, subbing and glorious camping expeditions.

■ Sue and Peter Elson, dear friends who threw open their Deal flat to us so that we could fulfil our dream of writing by the sea.

■ Professor Loic Lang-Lazdunski and his wife Alexandra for their continued advice, support and encouragement.

■ Kay Leitch, Lisa Castillo and Deborah and Angus Lawrie for their incredible proofreading help and encouragement.

■ Loren Jackson, John O'Dowd, René Kujan, Barbora Boušová, Cynthia Walley, Melissa Fehr, Jez Harris, Vacarmoh Varlee Sarnor, Dylan Harris, Luisa Yu, Ernestine Chan (@ernies.journies), Louise and Felipe Fernandes, Kristen Sarah, Danielle Cemprola, Felix Schlagwein, Anna Kiss, Andrew, Kieran, Bastien and Csaba for memorable travels (and quotes) shared.

■ Mark Jackson, Leoné Jackson, Yong-yi Chen, Ernest Gielink, Rod and Paul Williams-Young, Anna Britz, Alan Madine, Joan Ciacciofera, Ian Beach, Nadia Dawson, Bridget and Kent Robinson, David Butler, Bonnie Barber, Barbara Johnston, Faye Slater, Rose Shillito, Mark Chidlow,

Debbie Chapman, Tara Nathanson, Kate Donoughue, Mike and Siobhain Pothier, Michael and Sanober Thomas, Joe Mackie, Hilary Ivory, Sandy van Lingen, Helen Brown, Vanessa Brewster, Jackie Graveney, Christina Neal, Leanne Davies, Roger Robinson, Iona Bower, Antoinette Rendle, Dave Wise, Katy and Euan, Marissa Charles, Helena Charles, Belinda Carroll, Rachel Boston, Antoinette Strapp, Nicky Chrascina, Lyndel Costain, Juliet McGrattan, Sarah Loftus, Peter Kandralides, Karen Harverson, Karen Hatty, Allie Scott, Katherine Selby, Etta Bowden-Jones, Grace Lees, Sandy Lewis, Colette Harris, Antonia Kanczula, Torri Mundell, Laura Greaves, Andy and Marianne Schaffner, Heinz Haberzeth, Dawn Anderson, Tina Chantrey, Claire Hazleton, Emily Coltman, Loretta Reehill, Edward Chapman, Terry Keen, Cecy Montes, Kim McCallum, Eric Munro and Marifi Atsedro for their unstinting support and invaluable comments and suggestions.

■ Kelly Flood (kellyflood.co.uk), our enormously talented designer, who was always happy to do 'one more tweak'.

■ Adam Fletcher, the hugely talented author of *Don't Go There!* and *Don't Come Back!*, whose books were a constant source of inspiration, for his generous publishing advice.

■ Anna McNuff, for all her encouragement and for sharing her fab audiobook contact, Greg (soundshackstudios.co.uk).

■ All the wonderful people who wrote an endorsement for our two books: Vassos Alexander, Tony Wheeler, George Mahood, Jamie McDonald, Helen Foster, Phil Hewitt, Dave Cornthwaite, Kathrine Switzer, Elaine Griffiths, Diane Morgan, Anna McNuff, Suzy Walker, Esther Newman, Verna Brown, Jenny Janisch, Dion Leonard, Dylan Harris and Irene 'Ma' Williams.

■ All our Advance Readers for taking the time to read our books and to offer encouragement and suggestions.

■ The National Health Service, especially the devoted professionals at the Royal Marsden and University College Hospital London.

PRAISE FOR *TRAVEL SEEKNESS*

Travel Seekness is a non-stop litany of messes, misadventures and misfortunes. **Lonely Planet co-founder Tony Wheeler**

Travelogues are generally not like this! It made me laugh out loud. So funny. So personal. **Diane Morgan, comedian, actor & BBC Two's *Cunk on Britain* presenter**

A touching, honest and often hilarious collection of travel tales that will delight both seasoned travellers and armchair adventurers. **George Mahood, author of *Free Country* & *Travels with Rachel***

Despite their endless arguments, Lisa and Graham's passion for travel – and each other – comes across on every page. **Anna McNuff, adventurer, author of *Llama Drama* & winner of the 2020 Kindle Storyteller Award**

Heart-warming and inspirational, this book made me laugh out loud, and cry, too. **Suzy Walker, Editor-in-Chief *Psychologies***

Brilliant, poignant – and properly funny. **Esther Newman, Editor, *Women's Running***

If you're the type of traveller who thinks 'What's down that alley' or 'What's that, and can I eat it?' on a trip, you'll love *Travel Seekness* – just don't read the Cuban toilet story before dinner. **Helen Foster, travel writer and Differentville.com blogger**

A whirlwind adventure that will have you laughing and crying, Graham and Lisa's quest to find happiness in the hardest times of life's journey is an inspiring and heart-warming read. **Dion Leonard, author of *Finding Gobi***

PRAISE FOR *YOUR PACE OR MINE?*

Winner of three Running Awards and No1 Amazon best-seller in 'Running & Jogging'

This zestful romp of a book affirms life on every page. It's funny, wise, and full of vivid stories. Lisa claims to run slowly, but she writes with the spring and verve of a champion.
Roger Robinson, author of *When Running Made History* and co-author of *26.2 Marathon Stories*

An inspiring book. ***Red Magazine online***

An absolute tonic – and a very funny read. **Paul Tonkinson, comedian and *Runner's World* UK columnist**

I love the fact that Lisa's a real, normal woman who proves that anything is possible if you want it enough.
Gaby Huddart, Editor of *Prima* magazine

A terrific insight into the strange and strangely beautiful mind of a runner. We've all been there… although most of us have kept our clothes on! **Phil Hewitt, author of *Outrunning the Demons***

Lisa's tales of the runners she's helped and been helped by during dozens of challenging marathons are incredibly moving. **Lornah Kiplagat, three-time Olympian**

Aimed at motivating absolutely everyone to become passionate about running – without worrying about whether they'll be any good at it – Lisa's inspirational book is sure to start a chat-running craze. **Justine Roberts, founder of Mumsnet**

MORE PRAISE FOR *TRAVEL AGENTS*

Lisa and Graham's hysterical sequel to *Travel Seekness* is a laugh-out-loud tonic if you're suffering from Covid-related travel withdrawal. The (often squabbling) couple take you on trips to Central America, Zimbabwe, North Korea, Iran and many other places even intrepid travellers fear to tread. Along the way they encounter a cast of unforgettable characters – a voodoo priest with wandering hands, a cut-price clairvoyant, a Ghanaian 'fantasy' coffin maker and the Iranian secret police's 'man from Tehran' – who will either fascinate or repel you but never fail to make you chuckle. **George Mahood, author of *Free Country* & *Travels with Rachel***

An enthralling collection of travel stories, told with great warmth and humour. The Iran chapter had me in stitches and feeling incredibly anxious in equal measure! **Dylan Harris, Lupine Travel founder**

Lisa and Graham are travel nuts with an endearing talent for entertainment. Sure they have agency aplenty, empowered by travel of the most exotic, unusual and perilous kind. They are utterly extraordinary. Lisa's last words, 'Wow, it's been one hell of a ride', can be personally confirmed if you choose to join them on their daredevil ride around the world. The writers' informed eyes range from the refined to the raw, from the harmonious to the raucous. These are not simply travel tales but the portrait of a marriage, complete with gentleman's relish and lady's sauce. The spirited interchanges chart the give and take of gifted equals in barbed badinage and loving support. **Verna Brown, 5-star Amazon review**

I'm almost 91, and I've read a lot of books in my time. This is without doubt the very best of them. **Irene Williams, Graham's mother**

Printed in Great Britain
by Amazon

33767386R00149